EXPLORATIONS IN SOCIOLOGY

British Sociological Association conference volume series

and Stephen Wood (editors)

*Kate Purcell, Stephen Wood, Alan
Waton and Sheila Allen (editors)

*Jalna Hanmer and Mary Maynard
(editors)

22   *The Changing Experience of Employment:
Restructuring and Recession*

23   *Women, Violence and Social Control*

*Colin Creighton and Martin Shaw (editors)   24   *The Sociology of War and Peace*

*Alan Bryman, Bill Bytheway, Patricia Allatt and Teresa Keil   25   *Rethinking the Life Cycle*

*Patricia Allatt, Teresa Keil, Alan Bryman and Bill Bytheway   26   *Women and the Life Cycle*

*Ian Varcoe, Maureen McNeil and Steven Yearley (editors)   27   *Deciphering Science and Technology*

*Maureen McNeil, Ian Varcoe and Steven Yearley (editors)   28   *The New Reproductive Technologies*

David McCrone, Stephen Kendrick and Pat Straw   29   *The Making of Scotland: Nation, Culture and Social Change*

*Stephen Kendrick, David McCrone and Pat Straw (editors)   30   *Interpreting the Past: Understanding the Present*

*Helen Corr and Lynn Jamieson   31   *Politics of Everyday Life: Continuity and Change in Work and the Family*

*Lynn Jamieson and Helen Corr   32   *State, Private Life and Political Change*

*Published by Macmillan

State, Private Life and Political Change

Edited by
Lynn Jamieson

Lecturer in Sociology
University of Edinburgh

and

Helen Corr

Research Fellow in Sociology
University of Edinburgh

MACMILLAN

First published 1990

Published by
THE MACMILLAN PRESS LTD
Houndmills, Basingstoke, Hampshire RG21 2XS
and London
Companies and representatives
throughout the world

Typeset by Vine & Gorfin Ltd,
Exmouth, Devon
Printed in Hong Kong

British Library Cataloguing in Publication Data
Jamieson, Lynn
State, Private Life and Political Change.
(Explorations in sociology).
1. State. Socio-political aspects
I. Title   II. Corr, Helen   III. Series
306'2
ISBN 0–333–49368–0
ISBN 0–333–49369–9 pbk

193593

Contents

Acknowledgements

Notes on the Contributors

Introduction
Lynn Jamieson and Helen Corr

PART I   THE STATE, MASCULINITY AND SEXUALITY

1   'No More Heroes'?: Masculinity, Violence and the Civilising
    Process
    David H. J. Morgan

2   Sexuality and History Revisited
    Jeffrey Weeks

3   State Organisations and Men's Sexuality in the Public
    Domain, 1870–1920
    Jeff Hearn

PART II   THE DEVELOPMENT OF THE WELFARE
STATE REVISITED

4   The Second World War and the Welfare State in Britain:
    Sociological Interpretations of Historical Development
    Graham Fennell

5   Wartime Designs for a Welfare State: Australia and Britain
    in 1942
    Sheila Shaver

6   The Politics of Caring: The Case of Municipal Homemaking
    in Finland
    Leila Simonen

PART III NINETEENTH-CENTURY INTERVENTION AND REFORM

7   Women in the Factory: The State and Factory Legislation in Nineteenth-Century Britain
    Barbara Harrison and Helen Mockett

8   Women and the Inebriate Reformatories
    Geoffrey Hunt, Jenny Mellor and Janet Turner

PART IV LOCAL POLITICAL ACTION AND THE CENTRAL STATE

9   A 'Social Danger': The Contested History of Teacher – State Relations
    Jenny Ozga

10 Urban Politics and the Rise of the Labour Party, 1919–39
    Mike Savage

11 Women and Working-Class Politics in Scotland 1900–14
    Eleanor Gordon

Index

Acknowledgements

The chapters which follow were originally presented at the British Sociological Association Conference (BSA) 'Sociology and History' held at Edinburgh University in March 1988. This is one of four volumes to be produced and it reflects the high quality of the papers and wide-ranging response to the theme. The sister volumes are *Politics of Everyday Life: Continuity and Change in Work and the Family* (eds) H. Corr and L. Jamieson; *The Making of Scotland: Nation, Culture and Social Change* (eds) D. McCrone, S. Kendrick and P. Straw; *Interpreting the Past: Understanding the Present* (eds) S. Kendrick, P. Straw and D. McCrone.

We would like to thank all those who gave papers, the participants, and those who helped with the organisation, all of whom contributed to the success of the conference. We would like to thank the other editors of the conference, Terry Inkster and Lilianne Paterson for their efficient typing and administrative work in the Sociology Department, Mike Milotte and Ann Dix of the BSA for their helpful advice, and Sophie Lillington, editor, Macmillan, for her contribution towards the final stages in the production of this book.

Notes on the Contributors

Graham Fennel has been Lecturer in Sociology at the University of East Anglia since 1968 and is to be Head of the Department of Sociology and Social Administration at the Roehampton Institute from 1989. His publications include *Day Centres for the Elderly in East Anglia* (with Roy Amerson, Moyra Sidell and Andree Hague, Centre for East Anglian Studies, 1981); *Anchor's Older People: What Do They Think? A Study of Sheltered Housing* (Anchor Housing Association, 1986) and, with Chris Phillipson and Helen Evers, *The Sociology of Old Age* (Open University Press, 1988). He is currently completing with Moyra Sidell a report to the Alcohol Education and Research Council on a five-year longitudinal study of life-events and problem-drinking, with an especial focus on women.

Eleanor Gordon is Research Fellow in the Department of Economic History at Glasgow University. She is completing a book on *Women and the Labour Movement in Scotland 1850–1914* which is to be published by Oxford University Press. She is co-editor of two books on women in nineteenth-century Scotland to be published by Edinburgh University Press. Her current research interest is on political influences of industrial employers.

Barbara Harrison is a Principal Lecturer in Sociology in the Department of Social Sciences, South Bank Polytechnic, London. Her teaching and research interests are in the sociology of health and illness and women's studies. Her contribution to this book developed out of a current research project examining aspects of the history of occupational ill health in women in the period 1880–1914, and other publications are forthcoming. She has previously published in the field of race relations and educational sociology.

Jeff Hearn is Senior Lecturer in Applied Social Studies, University of Bradford and during 1988–89 Hallsworth Research Fellow, University of Manchester researching 'The political economy of men and masculinity in historical perspective'. His publications include *Birth and Afterbirth: A Materialist Account*

(Achilles Heel, 1983), *'Sex' at 'Work'*. *The Power and Paradox of Organisation Sexuality* (with Wendy Parkin, Wheatsheaf/St Martin's, 1987), *The Gender of Oppression*. *Men, Masculinity, and the Critique of Marxism* (Wheatsheaf/St Martin's, 1987), *Studying Men and Masculinity* (with David Ford, University of Bradford, 1988).

Geoffrey Hunt after acquiring a B. Sc. in sociology and an M. Phil in social anthropology at the University of London, joined the Sociology Department at the Polytechnic of North London as a lecturer and researcher. Since then he has carried out extensive research on a range of issues including the culture of drinking, immigration in Western Europe, the National Health Service, racism and unemployment and the culture of consumption.

Jenny Mellor obtained her first degree and her doctorate at the University of London. She then joined the School of Policy Studies and Social Resarch at the Polytechnic of North London where she is currently Head of Department. In addition to her teaching duties she has conducted research on alcohol advice agencies, girls in Borstal, race relations in Britain and the National Health Service.

Helen Mockett has been a Researcher in Sociology at the South Bank Polytechnic since 1983. Her research interests are in the field of women and the state, and she is hoping to complete her Ph.D. thesis on women, the state and factory legislation 1830–80 later this year.

David H. J. Morgan has been Senior Lecturer in Sociology at the University of Manchester from 1975. His main interests include the sociology of the family and the study of gender with particular reference to masculinity. Publications include: *Social Theory and the Family* (Routledge & Kegan Paul, 1975); *The Family: Politics and Social Theory* (1985) and *It Will Make A Man of You: Notes on National Service, Masculinity and Autobiography* (University of Manchester, Studies in Sexual Politics No. 17). Current research interests include further developments in the study of masculinities and violences and (with Jane Lewis and David Clark) a study of marital problems and marital agencies.

Jenny Ozga is a member of the Centre for Sociology and Social

Research in the School of Education at the Open University. She previously taught at Strathclyde University and worked in the Education Department of the National Union of Teachers. Her main research and writing interests are in the areas of teachers' work, teacher history and the post-war 'partnership' in education.

Mike Savage is a British Academy Research Fellow at the University of Sussex. His research interests are in urban sociology and in historical sociology. His main publications are: *Localities, Class and Gender* (with other members of the Lancaster Regionalism Group, Pion, 1985) and *The Dynamics of Working Class Politics* (Cambridge, 1987). He is currently working with Alan Warde on a textbook to be published by Macmillan on the 'new urban sociology'.

Sheila Shaver is a Senior Lecturer at Macquarie University, Sydney, where she has taught since 1975. Her research interests centre on the political sociology of social welfare, and in particular on class and gender politics in the Australian welfare state. She is joint author of *Who Cares? Family Problems, Community Links and Helping Services* (with Jean McCaughey and Helen Ferber, Macmillan Australia, 1977), and is currently writing a book provisionally titled *Whose Welfare State? Class, Gender and Community in Australian Welfare Politics*.

Leila Simonen has been researcher of the Academy of Finland since 1982. Currentlly she holds an assistantship in the Research Institute for Social Sciences at the University of Tampere. She also serves as coordinator for Women's Studies in her home university. She is co-editing a Finnish anthology on feminist perspectives on women and the welfare state. She is writing a book on *Gender and Caring: The Case of Municipal Homemaking in Finland*.

Janet Turner graduated in society and technology at Middlesex Polytechnic and then joined the alcohol research team at the Polytechnic of North London. She is currently employed as a researcher in the Department of Sociology at the University of Aberdeen working on a race relations project.

Jeffrey Weeks works in academic administration in London and is a visiting research fellow at the Universities of Kent and

Southampton. He has published widely in the history and social organisation of sexuality, and his publications include *Coming Out* (Quartet, 1977), *Sex, Politics and Society* (Longman, 1981; 2nd ed 1989), *Sexuality and its Discontents* (Routledge & Kegan Paul, 1985) and *Sexuality* (Tavistock, 1986). He is currently working on a book of essays on sexuality, history and politics and on a book on value debates in contemporary politics.

Introduction

Lynn Jamieson and Helen Corr

This book is about the interplay between everyday lives and 'the state'. Throughout the book, authors grapple with fundamental questions about the nature of the state and our relationship to it. Even our sexuality, which we have learned to view as private and profoundly personal, cannot be understood without reference to this complex conglomerate, as the first contributions demonstrate. These three chapters provide a particularly poignant sense of how bound up the development of 'the state' and our personal lives are.

Since the nineteenth century, the modern states of capitalist societies have been vigorously expansive, touching more and more of people's lives. After the Second World War the elaboration of state health and welfare provision resulted in the term 'Welfare State'. Just as there is more than one theory of the state, so there have always been competing accounts of these developments. The second set of chapters allows the reader to think again about the politics of the emergence of the Welfare State (particularly the relationship between warfare and welfare) and the ensuing gains and losses for everyday lives. Two further chapters provide a valuable juxtaposition between twentieth-century state welfarism and nineteenth-century protective and reforming legislation.

The final set of three chapters concerns the relationship of ordinary men and women to the state through their everyday political participation. All the contributions to this volume explore the boundaries of the state, reassessing who is 'in' and who is 'against' the state. Whereas some contributions do this by exploring the sources of motivation, momentum and opposition to particular state measures, these chapters are concerned with the political doings of particular sectors of the community: teachers, the labour movement, working-class people and in particular employed working-class women.

Before making some general remarks about the value of the chapters, and then summarising each in turn, it might be helpful to define the state. It is a complex conglomeration of agencies and

1

institutions claiming ultimate authority. The conventional Weberian definition further clarifies this 'ultimate authority' by referring to the monopoly of legitimate use of force in a given territory. Abstract definitions of the state allow some degree of freedom as to precisely who and what makes up this conglomerate. Obviously 'the government' and devolved forms of local government are the legislative core. Central to the state also, because they are established by and preoccupied with the work of government, are the Civil Service or equivalent administrative institutions. Thereafter there is a gradation of institutions and agencies more or less closely tied into the state. The police and legal officials are generally regarded as uncontroversially part of the state as they enforce its laws. Even more emphatically the armed forces are part of the state as they underwrite its sovereignty with the threat of force. But many institutions concerned with education, health and welfare could also be called aspects of the state. They are established by government legislation and run with government money, although how preoccupied these agencies are with state business is more controversial. The chapter by Ozga explores this issue with reference to teachers.

How much the state should impinge on 'private life' has long been a question for politicians and the public. This volume demonstrates that there is no simple answer. Perhaps this is not surprising, since much recent work has emphasised the complexity of the state. It is not a unitary category acting with one mind and no single state action typically has a simple motivation or one intended effect. Hence parts of the state can have contradictory interests and be more or less open to pressure 'from below' and what is oppressive interference for one set of citizens can be fought for or eagerly received relief for another.

In Britain, the Thatcher government is on record as being committed to 'rolling back the state'. Nineteenth-century rhetoric of *laissez-faire* individualism is currently in vogue. For example, the term 'nanny legislation' has gained a new popularity among Conservative politicians meaning that the legislation is unnecessarily over-protective and interfering. At the same time, commentators like Stuart Hall see an increasing loss of civil liberties in British society as a result of a state obsessed with control. This is exhibited through an emphasis on law and order, with attendant moves to more military style policing and greater censorship. It is also effected through the appropriation of local government power by central government.

In Britain, a broad range of the political spectrum is prepared to defend 'the welfare state' in the face of government which, in nineteenth-century style, caricatures welfare provision as sapping individual self-reliance and weakening 'the moral fibre' of the nation. As Fennell reminds us, this spirited defence is not without its ironies. Recent instances of odd alliances abound. A 1988 example was provided by the freezing of child benefit – state income support for dependent children paid to the carer, usually the mother. Establishment figures in the form of bishops, members of the royal family and 'wet' Conservatives combined in opposition with socialist and feminist political activists. But even more striking is the fact that the vigorous defenders include those who were previously among its most serious critics – although again this is not really surprising given the complexities of the state/society relationship. Many Marxists and feminists have remained cynical about the historical origins and aims of *aspects* of welfare reform, believing they emanated from an interest in reproducing healthy socialised bodies which could be slotted into place in systems of unequal class and gender relations. But historical work also tells us about the other side of the story; some welfare provisions, like child benefit, were fought for long and hard by ordinary people with the interests of ordinary people at heart.

Careful empirical work often shows that the two sides of the coin – the self-interested, controlling, constraining and sometimes crushing state and the conceding, giving, caring state – are often muddled up in practice. This is presented particularly clearly in the chapters on nineteenth-century state intervention and reform (Harrison and Mockett; Hunt, Mellor and Turner) although it comes through in all the empirical contributions. In general, the volume allows the reader to consider the subtleties of the interplay between everyday lives and the state. It demonstrates the need for considerable theoretical sophistication. Each chapter takes steps towards deepening our understanding and makes some contribution to equipping us to deal with the political realities of today.

Most contributions directly address the question of how history can help us to understand the present. The Morgan, Weeks and Hearn chapters on the interplay between the state, sexuality and masculinity help us to understand present-day developments like the emergence of the 'wimp' and his political cousin 'the wet'. They offer a sense of how our current notions of 'normal' sex and 'real men' have been distilled from the history of a variety of

sexualities and masculinities. This in turn sensitises us to
distortions and blindness to history in the present, like the appeal
to Victorian values, and the discussion of AIDS linking the
disease to immoral sex. Other chapters raise the question – could
the present be otherwise? The chapters on the history of the
Welfare State allow space for a more specific question – how could
it have been better? This is not done simply through scrutiny of
twentieth-century Britain but also through comparison with
Sweden, Australia and Finland in Fennell, Shaver and Simonen.
These alternative histories indicate an affirmative answer.
Similar lines between the past and the present are traced in the
chapters dealing with the political doings of particular sections of
society, with Gordon and Savage referring directly to the current
lack of fortune of the labour movement and the Labour Party, and
Ozga addressing the current tussle between the government and
teachers.

All chapters address the maintenance of unequal relationships
between men and women. It should not be otherwise, given that
gender inequality manifests itself in every aspect of everyday life.
Most chapters take the view that class and gender relations are
inextricably linked. This is a theoretical stance developed from
empirical work. Contributions document the consequences of the
ebb and flow of power in the struggle between classes for the
struggle between the sexes and vice versa. For example, Shaver
describes how the Australian Labor Party's stance against
contributory social security schemes resulted in a less deeply
entrenched sexual division of labour than that enshrined in the
British Welfare State; the chapter by Hunt, Mellor and Turner
documents how state concern with working-class drunkenness
and disorder resulted in the predominance of inebriate reformatories for women, rather than men; Harrison and Mockett's
account of 'protective' legislation shows how this concentration
on the problem of 'the weaker sex' focused concern away from the
conditions of work and the means of production to the detriment
of all.

THE STATE, MASCULINITY AND SEXUALITY

Morgan explores the connections between combat, the heroic and
masculinity. Central to this account is the development of the

modern patriarchal state which both monopolises the means of violence and legitimates violence perpetrated in its name. He starts to unpack some of the complex and deep seated connections between state power, masculinities and violence which emanated from the fact that the arms of the state, in inception and development, are dominated by men.

Weeks is concerned with the expansion of the study of sexual history which he refers to as 'the new sexual history' – new, not simply in the sense of recent, but also in terms of a break with a more traditional style of analysis. Authors draw on a range of disciplines and perspectives which share the conviction that sexuality is a social and historical construct. The work of the social scientist is then to document how and why sexuality is constructed in particular ways at particular times. This inevitably results in a focus on the state as it has become more and more involved with the sex lives of its members, constituting the permissible and the impermissible, the pure and the obscene. Again he reminds us that the state is not a unitary actor acting with one mind. Moreover, whatever the (sometimes contradictory) concerns of legislators and state agents – moral uniformity, economic well-being, national security or hygiene and health – interventions do not always have their intended outcome.

State intervention is most easily documented by tracing the intentions and outcomes of legislation. More ambitiously, Hearn is not only concerned with laws to do with sex but also with how the form of state organisations, such as the Civil Service and local government, has shaped male sexuality in the public domain. This is an area of work which has been previously almost entirely neglected. Attending to the stages of capitalism, patriarchy and state development, he identifies the period 1870–1920 as a key phase in shaping modern masculinities. This is the period of a first wave of legislation directly addressing sexuality but it is also the formative years for gender relations and sexualities in many incipient state bureaucracies. The processes culminated in the retrenchment of gender hierarchies, for example, the male supervision of female secretaries. These same processes were also materials for men's sexuality. Cinema representations of women as the modern sexually available slave was a fantasy constructed from power relations in the office.

THE DEVELOPMENT OF THE WELFARE STATE REVISITED

Fennell notes that ideas about the nature of the Welfare State seem entangled with hypotheses about how it came about. He discusses not only different general assessments of the Welfare State but specific competing hypotheses concerning the relationship between warfare and welfare. On the one hand, there is a battery of arguments concerning the ways in which warfare promotes welfare, but on the other is the fact that the British Welfare State was born into a post-war economic climate that was highly disadvantageous to its future. Comparisons with Sweden sharpen the sense that the British system is not all that it might have been.

Shaver offers a comparison between the British and Australian war-time planning exercises which profoundly affected post-war social policy, the British Beveridge report and the Australian Joint Parliamentary Committee on Social Security. Despite occurring in very similar ideological contexts, they reached radically different conclusions. The Australian Committee rejected Beveridge-style contributory systems of social insurance (strongly opposed by the Australian Labor Party) in favour of funding through a graduated tax on incomes. These differences had potential for producing radically different outcomes in the two national systems. For example, Australia's non-contributory framework gave women comparatively direct access to social security, their claims being independent of their husbands' insurance status. But in practice the Australian system has never fully realised its more radical potential for levelling both class and gender inequalities.

The wartime situation, the need for speed and consensus, assisted the resistance to contributory schemes by the Labor Party in Australia, at a time when the British labour movement had already accepted them.

The sting at the end of Shaver's tale is the suggestion that the more radical basis of the Australian welfare state does not wholly escape the classism and patriarchy of the British system.

Simonen offers more of a success story (although not without qualification) in her case history of a particular twentieth-century welfare provision – the Finnish municipal homemaker. In comparison to the British home help, this is a full-time trained post with pay and status equivalent to nursing. The more generous Finnish provision of home help type back-up to households certainly does not break down the sexual division of labour. Home-carers are predominantly women and predominantly stand in for or assist other women carers. But in Finland there is a state organised infrastructure of paid women carers rather than a partial, part-time, under-resourced welfare state where women do the bulk of the caring unpaid. Simonen argues that this is empowering for women and partially an outcome of political intervention by women (although again a complex interplay of more and less radical factions was involved).

NINETEENTH-CENTURY INTERVENTION AND REFORM

Harrison and Mockett examine state intervention in industrial work in the period 1830 to the early 1900s focusing on legislation limiting women's hours of work and their participation in 'the dangerous trades'. They weigh up the extent to which a patriarchal state was enforcing a particular sexual division of labour in the interests of men against feminist involvement in the legislation and the benefits to working-class women from the legislation. Nineteenth-century government investigators were concerned with the morality of women's work outside the home and drew heavily on the notion of 'the weaker sex's' particular vulnerability and special need for 'protection'. Feminists of the time were divided on the issue of 'protection'; although agreeing at theoretical level that women should have the right to work, some wanted immediate practical relief for women from the degrading conditions of their employment. However, the actual legislative restrictions failed to match the nature and extent of the problems identified. In concentrating on the particular problem of women rather than the conditions of labour and the means of production, it failed to address the many hazards facing workers. By asserting the primacy of women's domestic labour over waged labour, they argue, it consigned employed women for ever to the 'double shift'.

Although using an early twentieth-century case study, Hunt, Mellor and Turner are also concerned with a piece of nineteenth-century legislation, the 1898 Inebriates Act. This Act resulted in a predominance of reformatories for women rather than men, despite their lower rate of drunkenness. This is intelligible in the context of a period of moral panic about working-class women which spawned a number of measures aimed at reclaiming them as wives and mothers of a healthier imperial race. Their study of Farmfield certified reformatory also suggests another twist to what is otherwise a story of a self-interested repressive state controlling women's lives; they also present evidence which indicates that some women may have benefited from the institution.

LOCAL POLITICAL ACTION AND THE CENTRAL STATE

Ozga takes issue with approaches to teacher–state relations which cast teachers simplistically as sharing and acting in the interests of a ruling-class state. While accepting that the state motivation for the expansion of education was management of the working class in the interests of the state, her survey of the state system of education in England and Wales reminds us of 'lost' aspects of teacher history: alliances between teachers and working class, conflict between teachers and the state. She demonstrates how governments have required compromise management strategies to reduce the 'social danger' presented by some teachers. Swings between state recognition of professional autonomy and government efforts to regain more centralised control can be understood in terms of management strategies. This analysis clearly has relevance to the present as well as the past.

Savage turns to the history of the rise of the Labour Party in Britain arguing that this has always been mistakenly over-identified with the fortunes of the trade union movement. Savage argues that in the inter-war years political struggles arising out of service provision by the local state, struggles which often involved women, were crucial for Labour Party support. Also the extent to which the Labour Party took 'women's issues' seriously in itself affected their support. This is documented through two case studies of local politics and Labour Party fortunes in Preston and Slough. Issues around housing, health care, schooling, and other municipal provisions such as public baths were as relevant to the Labour Party's political health as the state of the trade union movement. His account has important implications for analyses of the contemporary decline in the fortunes of the Labour Party which primarily link this demise to the decline in militant unionised male workers.

Gordon's piece tackles the history of women's relationship to working-class politics directly. Her argument is that insufficient attention has been paid to the failure of the labour movement to provide consistently a supportive framework for women's political involvement. Focusing on Scotland, she documents working-class women's political activism through organisations such as the Co-operative Women's Guild, Women's Labour League, the Independent Labour Party and the smaller socialist parties. The women attracted by and sought out by these organisations were almost exclusively working-class housewives despite the facts of political activism and support for women's suffrage among women waged workers. Gordon argues that the reasons for the absence of employed women lies in the policies and practices of the socialist movement. Women were related to in their capacity as homemakers, with women's employment being regarded as a temporary deviation from the 'natural' division of labour between the sexes. Sexual equality meant recognition of the equal value of motherhood – women's work – to that of paid employment, which was viewed as primarily man's work, hence the ILP's frequent support for sectional trade union struggles to exclude women. Working women's own defence of their right to work for a living wage was not necessarily a challenge to the ideological primacy given to domesticity for women or the ideology of the family wage, but a pragmatic plea born from economic necessity.

To sum up, then, the book offers considerable insight into the ways in which our personal lives and the state are bound up. A simple 'them' and 'us' view of the relationship between the state and our everyday lives is clearly inadequate, not least because neither the 'them' nor the 'us' are simple categories with common interests. To take a topical example from earlier work, with reference to child abuse, Linda Gordon (1983) notes that, historically, outrage over intervention into the family was often outrage over a territorial violation that was a challenge to male authority, while women sometimes sought out intervention to bring relief from male violence. The interplay of conflicting interests she sketches is further mapped out by each empirical contribution here.

State actions are not all of a type in intention or outcome; state intervention can be experienced as empowering and caring as well as constraining and penalising. Even a government which is expanding its constraining and penalising functions while denigrating as 'wet' and 'wimpish' its caring side will spawn idiosyncrasies, contradictory policies and unintended consequences. Recent work on the state has generally recognised these complexities but the complications of class conflict have been more consistently addressed than those of gender divisions. All the chapters in this book address the fact that both class and gender relations shape and are shaped by how 'the people' are represented in and by the state.

FURTHER READING

Bean, P., Ferris, J. and Whynes, D. (eds) (1985) *In Defence of Welfare* (London: Tavistock).

Gordon, L. (1985) 'Child Abuse, Gender and the Myth of Family Independence: A Historical Critique', *Child Welfare*, vol. LXIV.

MacKinnon, C. A. (1983). 'Feminism, Marxism, Method and the State: Toward Feminists Jurisprudence', *Signs*, vol. 8, no. 4.

McLennan, G., Held, D. and Hall, S. (eds) (1984) *State and Society in Contemporary Britain: A Critical Introduction* (Cambridge: Polity Press).

Part I
The State, Masculinity and Sexuality

1 'No More Heroes'?: Masculinity, Violence and the Civilising Process

David H. J. Morgan

INTRODUCTION: THE PROBLEM STATED

Giddens, referring to a variety of factors such as a growing professionalism, the use of conscription and the wearing of more functional uniforms, writes of the 'decline of the traditional warrior ethic' (Giddens, 1985, pp. 228–30). This theme is found in a variety of other sources, especially those dealing with the history of the military. Keegan writes of a decline of the gentlemanly codes of warfare and killing, arguing that it becomes less and less possible to have combat between men of more or less equal status (Keegan, 1978, pp. 322–3). His more recent study of military leadership concludes with a chapter on the 'post-heroic' (Keegan, 1987). This theme is also found in McNeill's influential history of warfare (McNeill, 1983, pp. 105, 130) and a popular history of the British officer (Turner, 1956, pp. 68–70).

Statements of this kind point to a particular nexus linking combat, the heroic and masculinity, although the masculine gender theme is sometimes muted. Moreover, it is argued in statements of this kind that this nexus has, for a variety of reasons, become weakened over the centuries. A variety of complex issues are beginning to emerge here. First, the heroic is a gendered construction. The dominant version would have it that the hero is someone possessing characteristics conventionally understood as masculine. These masculine heroic qualities are conventionally understood in opposition to or in contrast to feminine character-istics, those to do with vulnerability, tenderness or a need for protection. Second, the construction of the hero is usually, although not exclusively, around matters of combat and violence between men (Connell, 1987, p. 249). These constructions of the

13

heroic and their strong associations both with masculinities and violences do not imply an unlimited or uncontrolled use of violence. Constructions of the heroic are as much to do with the control of violence and of self as of its direct expression or deployment in the field of battle.

Part of the continuing construction of the heroic is the symbolic linking of present-day heroes, real or fictitious, with their counterparts in the past, often the distant past. The use of terms such as 'Homeric' or 'chivalric' (Girouard, 1981) shows this process quite clearly. However, it is also possible to argue that while the construction of the heroic often embraces the rhetoric of continuity (and hence an ideology of unchanging masculine virtues and strengths), the reality may be somewhat different. To Connell (1987), there has been a kind of debasing of the concept of the heroic from the early heroic epics, where violence was also 'posed as a moral and human issue', to Bond, Rambo or the Man with No Name.

Whether or not the ideal typifications of the heroic have declined in the way Connell has suggested or whether, as the military historians argue, the opportunities for heroism on the field of battle have declined, one thing remains clear. Even in the earliest times, although heroic combat might be direct violence in the sense of an exchange of blows and injuries between parties in full view of each other, it was never unmediated. In other words, the accounts of violence are placed in wider frameworks of interpretation and evaluation. One important framework is to do with the notion of 'honour':'Honour . . . was for the British officer of 1815 an almost wholly abstract ideal, a matter of comportment, of exposure to risk, of acceptance of death if it should come, of private satisfaction – if it should not – at having fulfilled an unwritten code' (Keegan, 1978, p. 194). Goffman's notions of 'action' and 'character' (Goffman, 1967) extend these constructions beyond the military to other masculine spheres of activity especially gambling. The man of character is associated with courage, gameness, integrity, gallantry, composure, presence of mind, dignity and stage confidence!

A somewhat indirect perspective on these themes of masculinity, violence and character is provided by the current widespread use of the term 'wimp'. In the first place, it is 'used only as a term of abuse or contempt' (*OED* Supplement) although Woody Allen, among others, has made something of a career renegotiating 'the wimp as hero'. Second, in the overwhelming majority of cases, the term is applied to men only. It refers, therefore, to some sense of failure as 'a man' and has, therefore, some affinities with weeds and wankers. Finally, and most interestingly, the opposite is relatively ill-defined. The opposition, implied in several accounts of the Hungerford shooting, was between the wimp and 'Rambo'. However, the fact that 'wimp' clearly has a minus sign against it does not mean that 'Rambo' has a plus sign, certainly not in the Hungerford context. What does seem to be the case is that the negative term 'wimp' appears to be currently in sharper definition than any contrasting positive term. Real men are *not* wimps, clearly; but what *are* they? For the time being perhaps all we can say is that 'wherever the action is, wimps are not'.

'THE CIVILISING PROCESS'

We have, therefore, a cluster of related themes. These include some problems around the public definition of masculinity in the 1980s reflected in the use of the word 'wimp', arguments about the weakening of the links between combat, heroism and masculinity, and theories about 'action' and 'character' which provide some elements of continuity allowing for manly qualities to be displayed in arenas other than the field of battle. While it cannot be pretended that all these can be neatly tied together in one functional packet, there appear to be some affinities, certainly enough to warrant further investigation.

One possible framework for understanding, or at least formulating, these links has been provided by the various works of Elias and his associates on 'the civilising process'. The most general statement is in the following quotation: 'The change in drive-control and conduct that we call 'civilisation' is very closely related to the growing interweaving and inter-dependence of people' (Elias, 1982, p. 52). At a slightly less general level, we can look at the shifting conduct of the upper classes at different stages of European history: the warriors/knights, the courtiers and the bourgeoisie (Elias, 1978, p. 186). The development of the court societies and absolutist monarchies represented major spurts in the civilising processes to do with the growing control and monopoly of the means of violence and the theme of self-control.

Castiglione's (1478–1529) *The Book of the Courtier*, for example, is frank in its recognition of the importance of martial skills and the use of arms but also quite clearly distances the uncontrolled deployment of these skills from the model of the ideal courtier (Castiglione, 1976, pp. 58–9). Another major 'increase in reserve and self-restraint' was associated with the rise of bourgeois society (Elias, 1978, p. 186). Restraint, not simply in the resort to violence, but also in the expression of emotion, passions and animalities of any kind become the hallmark of the bourgeois, often indeed to the point of stereotype.

Some support for this model might be found in Stone's account of the aristocracy in the sixteenth and seventeenth centuries where he draws attention to the growing monopolisation of the use of violence and the deployment and ownership of weaponry by the state and its agencies (Stone, 1965, p. 231). Certainly, the emphasis in many accounts is on the role of the state and the growing incompatibility between the rational bourgeois conduct of business and government and the privatised expression of violence and the passions. Perhaps, however, we should allow some part also for the growing and articulated opposition to warfare itself. Hale, for example, argues that war was more or less taken for granted up to around the fifteenth century but that, in the light of developing religious perspectives from Hussites and Anabaptists together with a more humanistic pacifism, during that century war and its morality became the subject of some intense debate (Hale, 1962).

What, then, is the civilising process? The key word is 'control', a linked set of processes concerned with the growth and extension of agencies of state control over the use and the means of violence together with and interacting with a growing concern over and monitoring of the 'internal' self, a distancing from what might be defined as 'the animal'. Elias makes it clear that this is not a straightforward or smooth progression. There may be particularly strong spurts in the civilising process at certain times and in certain places just as there may be, at certain times, reversals, a kind of 'decivilising process'.

One important feature of this whole approach to the civilising process is in the explicit linking of gender relationships and constructions of gender identities to this wider societal analysis. Thus, in Dunning's model of 'segmental bonding' (part of a wider discussion of soccer hooliganism) there is a high degree of conjugal role segregation, an authoritarian father, high physical violence in relations between the sexes and an overall pattern of male dominance. These are related in his model to the 'norms of aggressive masculinity' and the patterns of inter-group rivalry and violence that characterise much soccer violence (Dunning in Elias and Dunning, 1986). Elias, himself, sees the civilising process as something that accompanies moves towards greater equality between sexes. He argues, where a warrior class (such as the knights of the ninth and tenth centuries) is influential, male dominance and male culture are also firmly established. In contrast, the court society offered the chances for greater equality between the sexes: 'wherever men are forced to renounce physical violence, the social importance of women increased' (Elias, 1982, pp. 78–81). This argument about the inverse relationship between sex equality and warrior culture does receive some confirmation in cross-cultural studies (Sanday, 1981).

An instructive illustration is provided by the history of duelling in European society (Kiernan, 1988). Here is a type of violence which is highly formalised and controlled with strong connections with constructions of gender identity which are firmly anchored in particular social orders and hierarchies. Moreover, the shifting nature and significance of duelling in different countries between the sixteenth and nineteenth centuries illuminate some of the themes to do with the 'civilising process' while also suggesting some ambiguities and difficulties with the concept.

The duel represented both the expression of and the control of 'masculine' attributes. Far from being a straightforward expression of aggression, it represented the suppression or control of the spontaneous or the 'natural'. The mediating concept was, of course, that of 'honour'. Honour was not simply a matter of being brave enough to defend one's reputation with one's life if necessary. It was as much a matter of the willingness to conform to the code by which satisfaction was sought and obtained, a matter of style as well as of substance. Bryson argues that to surrender was not necessarily to be dishonoured. It was, in fact, sometimes more cowardly to be seen to prefer death to surrender (Bryson, 1938, p. 65).

This particular mix of class and gender found in the construction of 'honour' was not necessarily stable or constant. In the case of the resurgence of duelling in nineteenth-century Germany a new kind of masculinity seemed to appear. Here, participation in

a duel seemed to be a particular form of male initiation or
bonding, where the emphasis was to be *seen* to have a scar on one's
face (Baldick, 1965, pp. 148–9). This is some distance from the
idea of a mature defence of one's honour.

It is also important to stress that the 'golden age' of duelling
lasted for a relatively short period of European history and that it
was never fully legitimated, with periodic attempts to control or
suppress it by different authorities. Pressures to ban duelling
altogether grew during the eighteenth and nineteenth centuries
and, interestingly, the debate about duelling was also a debate
about the nature of masculinity.

Even before the eighteenth century, duelling in England was
opposed on religious grounds but increasingly the debate focused
on the true nature of honour (Andrew, 1980). True honour was a
matter of a whole life, not something that turned on a single act.
The code of honour itself increasingly came to be seen as a relic of
an earlier barbarism. Moreover, the attack on duelling became in
part the critique of the life-style of a particular class, the challenge
on the part of Evangelicals and men of commerce on privilege and
corruption (Andrew, 1980). In the early nineteenth century the
debate came to be seen as one between an older code of
masculinity and a newer, religiously inspired, life of true manliness (Davidoff and Hall, 1987; Mangan and Walvin, 1987).
Attempts to redefine and give a new value to the concept of
chivalry were part of the same series of debates (Girouard, 1981).

This ambiguous relationship between duelling and masculinity
also points to a shifting relationship between duelling and the
civilising process. Up to a point, the practice of duelling might be
seen as a 'stage' in the civilising process. It entailed a sharp
distancing between performance and the passions. The institution of the duel limited the combat between two people (usually)
and allowed for an opportunity for reconciliation without loss of
honour or life. It may be, as was sometimes maintained, that the
duel had a good effect on manners as it meant that one did not call
another man a liar without some consideration (Andrew, 1980,
p. 414). Nevertheless lives were lost and injuries sustained as a
result of duelling and the very code that was meant to regulate
such losses also probably encouraged young men to defend their
honour, often in the face of the most trivial of slights (Stone, 1965).
If the development of regulations such as the *code duello*
represented the civilising process in one century, the growing

opposition to and outlawing of duelling represented it in later centuries.

STATE, GENDER AND VIOLENCE

It can be seen that the civilising process is bound up with the development of the state. In various ways and to various degrees, the state claims the legitimate use of violence in relation to other states while claiming an increasing monopoly of the exercise and means of violence internally. These processes are also, therefore, clearly bound up with the history of armies and of policing.

There is general agreement as to the importance of the monopolisation of force in the processes of state formation. A variety of terms are used – force, violence or coercion – but the arguments all point in the same direction, that is to the mobilisation of actual or potential force for the maintenance or extension of boundaries externally in relation to other similarly constituted states and the simultaneous control over the use and deployment of violence within the area covered by the state. This is rarely a straightforward process and never a once-and-for-all accomplishment. A comparison of the debates surrounding the possession and use of firearms following the Hungerford shooting with similar debates in the United States will highlight the point that different societies understand the theme of the monopolisation of the means of violence in somewhat different ways.

What has been ignored in most of these accounts of the state and its relationship to institutionalised violence has been its gendered character. Among the major male theorists of the development of the state, Elias is almost alone in attempting to incorporate a gender dimension into the analysis, although there are also brief hints in Poggi (1978). The recognition of strong connections between the state and patriarchy or male power came with feminist writers (see, for example, MacKinnon, 1982, 1983; Burstyn, 1983) and has recently been taken up by men whose works have been influenced by feminist thought. Connell, for example, stresses the importance of understanding the state in gender as well as in class terms (Connell, 1987, pp. 127–8). In keeping with his overall orientation he argues for a dynamic model of the patriarchal state, one which emphasises process and contestation. Hearn makes the connections with violence quite explicit: 'Those parts of the state that are more concerned with repression and violence are more fully male-dominated and male-membered than those parts which are concerned with caring, welfare and reproduction which are usually male-dominated and female-membered' (Hearn, 1987, p. 94). The suggested distinction between domination and 'membering' is a useful one. Thus it is useful to be reminded of the obvious fact that throughout the world, armies and police forces are both predominantly male-membered and almost wholly male-dominated, and that even where there may be some shift or variation in the former this is not accompanied to any significant extent by any movement in the latter (Enloe, 1983). The same analysis could, of course, extend to the legal apparatus and to the membership of legislative assemblies.

This is not simply a numerical domination or a question of who occupies the higher positions in the state, especially those positions associated with the exercise and control of violence. The gendered character of the state and state institutions is equally to do with the ideological and the symbolic. In the case of military institutions or police forces, for example, we cannot keep separate the actual practices of keeping, or seeking to keep, women away from direct association with violence or combat and the legitimations which are provided in order to justify these practices. A man in uniform is simultaneously an individual occupying a particular role associated with the legitimised and controlled exercise of violence and a symbol of state power and national identity. There is a complex and deep nexus linking themes of state power, masculinity and violence, one which is enhanced by the growth of nationalisms. Poggi, following Weber, argues that the modern state, like religion, has the ability to give meaning to death. In a variety of ways – through uniforms, parades and public speeches – the state deploys the imagery of the heroic death in order to encourage young men to die on the battlefield (Poggi, 1978, pp. 99–100).

The nature of the three-cornered relationship between state, masculinity and violence may now be summarised. Internally and externally, the state is involved in the control and the legitimation of violence. Men are doubly involved as both the main authors and subjects of this violence. They are subjects in two senses, in that their identity is in some measure bound up, directly or indirectly, with this controlled and legitimated violence and, secondly, in that they are often the direct victims of this violence. This relationship is not static or clear-cut and is subject to change and challenge.

This account of the three-cornered relationship between violence, the state and masculinity has so far left out women. There are all kinds of reasons why such an account would be incomplete. In the first place, the ideological nexus that weaves together patterns of legitimised violence and constructions of dominant masculinities simultaneously defines notions of women and femininities. These understandings revolve around distinctions between the protectors and the protected, distinctions which are heightened at the times of actual conflict. (See, for example, the Glasgow Media's account of the Falklands/Malvinas conflict; Glasgow University Media Group, 1985.) In the second place, definitions of masculinity and femininity often revolve around questions of aggression and violence, linkages often made in scientific as well as in popular understandings. What this means is not that women are incapable of violent or aggressive behaviour but that their manifestations of violence are often treated or seen as problematic in gender terms. Finally, there is the important question of violence of men against women in the context of the state. This is where the 'male-dominated and male-membered' character of many of the relevant state agencies comes to be of crucial importance, contributing, for example, to the trivialisation of rape and the marginalisation of 'private' violence within the home. This is also, it should be noted, an area where the sense of contestation and challenge is also marked.

WAR AND SOLDIERING

Very generally, the history of warfare in European society may be described as a process of rationalisation, a process connected with but not wholly determined by the growth of the nation state. This rationalisation process would include:

(a) The development of large, sometimes mass, standing armies with a clear national territorial base;
(b) The development of the idea of military career and a process of professionalisation, eroding if not completely replacing the

identification of soldiering with a particular stratum in society;

(c) The growing ordering and disciplining of large bodies of men as symbolised by drill and uniforms;

(d) The increasing use of weapons with much greater destructive power and technical sophistication, establishing greater distance between combatants.

What has this process of rationalisation to do with gender and violence? First, in even raising the question about whether war and soldiering has become more or less violent we highlight the need to pluralise the term, to talk about violence*s*. If by violence direct hand-to-hand combat is meant then it is probable that wars have become less violent. It is also the case that the development of the state and the rationalisation of warfare have meant a dwindling scope for the exercise of legitimated inter-personal violence. It is likely also that much of the legitimised violence within the military – the floggings and more violent means of disciplining, for example – together with some, if not all, of the more violent forms of horseplay have declined. However, if we are considering violences in terms of the numbers of people killed or maimed in war especially in terms of formally non-combatants, the picture becomes much more contradictory. It is also likely that this increase in the scale and character of slaughter has augmented a sense of revulsion against and opposition to the very concept of war.

If the connections between war and violence have become more complex or contradictory, what of masculinity? The conventional view as we have seen seems to point to an overall weakening of the connections between war, soldiering and masculinity. We have already considered some of the factors that, it has been assumed, contributed to the decline of this traditional 'warrior ethic' or particular close identification with 'masculine' values. All these seem to entail the decline of the scope for individualised deeds of heroism on the battlefield.

However, it can be seen that what is being deployed here is a more or less one-dimension model of masculinity, one associated with a warrior ethos, with personal courage, fighting prowess and so on. Particular constructions of masculinity are being used as a resource in order to tell, in a circular fashion, a particular story about the topic of masculinity and its decline. Take, for example,

McNeill's contrast between pecuniary calculation and his description of sixteenth-century war as dealing with 'honour, prestige, heroic self-assertion' (McNeill, 1983, p. 105). It is true that there is a contrast here but it would not be correct to read this, as some might do, as simply a statement about a challenge to masculine skills and virtues. Equally it might be seen as a kind of contradiction between two different styles or constructions of masculinity, a contradiction that, in various guises, persists to this day.

Even if we continue to argue that there are particular associations to be made between soldiering and war and masculinity, the connections are not simply between masculinity and combat or martial values. There are other connections which need to be considered as well. We have already mentioned military discipline and the often brutal floggings that were inflicted upon lower participants in military organisations. Even ignoring some of these excesses, being able to 'take it like a man' was, and continues to be, part of the military experience with its particular emphasis on a whole range of deprivations, from harsh and sometimes all-embracing disciplines to cold water, hard beds and lack of sleep. We also need to remember that armies have been the locales for other kinds of violence, including bullying, rough horseplay and initiation rituals, with their connotations of masculinity, sexuality (and homosexuality), defilement and, once again, being able to 'take it'.

Further, the army may be seen as a locale for the development of male cultures which do not have a direct connection with fighting on the field of battle. Dubbert, for example, argues that the American Civil War offered young men the opportunity for a variety of 'manly' pursuits other than fighting including swearing, gambling, drinking and sexual adventure (Dubbert, 1979, pp. 64–5). Elkin emphasises the relative freedom from social constraints which permits the elaboration of patterns of masculine solidarity, culture and language, a feature taken up in many other accounts (Elkin a and b, 1946; Royle, 1986). Hockey describes the trinity of 'birds, booze and brawling' among the leisure-time activities of modern-day regulars (Hockey, 1986) while I have described similar patterns for National Servicemen (Morgan, 1987).

In talking about military settings as providing the opportunities for the development and expression of 'masculine' characteristics other than simple warlike or fighting skills, we are also reminding ourselves that gender is a relational property, that masculine cannot be considered apart from feminine. The army unit, with its emphasis on the male solidary group, both provides the setting for the constructions of femininities and the use and deployment of commonly held images of women. It is unlikely, for example, that the use of derogatory or negative images of women during the basic training process is something peculiar to this century. Men, for example, might be told that they are marching like 'a bunch of women' (Hockey, 1986; Morgan, 1987). Sex is both a frequent topic for conversation and a resource for metaphors and language with which to understand the military environment (Elkin, 1946).

Such orientations to women are not, of course, purely meta-phorical. The romantic image of the young woman falling for the dash and glamour of the uniform (Hichberger, 1988, pp. 165–6) may be counterposed to the more frequent realities of seduction and abandonment, prostitution and rape (Brownmiller, 1976). While the presence of organised armies in society might not always and necessarily lead to the domination of women in other spheres (Connell, 1987, pp. 152–3), there seems, at least in the modern armies that have developed from the sixteenth and seventeenth centuries, to be a strong set of relations linking the monopolisation of violence, the harsh military discipline, the development of primary male groups and stereotypical and often aggressive constructions of women and sexuality. In this context, rape and protection may be seen as two sides of the same coin.

So far, then, the model is of a decline of the links between masculinity and heroism on the field of battle, although in terms of other aspects of masculinities the links between soldiering and gender might seem to remain quite strong. However, there are other reasons for a measure of scepticism about the 'decline of the heroic' model. In the first place, it is likely that those who argue for this theme have in mind some kind of military élite. The heroes, by and large, are also leaders and the ordinary soldiers are sometimes missed in the heroic poses and the panoramas of battle. In this respect it might be less true to talk of 'the decline of the heroic', simply because there was not a great deal of it there in the first place. Keegan, for example, asks: 'What sustained men in a combat like Agincourt, when the penalty of defeat, or of one's own lack of skill or nimbleness was so final and unpleasant?' (Keegan, 1978, pp. 114–16). He suggests a whole host of factors, some with particular relevance to Agincourt and others of more general relevance, including alcohol, the presence of the King strengthening the bond between leaders and followers in martial societies, religion, the prospect of enrichment as a result of ransom and looting, compulsion and coercion and a wider tolerance for and acceptance of violence in society. There is enough here to suggest, at least for the ordinary soldiers, a continuity of the relatively unheroic rather than the decline of the heroic.

This is not to say that the soldier, and the non-commissioned one at that, does not continue to be constructed in heroic terms. Indeed, the growth of the modern nation state and the development of imperialism in the nineteenth century may have contributed to a kind of democratisation of the heroic, the ideological construction of the ordinary soldier as someone who, rather than being feared by the civil authorities, was the subject of praise and adulation. The aristocratic notion of 'honour' was given a much wider referent in the nineteenth century. This may be done retrospectively as in, for example, the boys' novels of Henty (Arnold, 1980) or, more poignantly, in war memorials (Inglis, 1987) or Remembrance Day ceremonies or, further, in the celebration of the ordinary soldier, Tommy Atkins, in fiction, poetry, paintings and the music hall (Hichberger, 1988; Mackenzie, 1986). Nevertheless, accompanying this celebration of the ordinary hero, there is a growing and often bitter recognition of the gulf between ideal and reality.

Even for the officer ranks, the motivation might be more a question of not wishing to be seen to be a coward than a desire to be a hero. Hence, the importance of the wider network of group relationships which provides an audience for one's conduct in the face of the enemy (Keegan, 1978, pp. 71–2). This concern with how one appeared in the eyes of fellow officers and the wider code of honour is reflected in a stress on wounds received rather than enemy slain.

What we are pointing to is a much more complex and often contradictory pattern of relationships between the military, the heroic and the masculine. We see that military organisations facilitate the creation of male solidary groups, at all levels. These groups may, to some extent, draw upon and build upon previous groups' experiences in schools (especially public schools), peer groups and gangs but will have some of their own particular features. Nor are these features always to do with violence, hardness, aggression and other constructed masculine features. The groups may also engender tenderness and mutual concern as many accounts of life in the army testify (Hearn and Parkin, 1987, pp. 76–7, 159–60). A recent account, for example, notes: 'There's no mention of love in the recruiting ads, but these lads have found it here; in each other's grins, in the poky, warm, muscular fug of their barrack room' (John Sweeney, *Observer*, 24 January 1988). Sometimes, indeed, these solidarities may run counter to wider military values.

The association, therefore, between the military, war and masculinity is a complex and multi-stranded theme. Farrar attempts to look at the processes by which war is constituted as male. He argues that we must look – as has been attempted here - at nationalism and, for Britain and some other countries, imperialism, and the processes by which these are bound up with the constitution of the male subject. He also refers to the 'unique intensity of experience' (linked to constructions of male desire) associated with war (Farrar, 1985, pp. 65–6). This intensity of experience may, with some distortion perhaps, be removed from a single location on the field of battle to the periods of training, the relationships in the billet or the bar, the solidarities and mutual support in opposition to officers and NCOs. What we are pointing to, therefore, is not a simple 'decline of the heroic' in the face of the rationalisation of war and the army but rather a reformulation of the heroic in the face of nationalism and imperialism and the pressures to mobilise large numbers of men from civilian backgrounds.

CONCLUDING REMARKS

This chapter has attempted to explore one aspect of the changing understandings and constructions of masculinities through the argument that changes in the social control of violence and the rationalisation of warfare have brought about a decline in the opportunities for heroic display. Following Elias, this may be seen as an aspect of the 'civilising process'.

At the very least, the argument is open to some modification. In the first place, the class limitations of the original formulations should be noted; the constructions of the heroic which lay behind many of the accounts of its alleged decline were focused upon the activities, values and life-styles of particular élites in society. In the second place, there remains a great deal of analysis to be done, especially in relation to questions of causality. In particular, a more active model of social change needs to be elaborated, one which looks at masculinities as constructions which are open to challenge, negotiation and contest rather than as being (as would appear to be the case in models of the civilising process) simply dependent variables. One particular important aspect of this is the process whereby the concept of the 'heroic' became renegotiated to displace it from the field of battle to more civilian and non-violent pursuits.

I found Elias' account useful in drawing my attention to some of the possible connections between the different patterns of violences in society, the development of the nation state and changing gender relationships and identities. This sense of a shifting set of configurations might, for example, cast an ironic light on our own times. The elaboration of more and more sophisticated means of destruction seems, on the face of it, to be far from the idea of the 'civilising process'. However, to say that modern nuclear strategy is an extreme and possibly one-sided development of the civilising process is to point to an ever-growing distancing, through the processes of state control and scientific rationality, of the means of violence from what are conventionally understood to be primal or basic emotions of anger or aggression. The way in which strategists and defence experts distance themselves from the destructive implications of their activities is not only an impressive demonstration of this aspect of the civilising process but also of the elaboration of a new model of masculinity (Cohn, 1987).

Yet, in the last analysis, it is perhaps this supposed link in Elias' work between the civilising process and the improved position of women (or negatively between militarism and gender equality) that is most open to question. Such shifts that may be discerned from time to time in the position of women may be seen as being relatively minor as compared with the continuing presence of patriarchal institutions and male dominance. In particular, the continuing evidence of domestic violence and rape might provide a severe limitation to any general theory of the civilising process. If, as might be argued, there is some greater awareness of and sensitivity about sexual and domestic violence, this may be as much due to the activities of women themselves than of any more abstract motion of the 'civilising process'.

It is important, undoubtedly, to continue to explore the changing constructions of masculinities especially in so far as this search undermines any essentialist or biologistic constructions. However, in the last analysis, it is impossible to talk of masculinities and men without also talking of femininities and women. It is true that these different identities have their own relatively autonomous histories and that, in the case under discussion, this relative autonomy is heightened by the largely all-male and often relatively closed institutions with which we are dealing. Yet these shifting patterns of masculinities take place in a wider context of structured gender inequalities. The full story about the relationships between violence between men and violences between men and women must be told elsewhere but we have seen hints at various points in this chapter, including the various ways in which women service military men, the associations between rape, prostitution and military orders and the overall hypothesised relationships between militaristic cultures and gender segregations and inequalities. There is, as has so often been pointed out, a relatively hidden history of women running alongside but related to the more public histories of men. In the wider context the cry may not so much be a partially nostalgic one of 'no more heroes' but rather the more affirmative claim that 'we don't need another hero'.

REFERENCES

The project is supported by an ESRC Personal Research Fellowship for the year 1987–8. I am grateful to the ESRC for providing me with the opportunity to develop these themes. I am also grateful to Lynn Jamieson for her most helpful comments.

Andrew, D. (1980), 'The Code of Honour and Its Critics: The Opposition to Duelling in England, 1700–1850', *Soc. Hist.*, 5 (3).
Arnold, F. (1980), *Held Fast for England: G. A. Henty, Imperialist Boys' Writer* (London: Hamish Hamilton).
Baldick, R. (1965), *The Duel* (London: Chapman & Hall).
Brownmiller, S. (1976), *Against Our Will: Men, Women and Rape* (Harmondsworth: Penguin).
Bryson, F. R. (1938), *The Sixteenth-Century Italian Duel* (University of Chicago Press).
Burstyn, V. (1983), 'Masculine Dominance and the State', *The Socialist Register* (London: The Merlin Press).

Castiglione, B. (1976), *The Book of the Courtier* (Harmondsworth: Penguin).
Cohn, C., (1987), 'Sex and Death in the Rational World of Defence Intellectuals', *Signs*, 12 (4), pp. 687–718.
Connell, R. W. (1987), *Gender and Power* (Cambridge: Polity Press).
Creighton, C. and Shaw, M. (eds) (1987), *The Sociology of War and Peace* (London: Macmillan).
Davidoff, L. and Hall, C. (1987), *Family Fortunes* (London: Hutchinson).
Dubbert, J. L. (1979), *A Man's Place* (Englewood Cliffs, N. J.: Prentice-Hall).
Elias, N. (1978), *The Civilising Process: The History of Manners* (Oxford: Basil Blackwell).
Elias, N. (1982), *The Civilising Process: State Formation and Civilisation* (Oxford; Basil Blackwell).
Elias, N. and Dunning, E. (1986), *Quest for Excitement* (Oxford: Basil Blackwell).
Elkin, H. (1946a), 'Aggression and Erotic Tendencies in Army Life', *Am. Journ. Soc.*, 51, pp. 408–13.
Elkin, H. (1946b), 'The Soldier's Language', *Am. Journ. Soc.*, 51, pp. 414–22.
Enloe, C. (1983), *Does Khaki Become You?* (London: Pluto Press).
Farrar, A. (1985), 'War: Machining Male Desire', in P. Patton and R. Poole (eds), *War/Masculinity* (Sydney: Intervention Publications).
Giddens, A. (1985), *The Nation State and Violence* (Cambridge: Polity Press).
Girouard, M. (1981), *The Return to Camelot* (Yale University Press).
Glasgow University Media Group (1985), *War and Peace News* (Milton Keynes: Open University Press).
Goffman, E. (1967), 'Where the Action Is', in *Interaction Ritual* (New York: Doubleday Anchor Books) pp. 149–270.
Hale, J. R. (1962), 'War and Public Opinion in the Fifteenth and Sixteenth Centuries', *Past and Present*, Vol. XXII, pp. 18–35.
Hearn, J. (1987), *The Gender of Oppression: Men, Masculinity and the Critique of Marxism* (Brighton: Wheatsheaf).
Hearn, J. and Parkin, W. (1987), *'Sex' at 'Work'* (Brighton: Wheatsheaf).
Hichberger, J. W. M. (1988), *Images of the Army: The Military in British Art 1815–1914* (Manchester University Press).
Hockey, J. (1986), *Squaddies: Portrait of a Sub-Culture* (University of Exeter).
Inglis, K. (1987), 'Men, Women and War Memorials: Anzac Australia', *Daedalus*, Fall, pp. 35–60.
Keegan, J. (1978), *The Face of Battle* (Harmondsworth: Penguin).
Keegan, J. (1987), *The Mark of Command* (London: Jonathan Cape).
Kiernan, V. G. (1988), *The Duel in European History* (Oxford University Press).
Mackenzie, J. M. (ed.) (1986), *Imperialism and Popular Culture* (Manchester University Press).
MacKinnon, C. (1982), 'Feminism, Marxism, Method and the State: An Agenda for Theory', *Signs*, 7 (3), pp. 515–44.
MacKinnon, C. (1983), 'Feminism, Marxism, Method and the State: Toward Feminist Jurisprudence', *Signs*, 8 (4), pp. 635–58.
McNeill, W. H. (1983), *The Pursuit of Power* (Oxford: Basil Blackwell).
Mangan, J. A. and Walvin, J. (eds) (1987), *Manliness and Morality* (Manchester University Press).
Mann, M. (1986), *The Sources of Social Power: Vol. 1, A History of Power from the Beginning to AD 1760* (Cambridge University Press).

Mann, M. (1987), 'War and Social Theory: Into Battles with Classes, Nations and States', in C. Creighton and M. Shaw (eds) (1987) pp. 54–72.

Morgan, D. (1987), *It Will Make a Man of You: Notes on National Service, Masculinity and Autobiography*, Manchester, Department of Sociology Studies in Sexual Politics, No. 17.

Poggi, G. (1978), *The Development of the Modern State* (London: Hutchinson).

Royle, T. (1986), *The Best Years of Their Lives* (London: Michael Joseph).

Sanday, P. R. (1981), *Female Power and Male Dominance* (Cambridge University Press).

Shaw, M. (1987), 'The Rise and Fall of the Military-Democratic State: Britain 1940–85', in C. Creighton and M. Shaw (eds) (1987) pp. 143–58.

Stone, L. (1965), *The Crisis of the Aristocracy 1558–1641* (Oxford University Press).

Theory, Culture and Society (1987), Edition on 'Norbert Elias and Figurational Sociology'.

Turner, E. S. (1956), *Gallant Gentlemen: A Portrait of the British Officer, 1600–1956* (London: Michael Joseph).

2   Sexuality and History Revisited

Jeffrey Weeks

WRITING ABOUT SEX

Writing about sex can be dangerous. It makes you, as Ken Plummer put it, 'morally suspect' 1975, p. 4). Until recently, in the academic world at least, it marked you also as marginal to the central intellectual preoccupations of the major disciplines.

Nearly forty years ago, the young William Masters felt sufficiently inspired by the example of Alfred Kinsey to want to pursue a career in sex research. He was advised by his obviously more worldly wise supervisor to do three things first: to complete his medical qualifications; to establish his reputation in another field; and to wait until he was 40 before venturing into these treacherous waters.

This little anecdote tells us quite a lot about the moral climate in post-war America, and probably about the present too. Here we find, for example, the hegemony of medicine which has dominated most 'respectable' discussions of sex over the past century. Then there is the emphasis on reputation and credentials, a positive underlining of the importance of a student in this field demonstrating his or her objective, scholarly interest in the subject before venturing into it. And, of course, reputation, credentials, respectability and objectivity are assumed to come with age.

It has always been possible to write about sexuality. But, to do so and be listened to, it has usually been necessary to work within the confines of an acceptable discourse. The authorised voices have been religious, medical, medico-moral, legal, psychological, pedagogical, and certainly 'official'. They have rarely been sensitive to the nuances of history or social variability. It is striking that the only social scientific research initiative with a direct relationship to sexual behaviour spontaneously launched

31

by the (British) Economic and Social Research Council has to do with yet another medico-moral problem, that associated with the tragic spread of AIDS.

Needless to say, quite a lot of writing about sexuality has gone on outside these parameters. But it is noticeable how, even today, many of us who venture into this field still feel the need to stress our academic credentials for doing so. If you look at any journal whose main concern is sexuality in some form you will find the title page full of the names of impeccably scholarly advisers, complete with a long list of their academic qualifications, from MDs to Ph.D. (Candidate). Academic awards permit us to speak with authority; and to make what we say acceptable.

To get back to my anecdote: the young William Masters followed the advice of his mentor absolutely. And who can say he was wrong? Alongside his partner and future wife Virginia he was to become half of the world-famous sex research and sex therapy duo, Masters and Johnson. Their popular success has always been underpinned by their 'scientific' reputation. The very turgidity of their writing style may be seen as a simulacrum of the scientific text.

Some things at least have changed. Since the early 1970s there has been a major expansion in the study of sexuality in general, and of sexual history in particular. We now know a good deal about marriage and the family, illegitimacy and birth control, prostitution and homosexuality, changing patterns of moral, legal and medical regulation, rape and sexual violence, sexual identities and sexual communities, and oppositional cultures. Historians have interrogated old and discovered new documentary evidence; they have deployed extensive oral history sources; and all but exhausted the records of births, marriages and deaths (see Weeks, 1985).

Major scholars, whose reputations were, significantly, made elsewhere, have entered the field. To name just some of the best known: Lawrence Stone has exhaustively chronicled the (largely upper-class) family, sex and marriage in pre-modern England (Stone, 1977). Peter Gay is venturing into the complexities of the 'bourgeois experience' (Gay, 1984; 1986). Most influentially of all, Michel Foucault has essayed a genealogy of the Western apparatus of sexuality (Foucault, 1979; 1987; 1988). The subject has achieved an unprecedented range, depth and, dare I say it, respectability.

This signals an important and welcome shift. But it is vital that we understand its real significance, which lies not in who writes but what they write about. The really noteworthy point about the new sexual history lies in the fact that increasingly it is being recognised that far from being a minor adjunct to the mainstream of history, sexuality in its broadest sense has been at the heart of moral, social and political discourse. We cannot properly understand the past, let alone the present, unless we grasp that simple fact.

Two lessons for the historical enterprise flow from this. First, it is imperative to recognise not only the desirability but the absolute necessity of inter-, multi-, and cross-disciplinary approaches to the subject. The new sexual history has in fact been fed not only by new sources and new topics, but also by a multitude of approaches, from psychoanalysis to post structuralism and semiology, and nurtured by a number of disciplines, from the 'new social history' to sociology, philosophy and literature. They go far beyond the conventional intellectual tools of the traditional empirical historian. I would go so far as to say that the study of sexuality as a historical phenomenon fundamentally challenges the existing disciplinary boundaries, illustrating perhaps better than any other topic their contingent natures. Traditional historical methods have proved inadequate to the understanding of sexuality. The history of sexuality should not be studied by historians alone.

The second factor is that sexual history is to a high degree a politicised history, underlined by an energetic grassroots input into the study of sexuality. To an extraordinary degree, much of the most innovative historical work in this field has come from women and men whose initial concern was as much 'political' as purely 'academic'. Many of the pioneering feminist writers about sexuality in the early 1970s are now in often senior academic positions; their work has grown in empirical richness and theoretical sophistication. But their publications, while achieving the highest scholarly standards, are still clearly within a developing tradition of feminist writing (for example, Walkowitz, 1980; Taylor, 1983; Smith-Rosenberg, 1986). Similarly, within the area of lesbian and gay studies, important historical works have appeared which, though initially stimulated by the moral and political preoccupations of the authors, have begun to transform the wider intellectual debate (for example, Boswell, 1980; Bray,

1982; Freedman *et al.*, 1985). In the study of sexuality, it seems, scholarship and politics, broadly defined, are inextricably intertwined.

I want to devote much of the rest of this chapter to exploring the implications of these factors, concentrating on several interrelated questions. What, for example, is the impact of the new sexual history on our understanding of sexuality? Or, to put it another way, what is it we study when we say we are exploring the history of sexuality? What do our studies tell us about the relationship of the sexual to the social, to power and politics? In what ways do they illuminate our understanding of social and moral regulation, and the role of the state? How, in turn, does this affect our perception of the historic present in which we live? Why, in particular, has sexuality become so important in the contemporary political discourse of both left and right? My aim is not to supply the answers, but to sharpen the questions we must ask if we are to rethink the history of sexuality.

THE SUBJECT OF SEXUAL HISTORY

At the heart of the new sexual history is the assumption that sexuality is a social and historical construct. In the famous words of Foucault, 'Sexuality must not be thought of as a kind of natural given which power tries to hold in check, or as an obscure domain which knowledge tries gradually to uncover. It is the name that can be given to a historical construct' (Foucault, 1979, p. 105).

Leaving aside the ambiguities and problems with this statement, I want to emphasise the revolution in the approach to sexuality that this symbolised. Of all social phenomena, sex has been most resistant to social and historical explanations. It seems the most basic, the most natural thing about us, the truth at the heart of our being. This has been reflected until very recently in even the most sophisticated studies of sexuality. As pioneering sexual theorists sought to chronicle the varieties of sexual experience throughout different periods and different cultures they assumed that beating at the centre of all this was a core of natural sexuality, varying in incidence and power, no doubt, as a result of chance historical factors, the weight of moral and physical repression, the patterns of kinship, and so on, but nevertheless basically unchanging in biological and psychological essence.

Such an assumption governed equally the naturalist approaches of the early sexologists and the metatheoretical
approaches of such Freudo-Marxists as Reich and Marcuse. It
dominated the thoughts of functionalist anthropologists with
their commitment to cultural relativism as much as the evolution-
ists they displaced. It lurked as effortlessly behind the sexual
writings of cultural radicals as the work or moral conservatives. It
was the taken-for-granted of sexual studies (see Weeks, 1985, Part
2).

The new sexual history has changed that. Its origins are
disparate, owing, as I have already indicated, something to
sociology and anthropology (their emphasis on cultural relativism, social organisation and micro-studies: Gagnon and Simon,
1974; Plummer, 1975), something to psychoanalysis (especially
the challenge offered by the theory of the unconscious to fixed
gender and sexual positions: Coward, 1983), something to the
new sexual movements of the early 1970s (their critique of existing
social and sexual categories: Weeks, 1977), something to the new
social history (in as far as these diverse strands can be disentangled from the new history). Foucault's work made such an
impact in the early 1980s because, in part at least, it complemen-
ted and helped to systematise work already going on. Unifying the
new approach were several common themes.

First, there was a general rejection of sex as an autonomous
realm, a natural domain with specific effects, a rebellious energy
that the social controls.

Once you begin to see sexuality as a 'construct', as a series of
representations, as an 'apparatus' with a history of its own, many
of the older certainties dissolve. It is no longer appropriate to
state, as Malinowski did, that 'Sex really is dangerous', the source
of most human trouble from Adam and Eve on (Malinowski,
1963, p. 127). Instead, we are forced to ask: why is it that sex is
regarded as dangerous? We can no longer speculate about the
inevitable conflict between the powerful instinct of sex and the
demands of culture. Instead, we need to ask why our culture has
conceived of sexuality in this way.

Second, it followed that the new sexual history assumed the
social variability of sexual forms, beliefs, ideologies and be-
haviours. Sexuality has not only a history, but many histories,
each of which needs to be understood both in its uniqueness and
as part of an intricate pattern.

Third, it became necessary to abandon the idea that the history of sexuality can usefully be understood in terms of a dichotomy of pressure and release, repression and liberation. 'Sexuality' as a domain of social interest and concern is produced by society in complex ways. It is a result of diverse social practices that give meaning to human activities, of social definitions and self-definitions, of struggles between those who have the power to define, and those who resist. Sexuality is not a given. It is a product of negotiation, struggle and human agency.

The most important outcome of the resulting historical approach to sexuality is that it opens up the whole field to critical analysis and assessment. It becomes possible to relate sexuality to other social phenomena and to ask new types of questions (new at least to the field of sex research). Questions such as the following: how is sexuality shaped, and how is it articulated with economic, social and political structures – in a word, how is it 'socially constructed'? Why and how has the domain of sexuality achieved such a critical organising and symbolic significance? Why do we think it so important? If sexuality is constructed by human agency, to what extent can it be changed?

Questions such as these have produced an impressive flood of new work – and new questions – across a range of issues from the shaping of reproduction (eg Petchesky, 1986) to the social organisation of disease (eg Mort, 1987), from the pre-Christian origins of the Western preoccupation of the association between sex and truth (Foucault, 1987; 1988) to the making of the modern body (Gallagher and Laqueur, 1987).

I'll take a further example from an area which I myself have been particularly interested in – the history of homosexuality. Fifteen years ago there was virtually nothing in the way of serious historical studies of same-sex activity. Such writings as existed assumed an unchanging essence of homosexuality across cultures and over the millennia of human history, as if one could readily identify the experience of the modern gay sub-cultures with the socially sanctioned male inter-generational sexual patterns of ancient Greece or the institutionalised cross-dressing of certain pre-industrial tribal societies.

I became convinced (following McIntosh, 1968/1981) that this was an inadequate way of seeing this particular past, and my early researches persuaded me that there had been significant shifts in attitudes to, and the organisation of, same-sex erotic activities. In particular, it became clear that the idea that there was such a thing as a homosexual person, and an associated homosexual identity, was of comparatively recent origin, no more, in most Western cultures at least, than two or three hundred years old (Weeks, 1977). Other work carried on at the same time was reaching similar conclusions (see Smith-Rosenberg, 1975; Katz, 1976; Foucault, 1979).

Since the 1970s this approach has been much debated, and has occasioned a great deal of controversy. There is by no means unanimous agreement about it (Boswell, 1983). It has at the same time become the major hypothesis for the study of homosexual history. For example, a conference at the Free University of Amsterdam in December 1987 brought together over 500 people from all over the world to debate the relevance of 'essentialist' versus 'constructionist' perspectives in addressing the question 'Homosexuality, Which Homosexuality?' The history papers covered a wide range of topics, from Aristotelean philosophy to the sexual and emotional proclivities of Eleanor Roosevelt. But central to the majority of them was a sensitivity to historical context that illumined hitherto obscure issues, and largely confirmed the 'constructionist' hypothesis (HWH, 1987; Franklin and Stacey, 1988).

But sensitivity to context is one thing; doing away with a unifying concept of sexuality is quite another. One of the problems with the new sexual history is that it is in danger of becoming a history without a proper subject. The history of sexuality is at the same time a history of a category of thought, which, if we follow Foucault, has a delimited history; and a history of changing erotic practices, subjective meanings, social de-finitions and patterns of regulation whose only unity lies in their common descriptor. 'Sexuality' is an unstable category, in constant flux (Padgug, 1979).

It is, nevertheless, a vital one. All societies find it necessary to organise the erotic possibilities of the body in one way or another. They all need, as Plummer suggests, to impose 'who restrictions' and 'why restrictions' to provide the permissions, prohibitions, limits and possibilities through which erotic life is organised (Plummer, 1984). But they do so in a wide variety of ways. The study of sexuality therefore provides a critical insight into the wider organisation of a culture. The important question then becomes not what traditional disciplines such as history or sociology can contribute to our understanding of sexuality, but

rather what the study of the sexual can contribute to our grasp of
the historical, the social and the political.

SEX, POLITICS AND SOCIETY

This brings me to the second of the major issues I want to explore:
what indeed does the new history of sexuality tell us about the
relationship of sexuality to other elements of social life, and
especially what insights does it give to the nature of power and
politics in the modern world?

'To some', the feminist scholar Gayle Rubin has argued,
'sexuality may seem to be an unimportant topic, a frivolous
diversion from the more critical problems of poverty, war, disease,
racism, famine, or nuclear annihilation. But it is precisely at times
such as these, when we live with the possibility of unthinkable
destruction, that people are likely to become dangerously crazy
about sexuality' (Rubin, 1984, p. 267).

Why is this so? Why is sexuality so thoroughly bound up with
the modern play of power, as Foucault suggested (Foucault,.
1979)? What is it about sexuality that makes it so susceptible to
anxiety, conflict and moralising zeal?

The first point to make is that this is not always the case.
Although our culture attributes a peculiar significance to the
sexual, there is plentiful anthropological and historical evidence
to suggest that other cultures interpret the possibilities of the body
quite differently (Caplan, 1987). While all societies have to make
arrangements for the organisation of erotic life, not all do so with
the obsessive concern we show in the West. Different cultures
have varying responses to childhood sexuality, marriage, homosexuality, even reproduction. Some societies display so little
interest in erotic activity that they have been labelled more or less
'asexual'. Islamic cultures, by contrast, have developed a lyrical
view of sex with sustained attempts to integrate the religious and
the sexual – as long, that is, as it was heterosexual (Bouhdiba,
1985; Weeks, 1986, pp. 25–6).

We in the West are heirs of a Christian tradition which has
tended to see in sex a focus for moral anguish and conflict,
producing an enduring dualism between the spirit and the flesh,
the mind and the body. It has produced a culture which
simultaneously disavows the body while being obsessively preoccupied with it.

Michel Foucault was centrally concerned with this issue. He abandoned the original schema for his *History of Sexuality* and went back to the ancient Greeks and Romans in the two volumes published at the very end of his life (Foucault, 1987; 1988) precisely because of his growing conviction that the Western preoccupation with the relationship between sex and truth was of very ancient lineage, and crucial to the understanding of power and subjectivity. For the ancients, he argued, concern with the pleasures of the body was only one, and not necessarily the most important, of the preoccupations of life, to be set alongside dietary regulations and the organisation of household relations. We, on the other hand, seek the truth of our natures in our sexual desires. In the course of that shift, with pre-Christian as well as Christian origins, sexuality has emerged as a domain of danger as well as pleasure, emotional anxiety as well as moral certainty.

I do not wish here to assess the merits and defects of this argument. I cite it because it illustrates the major point I want to make. The new social history takes for granted that sexuality as an historical phenomenon is in fact a consequence of an obsessive social preoccupation with the body and its possibilities for erotic pleasure. As a result, far from being stubbornly resistant to social moulding, it is a peculiarly sensitive conductor of cultural influences, and hence of social and political divisions. [*]

There are five broad categories of social relations which are both constructed around and in turn shape and reshape sex and gender relations (Weeks, 1986; 1989). First, there are the kinship and family systems that place individuals in relationship to one another, and constitute them as human subjects with varying needs and desires, conscious and unconscious. Second, there are the economic and social organisations that shape social relations, statuses and class divisions, and provide the basic preconditions and ultimate limits for the organisation of sexual life. Third, there are the changing patterns of social regulation and organisation, formal and informal, legal and moral, populist and professional, religious and secular, unintended consequences as well as organised and planned responses. Fourth, there are the changing forms of political interest and concern, power and policies. Finally, there are the cultures of resistance which give rise to oppositional subcultures, alternative forms of knowledge and social and sexual movements.

These are quite general categories. They have had different weighting at different historical conjunctures. But their intricate and complex interaction in the West has produced a culture which assigns a critical role to sexuality in the definition of subjectivity and self, morality and sin, normality and abnormality.

Modern sexuality has been shaped and defined at the intersection of two absolutely central concerns: with who and what we are as human subjects and social individuals; and with the nature and direction of thes society as a whole. And as the state, as the organising focus of the social sphere has become more and more concerned with the lives of its members, for the sake of moral uniformity, economic well-being, national security or hygiene and health, so it has become more and more involved with the sex lives of individuals, providing the rationale for techniques of moral and legal management, detailed intervention into private lives and scientific exploration of the subject of sex.

As a result, sexuality has become an increasingly important political as well as moral issue, condensing a number of critical issues: with the norms of family life, the relations between men and women, adults and children, and the nature of normality and abnormality. These are central issues in any culture. The debate about them has become increasingly heated and bitter in recent years because debates about sexuality are debates about the type of society we want to live in. As sex goes, so goes society (Weeks, 1986, p. 36).

POWER AND THE STATE

This is another way of restating that issues of sexuality are at the heart of the whole workings of power in modern society. 'The state', broadly defined, clearly has a crucial role to play here. Through its role in determining legislation and the legal process it constitutes the categories of the permissible and the impermissible, the pure and the obscene. Through its symbiosis with the forces of moral regulation (from the churches to the medical profession) it can shape the climate of sexual opinion. Through its organisation of health and welfare it can help to determine the patterns of marriage, child-bearing, child-rearing, and so on.

Of course, the actual practice of the state varies enormously, depending on a variety of historical factors and contingencies. A would-be theocracy like modern Iran can make adultery a criminal offence, with draconian penalties. An ostensibly secular state might formally eschew a direct role in moral regulation (though all the evidence suggests that it is easier to make the declaration of disinterest than to carry it out when faced by the host of pressures to which the modern state is heir). The state can shape through its prohibitions and punishments. It can also organise and regulate through its positive will and injunctions, and influence through its omissions and contradictions.

But however critical the role of the state, both in the abstract and in real historical situations, it would be wrong to see its functions as either predetermined or necessarily decisive. One of the key achievements of the new sexual history is that it has helped us to understand the mechanisms through which sexuality is organised and produced in and through a host of different social practices. And in this complex process a variety of often interlocking power relationships are at play.

Take, for example, the question of gender and sexual difference. Various feminist writers have argued forcibly that the elaboration of sexual difference has been central to the subordination of women, with sexuality not only reflecting but being constitutive in the construction and maintenance of the power relationship between men and women. Sexuality is fundamentally gendered.

On the one hand, this can lead to an argument that all hitherto existing definitions of female sexuality (at least in recorded history) are male definitions, so that the category of sexuality itself is fundamentally corrupted by male power and the actual practices of 'masculinity' (Rich, 1984; Coveney *et al.*, 1984; Dworkin, 1987). On the other, the perception of the symbiosis between definitions of gender and of sexuality can lead to careful analyses of the play of definition and self-definition, power and resistance (eg Coward, 1984). In other words, it becomes a sensitising device which allows us to explore the complexities of practices – theoretical as well as social and political – which have given rise to the relations of domination and subordination that characterise the world of gender.

This has enabled Laqueur, for example, to argue that: 'the political, economic, and cultural transformations of the eighteenth century created the context in which the articulation of radical differences between the sexes became culturally imperative' (Laqueur, 1987, p. 35). The hierarchical model that held sway from ancient times interpreted the female body as an inferior and inverted version of the male, but stressed nevertheless the generative role of female sexual pleasure. The breakdown of this model, in political as well as medical debates, and its replacement by a reproductive model which stressed the radical opposition of male and female sexualities, the woman's automatic reproductive cycle, and her lack of sexual feeling, was a critical moment in the reshaping of gender relations.

It did not arise straightforwardly from scientific advance. Nor was it the product of a singular effort at social control by and through the state. The emergent discourse about sexual difference allowed a range of separate, and often contradictory, social and political responses to emerge. But this new perception of female sexuality and reproductive biology has been absolutely central to modern social and political discourse. Its effects can be discerned in a vast range of political practices, from the legal regulation of prostitution to the social security structures of the Welfare State (Weeks, 1989).

If gender is a key variable in the organisation of sexuality, class is another. Class differences in sexual regulation are scarcely unique to the modern world. In the slave societies of the ancient world, moral standards varied enormously with social status. But in the modern world class definitions of appropriate sexual behaviour have been sharply demarcated. It has, in fact, been argued by Foucault (1979) that the very idea of sexuality is an essentially bourgeois one, which developed as an aspect of the self-definition of the class against the decadent morals of the aristocracy and the rampant immorality of the lower classes in the course of the eighteenth and nineteenth centuries. It was a colonising system of beliefs which sought to remould society in its own emerging image.

Undoubtedly, the respectable standards of family and domestic life, with its increased demarcation between male and female roles, a growing ideological distinction between private and public life, and a marked concern with moral and hygienic policing of non-marital, non-heterosexual sexuality, were increasingly the norm by which all behaviour was judged (Davidoff and Hall, 1987).

This does not mean, of course, that all or even most behaviour conformed to these norms, or that the state acted in a uniform way to institutionalise acceptable forms of behaviour. There is a great deal of evidence that the sexual lives of the working class remained highly resistant to middle-class mores (Weeks, 1989). What one can say with confidence is that the complex sexual and moral patterns that exist in the twentieth century are the product of social struggles in which class played an important part.

Not surprisingly, the imagery of class has become a key element in sexual fantasy (Davidoff, 1983; Marcus, 1967). At the same time, the impact of formal regulation of sexual behaviour through the law and social policy is inevitably coloured by class-bound assumptions. In the 1860s and 1870s the Contagious Diseases Acts, ostensibly directed against prostitutes, were perceived to be aimed at working-class womanhood in general. This fuelled the feminist and labour opposition to them, and helped to shape the new sexual regime that followed their repeal in the 1880s (Walkowitz, 1980). More recently, it is impossible to understand the significance of the liberal sexual reforms of the 1960s in Britain without relating them to the re-formation of social boundaries, including, crucially, those of class (Weeks, 1989). Class does not determine sexual behaviour, but it provides one of the major lenses through which sexuality is organised and regulated.

Categorisations by class intersect with those of ethnicity and race. Euro-centric concepts of correct sexual behaviour have helped to shape centuries of response to the non-European world. So in the evolutionary model of sexuality dominant until the early twentieth century, the black person was classed as lower down the evolutionary scale, closer to nature than the European. This view has survived even in the culturally relativist work of twentieth-century anthropologists, who in their eagerness to portray the lyrical delights of other cultures take for granted that this is because the natives are somehow more 'natural' than modern 'civilised' peoples (Coward, 1983).

One of the most abiding myths is that of the insatiability of the sexual needs of non-European peoples, and the threat they pose to the purity of the white races. This has been constitutive of real effects in shaping sexual codes. A fear of black male sexuality was integral to slave society in the American south, and has continued to shape public stereotypes to the present. In South Africa, fear of inter-marriage and miscegenation is at the heart of apartheid legislation. In Britain, immigration policy is shot through with a dense network of assumptions where race, sex and gender are inextricably linked.

As European societies become more ethnically and racially

diverse, so dominant racial assumptions shape responses to manifest cultural differences, in family patterns, gender relations and sexual assumptions (Amos and Parmar, 1984). Sexuality here, as elsewhere, becomes a battleground for competing notions of what constitutes proper behaviour.

The boundaries of race, gender and class, as of other social divisions like age or disability I could have discussed, inevitably overlap. They are not clear-cut categories. The essential point is that sexuality is constructed and reconstructed through a complex series of interlocking practices, all of which involve relations of power – and of challenges to that power. In this dialectic of power and resistance, definition and self-definition, the formal bodies of the state inevitably play a crucial part. The state can organise the terrain of sexual struggle through its patterns of legal regulation, its political interventions and social policies. But the state is itself a locale of struggle over the meaning of sexuality: its impact can be highly contradictory as its different organs adopt conflicting policies. There is no functional fit between state intention and sexual regulation. On the contrary, the historian of sexuality must stand amazed at the unintended consequences of state action: laws designed to outlaw homosexuality which encourage it; injunctions to parents to bring forth children for the greater good of the community which are followed by a drop in the birth rate; and attempts to limit child birth (for the greater good . . .) which lead to an exponential increase in live births.

The major lesson we can draw from all this is that there is no simple way to understand the social organisation of sexuality. Instead of seeing sexuality as a unified whole, we have to recognise that there are various forms of sexuality, that there are in fact many sexualities: class sexualities and gendered sexualities, racially specific sexualities and sexualities of struggle and choice. The historian of sexuality must try to understand these, both in their distinctiveness and in their complex interactions.

HISTORY AND THE PRESENT

This brings me to the final theme I want to pursue: the implications of the new sexual history for our understanding of the historic present. As I suggested earlier, a major stimulus to the study of our sexual pasts has come from preoccupations that were clearly located in the present. Feminist history is, for example, by definition a history that has current political concerns at its heart. Thus a book produced by the London Feminist History Group, called *The Sexual Dynamics of History*, observes that 'Our link with contemporary political struggles gives our work as historians a special edge, because our analysis is constantly being reworked and developed' (London Feminist History Group, 1983, p. 1). At the very least this implies that the questions that are asked of the past are prompted by the concerns of the present. Sometimes these questions can lead to the exploration of new or neglected themes. A good example here is the interest in the history and politics of male violence against women, whose starting point is very much recent experience (for instance, Cameron and Frazer, 1987; Theweleit, 1987; 1990). Sometimes the result is a re-examination of well-worn but controversial subjects in new ways. For example, Boswell's (1980) work on attitudes to homosexuality in the early Christian church is a work of great (traditional) scholarship, but is clearly also part of a fierce debate within both the Roman Catholic Church and the gay community about the real implications of the Christian tradition's attitudes towards homosexuality.

But there is something more at stake than simply finding new or better ways of addressing the past. Sexuality is a highly contentious issue in contemporary society, and at the centre of some highly influential political programmes. I have mentioned feminism and lesbian and gay politics. Perhaps even more important today are the projects of moral regeneration that lie close to the centre of the politics of the New Right in some at least of its manifestations. In the resulting political struggles around sexuality the past is freely raided for its contemporary relevance – as, for example, in the capture by the Thatcher government in Britain of the idea of Victorian values (Walvin, 1987; Weeks, 1989). The new sexual history is important in so far as it contributes to these debates, and to the extent that it illuminates the present.

I do not mean by this that historians should only study the recent past, or concentrate on issues that are of current concern. But at the very least, if the perspectives I have described on the historical construction of sexuality have any merit, the new sexual history should be able to undermine the certainty with which the past is called in to redress the difficulties of the present. As we have seen, sensitive studies of sexual behaviour in other cultures (eg Caplan, 1987), or at other times within our own, serve to problematise the whole idea of a single history. Instead they direct our attention to the variety of forces and practices that shape sexual categories.

The historic present is a product of many histories, some of very ancient lineage, some very recent. What we can use the new sexual history for is to question the taken-for-granted, challenge our own culturally specific preoccupations, and to try to see whether what we assume is natural is not in fact social and historical. At the same time, we can explore the continuities and the discontinuities of our sexual histories.

Let's take as an example the ways in which our culture is responding to a crisis that is both personal and social, medical and moral, and also highly political – that relating to AIDS. This is a new problem in that it is a new, or at least newly discovered, disease or group of diseases. It is also a phenomenon that is very closely connected with sexuality, both because it can be sexually transmitted and because, at least in the West, the people most affected so far have been gay men.

What is most striking is the degree to which, in reacting to AIDS, people call on pre-existing discourses and shape them to the current crisis. As Frank Mort (1987) has shown, for example, there is a substantial medico-moral tradition, going back at least to the early nineteenth century, linking beliefs about health and disease to notions of moral and immoral sex, 'dangerous sexualities'. The linkage of AIDS with homosexual life-styles evokes a rich tradition that sees homosexuality as itself a disease (Weeks, 1977). Even the question of whether people with AIDS should be segregated and confined refers back to a heated debate in the late nineteenth century about whether the most effective means of controlling the spread of syphilis was by compulsorily testing and confining prostitutes (Walkowitz, 1980).

These are political and moral debates where more is at stake than mere historical accuracy. But it so happens that all the issues I have just referred to have been the object of investigation by the new sexual historians, who have effectively demonstrated the social conditions for the emergence of these discourses. It is too much to hope, perhaps, that their work would dispel illusions and prejudices. But at the very least it should force us to pause and ask about the conditions which are shaping our interventions. What their work underlines above all is the living nature of the past – and the historical nature of the present.

SOME CONCLUSIONS

To conclude, I want to offer just three brief observations. First, I want to underline my belief that the new sexual history has fundamentally transformed the way we interpret the sexual past and present. It is no longer possible to see sex as caught in the toils of nature, outside the bounds of history. It is a legitimate subject for historical investigation.

Having said that, it is worth stressing that the particular theoretical position I have adopted on the 'social construction of sexuality', while influential, is by no means dominant. As Carole Vance recently put it, 'Social construction theory may be the new orthodoxy in feminist, progressive, and lesbian and gay history, but it has made a minimal impact on mainstream authorities and literature in sexology and biomedicine' (Vance, 1987, p. 33). What this means in practice is that historians have been much more willing to recognise that homosexuality is 'socially constructed' than to examine the historical evolution of heterosexuality. A latent naturalism often survives in even the most advanced history. To my mind the great advantage of the deconstructionist approach outlined here is that it forces us to think beyond the boundaries of existing categories and to explore their historical production.

The second observation I want to make is that deconstruction should also imply reconstruction. There is no point in fragmenting the past into a series of disparate histories unless we deploy them for some purpose. What I have suggested is that an important outcome of the new sexual history is that it contributes to our understanding of the present. Increasingly we can see the present not as the culmination of an unproblematic past but as itself historical: a complex series of interlocking histories whose interactions have to be reconstructed, not assumed.

Finally, I want to suggest that the new sexual history may have a valuable political and ethical outcome. In demonstrating the sexual and moral diversity of the past it may lead us to be a little more accepting of the diversity of the present. Perhaps that is why writing about sex can still be dangerous.

REFERENCES

Amos, V. and Parmar P. (1984) 'Challenging Imperial Feminism', *Feminist Review*, No. 17, July 1984.

Boswell, J. (1980) *Christianity, Social Tolerance and Homosexuality* (University of Chicago Press).

Boswell, J. (1983) 'Revolutions, Universals, Categories', *Salmagundi*, No. 58/59.

Bouhdiba, A. (1985) *Sexuality in Islam* (London: Routledge & Kegan Paul).

Bray, A. (1982) *Homosexuality in Renaissance England* (London: GMP).

Bullough, V. (1976) 'Sex in History: A Virgin Field', *Sex, Society and History* (New York: Science History Publications).

Cameron, D. and Frazer, E. (1987) *The Lust to Kill* (Cambridge: Polity).

Caplan, P. (1987) *The Cultural Construction of Sexuality* (London: Tavistock).

Coveney, L. *et al.* (1984) *The Sexuality Papers* (London: Hutchinson).

Coward, R. (1983) *Patriarchal Precedents* (London: Routledge & Kegan Paul).

Coward, R. (1984) *Female Desire* (London: Paladin).

Davidoff, L. (1983) 'Class and Gender in Victorian England', in Newton *et al.* (1983).

Davidoff, L. and Hall, C. (1987) *Family Fortunes* (London: Hutchinson).

Dworkin, A. (1987) *Intercourse* (London: Arrow).

Foucault, M. (1979) *History of Sexuality: Vol 1, An Introduction* (London: Allen Lane).

Foucault, M. (1987) *History of Sexuality: Vol 2. The Use of Pleasure* (London: Viking).

Foucault, M. (1988) *History of Sexuality: Vol 3, Care of the Self* (London: Viking).

Franklin, S. and Stacey, J. (1988) 'Dyketactics in Difficult Times. A Review of the "Homosexuality, Which Homosexuality?" Conference', *Feminist Review*, No. 29, Summer.

Freedman, E. B. *et al.* (1985) *The Lesbian Issue* (University of Chicago Press).

Gagnon, J. and Simon, W. (1974) *Sexual Conduct* (London: Hutchinson).

Gallagher, C. and Laqueur, T. (eds) (1987) *The Making of the Modern Body* (University of California Press).

Gay, P. (1984) *The Bourgeois Experience: Vol 1. Education of the Senses* (Oxford University Press).

Gay, P. (1986) *The Bourgeois Experience: Vol 2. The Tender Passion* (Oxford University Press).

Howells, K. (ed.) (1984) *Sexual Diversity* (Oxford: Basil Blackwell).

HWH (1987) Papers of the 'History, Which History?' conference, Free University of Amsterdam, December.

Katz, J. (1976) *Gay American History* (New York: Thomas Crowell).

Laqueur, T. (1987) 'Orgasm, Generation, and the Politics of Reproductive Biology', in Gallagher and Laqueur (1987).

London Feminist History Group (1983) *The Sexual Dynamics of History* (London: Pluto).

McIntosh, M. (1968) 'The Homosexual Role', in Plummer (1981).

Malinowski, B. (1963) *Sex, Culture and Myth* (London: Hart-Davis).

Marcus, S. (1987) *The Other Victorians* (London: Weidenfeld & Nicholson).

Mort, F. (1987) *Dangerous Sexualities* (London: Routledge & Kegan Paul).

Newton, J. L. *et al.* (1983) *Sex and Class in Women's History* (London: Routledge & Kegan Paul).

Padgug, R. A. (1979) 'Sexual Matters', *Radical History Review*, No. 20, Spring/Summer.

Petchesky, R. P. (1986) *Abortion and Women's Choice* (London: Verso).

Plummer, K. (1975) *Sexual Stigma* (London: Routledge & Kegan Paul).

Plummer, K. (1981) *The Making of the Modern Homosexual*, (London: Hutchinson).

Plummer, K. (1984) 'Sexual Diversity', in Howells (ed.) (1984).

Rich, A. (1984) 'Compulsory Heterosexuality and Lesbian Experience', in Snitow *et al.* (1984).

Rubin, G. (1984) 'Thinking Sex' in Vance (ed.) (1984).

Smith-Rosenberg, C. (1975) 'The Female World of Love and Ritual', in Smith-Rosenberg (1986).

Smith-Rosenberg, C. (1986) *Disorderly Conduct* (Oxford University Press).

Snitow, A. *et al.* (1984) *Desire. The Politics of Sexuality* (London: Virago).

Stone, L. (1977) *The Family, Sex and Marriage* (London: Weidenfeld & Nicolson).

Taylor, B. (1983) *Eve and the New Jerusalem* (London: Virago).

Theweleit, K. (1987, 1990) *Male Fantasies*, Vols. 1 and 2 (Cambridge: Polity).

Thompson, E. P. (1968) *The Making of the English Working Class*, (Harmondsworth: Penguin).

Vance, C. (ed.) (1984) *Pleasure and Danger* (London: Routledge & Kegan Paul).

Vance, C. (1987) 'Social Construction Theory', in HWH (1987).

Walkowitz, J. (1980) *Prostitution and Victorian Society* (Oxford University Press).

Walvin, J. (1987) *Victorian Values* (London: André Deutsch).

Weeks, J. (1977) *Coming Out*, (London: Quartet).

Weeks, J. (1985) *Sexuality and its Discontents* (London: Routledge & Kegan Paul).

Weeks, J. (1986) *Sexuality* (London: Tavistock).

Weeks, J. (1989) *Sex, Politics and Society* (2nd edn) (London: Routledge & Kegan Paul).

3 State Organisations and Men's Sexuality in the Public Domain 1870–1920[1]

Jeff Hearn

THE PRESENT IN THE PAST

In this chapter I wish to draw together some of the changing historical connections between the modern development of state organisations, that is, organisations that are part of the state, and of men's sexuality in the public domain. Discussion will focus on events from 1870 to 1920, a period of immense social change, yet paradoxically that which forms the bedrock of contemporary experience.

The most obvious way in which men's sexuality and state organisations connect with each other is through state laws that explicitly deal with sexuality such as those on prostitution, sexually transmitted diseases, homosexuality, sexual slavery (Harrison and Mort, 1980), and incest and other sexual offences. Political activity and debates in and around the state on these issues, particularly concern with syphilis and gonorrhoea, was intense in the latter half of the nineteenth century. The Contagious Diseases Acts were passed in 1864, 1866 and 1869, and were followed in the 1870s and early 1880s by a period of campaigning against them. Contemporary examples of state intervention in men's sexuality include Clause 28 of the Local Government Act 1988, prohibiting the use of public funds to 'promote homosexuality', and the variety of state action around the AIDS crisis.

Less obvious connections between state organisations and men's sexuality have also developed through changes in the organisational form and structures of the state – in the Civil Service, local government, the Post Office, the police, the public utilities, education, and so on. Changes of this sort can be seen as part of very broad shifts in the social and economic structure of society, from a heavy manufacturing and industrial base to a growing services or tertiary sector, that have taken place since the late nineteenth century. In this view, the growth of the state can be understood as part of what is sometimes called the socialisation of reproduction. State organisations not only increased in size but also became more bureaucratised and more modern in their methods. A fundamental feature of this growth of the state has been the rise in the employment of men in central and local government. For example, employment in government increased from 564 000 in 1891 to nearly 2 million in 1921, of whom the vast majority were men. Even though the numbers of women were relatively small, towards the end of the period there were some rapid increases. In 1914 there were still only 65 000 women in the Civil Service, of whom nearly 90 per cent were in the Post Office non-clerical grades. By 1919 the number had risen to 170 000, spread throughout many departments. The increasing number of women in state organisations created novel situations, often sexual in meaning for the men there, such as whether they should work in the same or separate offices, and how social mingling in the offices should be conducted, albeit in the context of hierarchical divisions.

Similarly, the contemporary impact of the state on men's sexuality goes well beyond immediate laws on sexuality. Particularly since the oil crisis of 1973, the state has been subject to considerable restructuring, with relative and absolute cutbacks in welfare provision, expansion of the 'law and order' sector, and the increasing introduction of private sector managerial methods, and, sometimes, personnel in the state. All these changes have generic and sexual meanings, with reports of high levels of sexual harassment from surveys of women in local government, the sexist work culture of police forces, and the association of masculinism and management. Meanwhile, there have been modest gains in women's entry to middle and top management in the state, again raising novel situations for men, such as men's perception of heterosexual threat in what were formerly men's homosocial workgroups. State organisations were and are important sites of men's sexualities. In these and many other ways the state and private life are intimately related, and form a fundamental, yet neglected, aspect of politics and political change.

The rationale for looking to the past lies paradoxically in the present, and specifically in the need to understand and change men's sexuality, which has for so long been, and which remains, problematic. This chapter now goes on to look at the concept of patriarchy as a broad framework for understanding historical changes in men's sexuality.

MEN'S SEXUALITY, MODERN ORGANISATIONS AND PUBLIC PATRIARCHY

Debates about the nature and concept of patriarchy have led in recent years to either an abandonment of the concept, or have shifted to a concern with public (or social) patriarchy. The collective power of men, the metaphorical fathers, the collective fathers, the fathers of the public domain, and in particular the state, have been seen as more important than the aggregation of individual private fathers. Public patriarchy is centrally concerned with the power of the public domain, and men in the public domain. This in turn means that the understanding of public patriarchy involves an understanding of the major social forms of the public domain, that is the street (with its local variants, such as the crowd) and organisations.

Several further questions are raised by this line of thinking. For example, how is recent feminist theorising on the relationship of the public domain and the private domain, such as that of O'Brien (1981), who sees that division and relation are crucially determined in the patriarchal domination of biological reproduction, to be developed to the analysis of organisations (Hearn and Parkin, 1988)? How does the analysis of public patriarchy relate to or conflict with more orthodox marxist analysis? What are the implications of the historical development of public patriarchy for the development of (modern) masculinities? Furthermore, if sexuality is at the heart of patriarchy, men's domination and gender relations themselves (MacKinnon, 1982), how does the development of public patriarchy reinforce, alter, elaborate or challenge that centrality? And, what is the significance of any such development or change for the impact of organisations in construction of men's power, and the relationship of masculinity and sexuality?

The development of public patriarchy can be analysed in a number of ways through a focus on the family, the growth of the state, the family–state relationship, changing relations of the public and private domains, as well as changes in the form of public domain economic relations – all of which are no doubt important and relevant. In recent years several scholars have focused on the economic determinants of changes in masculinity, in the move from factory capitalism to monopoly capitalism at the turn of the century, and specifically some of the connections between capitalist organisations and men's sexuality at that time. It is important to emphasise that such 'economic changes' are not necessarily the most important: they are simply one element in the development of public patriarchy currently receiving considerable attention.

These accounts are mainly from the United States, and focus primarily on white men, and typically middle-class white men. They also very significantly typically focus on the economic development of the nation, with little regard to imperialist and other international relations. Pleck and Pleck (1980), for example, distinguish in *The American Man* between 'the commercial period' of 1820–60, in which industrial capitalism expanded, and the beginnings of separate spheres for women and men occurred, albeit within a system of patriarchal domination, to 'the strenuous life period' of 1861–1919. This saw a reassertion of the values of muscular Christianity 'pioneering' in theory rather than practice in sport, boy scout and other similar movements, and indeed, in contrast, the labelling of some men as effeminate. This has some parallels with Dubbert's (1979) analysis in *A Man's Place*, which refers to the 'Rise of Sport in 1880–1920' and discusses the 1890s in terms of the 'Bull Moose Mentality'. Kimmel (1987) has extended these analyses in terms of the impact of women and women's demands in producing a crisis of masculinity at specific historical periods of rapid economic and political change, namely Restoration England 1688–1714 and turn of the century United States 1880–1914. In the latter period men's responses to women included anti-feminist backlash, pro-male backlash and pro-feminist men. Such changes are seen by some as part of the change from precapitalist to capitalist patriarchy. A typical recent statement is that by Brod (1987, p. 13):

A transfer of power from the hands of the individual patriarchs to the institutions of capitalist patriarchy is an essential component of this shift. This transfer is part of the widening

depersonalisation and bureaucratisation of human relationships in the development of capitalism, which individuals
experience in and as various forms of alienation. Capitalism
increasingly creates a gap between institutional and personal
power. (citing Brown, 1981)

Writing on the economic class basis of the (ideology of the)
current 'men's movement' in the United States, Brod (1983)
suggests that this 'new' form of masculinity is actually a sub-
culture that fits into a certain class niche in American society.
Changes of men and masculinity arise from within not outside the
system. First, there is 'the pattern of twentieth century industrialisation in which more and more of everyone's personal life is
directly dominated by economic and political forces beyond their
personal control'. Second, there is the transformation of the
economic system from manufacturing to services, in the form of
information processing, public and private sector services, and so
on. Third, there is the transition from the work ethic to consumer
ethic, from production to consumption. All these changes are
particularly important for the middle classes and middle-class
men. Brod continues: 'the values espoused by the "new male" –
cooperation, self-expression, sensitivity etc – fit smoothly [sic]
into this new economic reality.'

These derive from several circumstances: the fact that the office
or service worker sells their (or in this context, his) self, as in the
public relations component of the job; the shift to the consumer
ethic has involved more energy being put into self-gratification
through leisure, loosening the rigidities of traditional masculinities, including moves to 'sexual liberation'; and self-definition
and identity more through consumer purchase rather than work
alone. According to Brod, these economic and social changes
produce new forms of masculinity. They can also be seen as the
basis of new forms of men's sexuality. For example, the selling of
the self may involve the selling of congeniality, but it may also
involve the selling of emotions, sexuality, and their interrelations.
Most important, the selling of the self means that even aspects of
the self that are not sold in specific forms of work, perhaps
including sexuality, may be mediated by that selling. These
current, modern developments of masculinity, and thereby men's
sexuality, have if not their origins, then at least their clearest early
development, in the 1870–1920 period.

A different kind of reference to capitalism is developed by Weeks (1977a). He begins his history of homosexual politics, *Coming Out*, with the statement: 'the late nineteenth century sees a deepening hostility towards homosexuality, alongside the emergence of new definitions of homosexuality and homosexual. I believe these developments can only be properly understood as part of the restructuring of the family and sexual relations consequent upon the triumph of colonisation and industrial capitalism.' He then goes on to examine the complexities of relevant medical, psychiatric, sexological, and political definitions and movements, and their interplay (see Mort, 1987).

A more precise statement is provided by D'Emilio:

> By the second half of the nineteenth century, [the] situation was noticeably changing as the capitalist system of free labor took hold. Only when individuals began to make their living through wage labor, instead of as parts of an interdependent family unit, was it possible for homosexual desire to coalesce into a personal identity – an identity based on the ability to remain outside the heterosexual family and to construct a personal life based on attraction to one's own sex. By the end of the century, a class of men and women existed who recognised their erotic interest in their own sex, saw it as a trait that set them apart from the majority, and sought others like themselves. These early gay lives came from a wide social spectrum. (D'Emilio, 1984, p. 144)

These types of accounts share a concern with the effects of economic change upon masculinities. They do, however, show marked differences. Brod is the most deterministic in causally connecting economic class change and the production of the 'self' of men. Kimmel is more eclectic in linking economic and other societal changes with demands from women for change, and then reactions from men to such demands. In this way he develops an interactionist account, in which the agency of (groups of) men figures strongly. D'Emilio's approach is structurally based yet encompasses the structural creation of space(s), spatial, social and metaphorical, within which different masculinities and sexualities of men may be enacted and developed.

Commenting on the difficulties of constructing histories of masculinities, Carrigan, Connell and Lee (1985, p. 589) note 'the technical superiority of the gay historians over the histories of masculinity and the "male role", to be found in the work of writers like Hoch, Dubbert, Stearns, and Pleck and Pleck'. They continue: 'conceptually, gay history moves decisively away from the conception . . . that history of masculinity is the story of modulation, through times, of the expressions of a more or less fixed entity.' Connell (1985, p. 263) has elsewhere noted the sociological problems of sex role approaches to gender, and in particular their inadequacy for the analysis of social change, except through externalised or internalised causes over the 'roled' (hypostatised) individual.

There are thus several problems with some of these 'economic' historical explanations of masculinities. There are methodological problems of relative economic determinism; the overarching causal emphasis on capitalism as the motor of change in masculinity; and the related question of the place of men's agency. There is a more general danger of attributing (simple) causes to (simple) effects. Economic explanations may also neglect more autonomous change in social relations, other than capitalist ones – of sexuality, fertility and procreation, nurture and violence, as in state development. For example, the shift from private patriarchy to public patriarchy, which certainly became intensified at the end of the last century, can be characterised by contradictory processes of desexualisation, whereby sexuality is excluded from formal organisations (Burrell, 1984) with the increasing separation of the private domain and the public domain; and increasing resexualisation, of a least certain sectors of organisational life (Hearn and Parkin, 1987, p. 152). This latter process is widespread, not least in the growth of the sex industry, the spread of sexual imagery in advertising and promotion, and the suffusion of the post-modern scene with 'panic sex' (Kroker and Cook, 1988).

Overly deterministic accounts of the historical development of masculinities may also shift attention away from qualitative change in organisations and organisational development, and its relation to qualitative change in men and men's experiences. Qualitative change in this context refers to the way in which men's experience and sexuality are subject to changes in the form of organisational development, not just the amount or extension of organisational growth. Qualitative change is a matter of process, not just quantity. Relevant developments of *both* organisations and men's sexuality thus included the growth of the film[2] and mass media organisations, and the accompanying media stars, mass popular pornography, the use of sexuality in advertising, public relations and 'girlie calendars'; the advent of typing, office technology and the female secretary, and her particular significance in male fantasy; as well as the expansion of sexology, the academic, medical and clinical study of sex, the sex hygienist movement and more popular sex manuals; the popularisation of sex scandals; the recognition of sexual harassment as a workplace issue; the rise of censorship and a vast range of public 'moral panics' and 'outrages'. The increasing power of all these public domain processes, in technology, imagery, law, and so on, upon the person necessarily contribute to modern forms of men's sexuality. This is specifically in the public domain and in organisations, and more subtly in men's psyche. The bombardment of the individual by the sexualisation of everything, and especially of (every) woman (MacKinnon, 1979; Haug, 1987) has become one element in their making of 'modern masculinities'.

Together all these changes form part of a broader change from private patriarchy to public patriarchy. Some indications of the impact of such changes on masculinity and men's sexuality are given in the studies cited – but there remains the danger of seeing even those organisational changes as external to men, rather than (re)produced by men. What I am talking of here is the construction of the *modern* experience for men, and the developing relationship of modernism, masculinities and men's sexuality. Consciousness of that sense of modern masculinity and men's sexuality, the ability to look at the male self and other men, and at women, at a distance, is largely derived from events at the turn of the century, including the increasing normalisation of an interplay of state organisations and sexuality.

The remainder of this chapter is directed towards the development of the state and state organisations, and their relationship to masculinities and men's sexuality. The period 1870–1920 was not only a time of major extension of state intervention in the family, child welfare, homosexuality and prostitution, it was also a time of major qualitative change in state organisations, and relations between state organisations and men's sexuality.

SEXUALITY AND STATE THEORY

Analyses of the relationship of the state and sexuality have been developed, or not developed, largely within the frameworks of political theory, with its own distinct ideologies. Accordingly state theory has been dominated by two major malestream traditions – liberal and marxist (Burstyn, 1983). In the first, the state is a social accumulation of powers, rights, duties and obligations from the previously unfettered individual of civil society – the personal freedom of the individual is lost to the contract of collective benefit; in the second, the state is a social structural form which contributes, sometimes determinedly, to the social constitution of classes, including individuals within them – collective freedom is gained or lost according to the particular domination of class relations within and indeed outside the state. In neither of these traditions does sexuality usually figure as a central element in either individual or collective freedoms or constitutions. Having said that, there is no obvious reason why the liberal tradition could not be elaborated in relation to sexuality; there are clear reasons around the pre-eminence of economic class why marxist theory of the state has difficulty with any gender-related facet, including sexuality, as a central element in theorising.

In contrast feminist scholarship on the state often makes questions of sexuality, and indeed violence, central, and this has been seen in specific disciplinary areas like feminist criminology and feminist jurisprudence and more generally in feminist political theory. Hartmann's (1979) work on marxism and feminism, though not exclusively on the state, has, by theorising patriarchy in terms of men's, restrictions on women's access to economically productive resources and on women's sexuality, been important in agenda-setting. Burstyn (1983), in what is one of the few marxist feminist direct assaults on the state as a system of male dominance, argues that 'women's labour and sexuality are the two most important things to control for any society of male dominance' (p. 64). For her, men's control of women's sexuality is a persuasive feature of the state, and 'capitalist states, like all other states, have functioned, in the final analysis, to preserve and in new ways extend masculine control' (p. 65), so that as much emphasis needs to be given to gender and class as economic class in their analysis.

MacKinnon (1982; 1983), writing from the perspective of feminist jurisprudence, has set out elements of a radical feminist analysis of sexuality, the state and society. For her, sexuality is fundamental, comparable to the status of work in marxist analysis. Thus sexuality is not just something to be controlled, as in Burstyn's theorising, but is 'that social process which creates, organizes, and directs desire, creating social beings we know as women and men, as their relations create society' (1982, p. 516). From this, what is called the state and state law follows, as structured areas of male dominance. She proposes that 'the state is male in the feminist sense'; 'the way the male point of view frames an experience is the way it is framed by state policy'; 'formally, the state is male in that objectivity is its norm' (1983, p. 644). And yet that state may be used politically on occasions to challenge dominant sexual practices such as sexual harassment, through the pursuit of feminist jurisprudence. If MacKinnon is correct in her approach, and I think she substantially is, we would expect to find a series of significant changes in the relationship of sexuality and the state in the move to public patriarchy.

STATE ORGANISATIONS AND MEN'S SEXUALITY

So what are the major ways in which the development of state organisations connects with men's sexuality in Britain during the period 1870–1920? I deliberately say 'connects with' rather than 'causally determines' as one of the lessons of the much recent feminist and other critical gender scholarship emphasises the multi-faceted and complex nature of social change in that period (eg Mort, 1985; also see Bland, McCabe and Mort, 1978). Indeed much of what follows concerns the mutual occurrence and mutal reinforcement of social phenomena at specific historical conjunctures. Inevitably state organisations and men's sexuality were subject to common historical forces, including enduring patriarchalism, developing feminism and widespread concern about the 'population problem'.

Feminism was clearly a major force in the transformation of the state at the end of the last century, especially from the 1880s (Durham, 1985). While many feminists from middle-class and upper-class backgrounds saw the state 'as an instrument for enacting their own class specific demands . . . many others rapidly became aware that the state itself was patriarchal' (Mort, 1985, p. 219). Christabel Pankhurst, a precursor of Catherine MacKinnon, considered 'the state was composed of men who not only denied women the vote but also tacitly condoned male immorality and sexual violence' (Mort, 1985). Pankhurst had a similarly clear view of men's sexuality as the basis of societal problems: 'What a man . . . really means is that women are created primarily for sex gratification of men and secondly for the bearing of children if he happens to want them' (Pankhurst, 1913, pp. 19–20, cited in Bland, 1986, p. 138).

Recognition of the 'population problem' was prompted by a combination of interests in the purity lobby, from medics and eugenicists, from the demands of war and militarisation, and from fears of international competition and insufficient 'national efficiency', particularly in comparison with Germany, Japan and the United States (Bland, 1982). Particular concerns at the turn of the century included the health of children, the 'fitness' of mothers, the physical state of men as workers and soldiers (in the Boer War and the First World War) and the appropriate measures for the mentally deficient and feeble minded (Simmons, 1978; Barker, 1983). Although these were not solely sexual questions, they were focused on the 'corrrect' use of the healthy body including sexual activities, albeit in ways different for men and women. Sexuality and health were both often seen within a 'racial' evolutionary framework, one consequence of which was the advocacy of sterilisation for the weak by eugenicists, such as Karl Pearson, and male avoidance of dissipatory sexualities. Stacey (1988, p. 73) sums up some of these ideas as follows:

> Men were 'driven' by strong sexual urges. They required an outlet for these. Hence the necessity of the occupation of prostitution; it went along with monogamy and was needed to sustain it . . . masturbation and night emissions were not only morally wrong, they were also medically pathological. Treatises from medical men such as Acton (1862) made this plain . . . Men were expected to exercise strong self-control over these urges . . . However, the temptations which they experienced were enormous and could be resisted only with the help of women. Thus it was the women's fault if men were overcome, and the particular sin of the prostitute was to tempt them.

Lewis (1984, p. 127) succinctly states: 'male virility could not be denied and within evolutionary thought was believed to be crucial to the progress of race and nation.'

These themes were influential in the development of the state and state organisations, in some rather contradictory ways. First, the period 1870–1920 was one of major, almost massive change in the interrelationship of state organisations and men's sexuality. Municipal and central government, especially *qua* administration, increasingly became centres of power at the expense of voluntary and philanthropic organisations, as in the Criminal Law Amendment Act 1885. Here a spurious compromise was offered between state organisations and purity groups, but in the event the resources and machinery for an equal partnership were not forthcoming and the state made further extensions in the control of 'vice'. Corporatism of the state was also a means to the modernist paradox of increased awareness of the self and yet overwhelming of the individual, including the sexual selves of men as state members, and as state clients: these transformations of state organisations and society were noticeably accelerated in the late nineteenth century liberal municipalism in the Liberal reforms of 1906–11, the beginnings of a welfare state, and in the centralisations/rationalisations of the First World War and post-war reconstruction bringing further growth of the Civil Service. Interestingly the 'population problem', with its racial–sexual subtext, was instrumental in moves to a more corporate governmental machinery, as in the interdepartmental Committees on Physical Deterioration (1903) and the Medical Inspection and Feeding of Children Attending Public Elementary Schools (1905).

Second, there is a profound sense in which change was faltering, gradual, diffuse and irregular. This is partly a reflection of the general level of development of state organisations at that time. Indeed the 'state' consisted of rather unfamiliar and locally variable collections of councils, boards, committees, royal commissions, legal apparatus, inspectorates and visitors, as well as a vigorous interplay of political actors, including lawyers, property owners, medics, purity lobbyists, feminists. Contrary to some current popular beliefs, the quango was a familiar expression of 'Victorian values'. This unevenness applied all the more so in the politics of morality and sexuality.

Each part of the state machinery had its own particular generic and sexual structure. For example, the royal commission, the prime unit of 'neutral' deliberation, was typically intensely male dominated. Edward VII, in 1909, was specifically opposed to female membership of the Royal Commission on Divorce and Matrimonial Causes (which reported in 1912) because 'the nature of the subject is one which cannot be discussed openly, and in all its aspects, in any delicacy, or even decency, before ladies' (quoted in Harrison, 1982, p. 284). In the event, just two women became members, and even its limited recommendations for new grounds for divorce were not enacted until 1937. Meanwhile, another part of the state machinery, the police, was involved, increasingly from 1907, in surveillance and control of suffragettes, including at times their violent control. Brian Harrison (1982, p. 63) comments that 'police and anti-suffragist manhandling made window-breaking seem attractive as a way of ensuring rapid arrest and consequent relative security'. Other distinctive parts of the state included the military and the law.

Under the Contagious Diseases Acts, a combination of men, as police, medics and justices, was able to enforce three months' detention in certain hospitals on women considered by them to be prostitutes in certain naval ports and garrison towns. Although these Acts may appear to be specifically about women and sexual procurement, they are, of course, not very implicitly about men's sexuality rather than women's sexuality – it is just that it was not seen as appropriate to control men, for example, by curfew, in order to control their sexuality, perhaps thought uncontrollable. Thus the Contagious Diseases Acts in fact enabled speech to be conducted on the unspeakable – men's sexuality. They are also about men's sexuality in a different way, as a documentary statement on the sexuality of a 'different' group of men, the enacters and implementers of the Acts as state organisational agents.

Arguments against state intervention in this arena came from a variety of quarters. Josephine Butler, the purity feminist, campaigned on the basis of the rewards of moral voluntarism, and the deleterious results of individuals not receiving the effects of their own behaviour through state protection. George Russell suggested in the House of Commons debate on prostitution (20 April 1883) that the Contagious Diseases Acts 'all but close the paths of regeneration against these women . . . we stamp them with the signet of the state, which marks them as the common prey of animal desire (presumably of certain men)' (quoted in Harrison, 1982, p. 399). The Acts were suspended in 1883 and repealed in 1886, superficially suggesting a withdrawal of state intervention in sexual matters. However, the previous year, the Criminal Law Amendment Act 1885 had raised the age of consent from 13 to 16, increased penalties for brothel keepers and, with the Labouchère Amendment, outlawed male homosexuality, institutionalising a heterosexual hegemony that still persists. In addition to legislation on divorce, separation and maintenance had been extended. From 1878 women were allowed to use cruelty as grounds for divorce, so recognising, albeit in a very limited way, a distinction between sexuality and violence. Even so, while by the end of the century married women had property rights formally equal to those of the husband, in practice legislation did little to undermine men's direct authority over their wives. Brophy and Smart (1982, p. 210) summarise the position as follows:

> She had no right to leave her husband without his permission and if she did he could physically restrain her. She had no right to maintenance if she could not prove her husband had committed a matrimonial offence . . . he could divorce her on a single act of adultery whilst she had to establish adultery combined with another matrimonial offence . . . Any challenge by a wife to his authority, or to the principle of sexual monogamy resulted in the courts refusing to grant her maintenance. The magistrates courts . . . treated adultery as an absolute bar to maintenance for wives. (See also Harrison and Mort, 1980.)

While state law may be an obvious focus of attention, it also has to be treated with some caution as a determining factor. According to Mort (1985, p. 210) the state was rarely the initiator in the move to criminalise sexual 'immoralities'. Furthermore, with regard to sexuality, there was no major expansion in direct state functions, state functionaries or incorporation of intellectuals into the state in this period, so that law was often the outcome of protracted political relations, particularly between feminists, purity groups and others, to which state agents reacted cautiously and usually patriarchally (pp. 210, 222).

In addition to state legal intervention directly attending to men's sexuality, there was a recurrent moral theme in other reports and parliamentary Acts (Bland, McCabe and Mort, 1978, pp. 106–7). Moreover it is not possible to abstract sexuality from the social construction of gender relations. Laws, policies and state policies in such areas as child-care, health and education are all relevant to the construction of men's sexuality.

Thus the extension of state operations into education, and subsequently into infant care, are particularly relevant in the constructions of gender and sexuality. Following the 1870 (Forster) Education Act introducing permissive board schooling up to ten years, compulsory attendance was enacted in 1876, school-leaving age was extended to eleven in 1893 and to twelve in 1899, and in 1902 the (Balfour) Education Act moved the state into secondary education, and its standardisation through local authorities. Bearing in mind that these innovations occurred before the advent of women's suffrage, it seems likely that the education of girls is more readily understandable as a means of reproducing gender divisions, including motherhood and female office labour, than in promoting female citizenship (Lewis, 1986; Brehony, 1985); even though the imitation of boys' education and single sex schooling for girls may also contradictorily challenge male hegemony.

Rather similarly from the 1890s onwards there was strong reinforcement of the division between the male breadwinner and female child-carer, especially for families headed by skilled workers. The Custody of Children Act 1891 introduced the concept of 'unfit parenthood', usually in effect meaning motherhood; the Notification of Births Act 1907 facilitated early visiting by health visitors; the infant welfare movement encouraged traditional notions of domesticity by municipal and voluntary clinics; national insurance, unemployment benefit and pension reforms contributed to the control of types of work open to women and limited women's access to cash benefits; and the First World War produced a systematic approach to childbirth and child welfare, and the inculcation of middle-class methods of child-rearing to the working classes, culminating in the Maternity and Child Welfare Act 1918, permitting local authorities to provide salaried midwives, health visitors, infant welfare centres, day nurseries and food supplements for needy infants and mothers (Lewis, 1980; Rowan, 1985; Lewis, 1986; Brookes, 1986). While confirming women's dependent status, these innovations also raised the status of motherhood against fatherhood and so contributed to the politicisation of (men's) sexuality.

Much of the discussion so far has focused on the extension of the state into sexual and related areas; these changes were not just a matter of increased legal controls upon men's sexuality, they were also significant in the qualitative construction of men's sexuality, as through the changing relations of the public and private domains.

Personal, private and sexual lives were more exposed to increasing numbers of state organisational agents acting upon men,
especially as fathers. These agents included the police, public
health and sanitary inspectors, child health and child cruelty
officers, health visitors, district nurses, midwives, school board
men and social workers, each occupation characteristically
clearly gendered. Some of these, such as the 'cruelty men' and the
'board men', were themselves typically men who in turn were to
participate in an effective reduction of the power of individual
fathers, especially among the working classes, as well as having
their own private and sexual lives (Ferguson, 1989; also see
Hearn, 1987, p. 95). Men thus did become dependent clients or
'visitees' in some cases, although often the process of change was
less direct, reinforcing established gender roles, with the mother
assumed to be the prime agent of the private domain, and the
father as a relative absentee. Men and indeed some women,
particularly as 'paramedics', acted as purveyors of state, para-
state and voluntary organisations, to inhibit the personal and
sexual autonomy of men as fathers; with this reduction of paternal
authority, there developed elsewhere in the public domain a
greater use and display of sexuality in some, especially capitalist
organisations.

The growth of state proto-bureaucracies brought a number of
changes for men's sexuality – the increased formalisation of
ranking in hierarchies, the mixture of men's desexualisation and
sexual authority, the creation of somewhat more egalitarian and
companionate marriages between state workers, such as teachers
(Copelman, 1986), the surveillance by men of women in lower
tiers, as secretaries, telephonists, telegraphists, and so on. In some
ways these conditions resembled the sexual dynamics of capitalist
organisations: men were subject to paradoxes of control, exemplified in F. W. Taylor's prescription for the control of others, time
and motion study, the 'management of men', and yet he himself
suffered recurrent 'nervousness' and difficulties of self-control
(Filene, 1986, p. 74). Bureaucratic organisational/sexual form
was also conducive to the establishment of stricter boundaries
to the state. This applied in the more precise stipulation of
'legitimate' and 'illegitimate' sexual practices of male, heterosexual and homosexual, behaviour (Weeks, 1977b, p. 151);
clearer separations between men within and men outside the
state, as boys, criminals and clients; and the increasing classifica-

tion of sexual diseases and states in psychiatric and related discourses.

Women entered the Civil Service in 1869 with the takeover of the Electric and International Telegraph Company by the Post Office formed in 1861 and rapid expansion of women Post Office clerks followed from 1871 (Walby, 1986, p. 145).

In 1872 the Post Office experimented in employing male and female staff *and putting them in the same room.* 'It was considered to be a hazardous experiment' wrote a senior official at the time, 'but we have never had reason to regret having tried it . . . it raises the tone of the male staff by confining them during many hours of the day to a decency of conversation and demeanour which is not always to be found where men alone are employed.' (italics in original) (Delgado, 1979, p. 39) (cf. Cockburn, 1983, p. 134)

This 'civil' approach was in contrast to practices elsewhere where workers were segregated by gender yet obliged to use the same lavatories. In 1889 a 'progressive' government department employing two women put them in an upper floor room and had a separate women's lavatory installed so they would be completely free 'from any danger or interference'. Other strategies in the Civil Service included locking a number of women in a room and serving meals to them through a hatch in the wall (Delgado, 1979, p. 39).

From 1870 recruitment to the Civil Service was moved towards so-called 'open competitive examinations', with the system more or less established in its entirety by 1890. However, the MacDonnell Commissioners, reporting in 1912–13, still considered that women should not be eligible for such competitions; that where women were employed, they should be segregated from men; and that the marriage bar, whereby women were required to resign on marriage, should be retained (Cohen, 1965). The First World War and the Sex Disqualification (Removal) Act 1919 changed this to an extent, though not conclusively (Walby, 1986, p. 157).

The place of women clerks and other workers in state organisations was certainly contested, in the eyes and practices of men (Walby, 1986, pp. 144–55), with women sometimes seen as sexually vulnerable (Anderson, 1976, p. 39), at others as sources of sexualisation.[3] These conditions and contradictions have provided materials for the development of men's sexuality, itself modern and fragmented (cf. Lunn, 1985, pp. 34–7). Not only may men portray women as asexual (virgin?)/sexual (whore?), but men's own sexuality may be founded on both the inclusion of women in heterosexual domination and the exclusion of women from men's homosocial social groups and homosexual subtexts (Wood, 1987).

CONCLUDING REMARKS

While a major theme in this discussion has been the increasing control of state organisations over men's sexuality, it must not be forgotten that state organisations were (and are?) not asexual or agendered: they were peopled largely by men, controlled by men and were the sites of various sexualities of men. State organisations were and are both patriarchal and patriarchally sexual. Superficially, capitalist organisations in this period might be seen as sexualising and state organisations as restraining, but this is altogether too simple a picture.

Men in the state appear to have acted, as men apart, to control the 'uncontrollability' of other men's sexuality, yet they themselves worked in, produced and reproduced their own sexual regimes in state organisations, and indeed often resisted legal interventions on men outside (Mort, 1985), perhaps fearful for themselves. Furthermore, and more subtly, state men contributed to that peculiar relation of power and transgression, whereby state control has reinforced modern sexualisation, exemplified in the interplay of pornography and censorship – the sexual as the Other. Film censorship was begun in 1912, and firmly established by the end of the First World War. In public patriarchy generally, and in and around state organisations in particular, these contradictions of supposedly desexualised state organisational power and supposedly sexualised individual men's transgression are at their most intense and profound – in men's experience. More specifically men's treatment of women clerks, secretaries and factory workers simultaneously shows desexualisation and sexualisation.

All these contradictions contribute to and are part of a broader change around the turn of the century in men's modern situation and sexuality. At the very least this involves a 'double-take' on reality, including masculinity (of self and others) and men's (our) sexuality, not just by intellectuals but by the mass of men. There is a 'public man' available for all to know and see, and a technology to show 'it'. The telegraph, the typewriter, and indeed the cinema, not only brought new employment and new gendered roles for women (such as the female secretary) and men, but broadcast them as materials for men's sexuality far and wide. New occupational roles placed women in relatively static positions in relatively clean working environments under the control of men bosses. Images were now available from this 'captive' group of workers – a new form of modern slavery. Women office workers, secretaries, typists were and are women who are static and located in one place, to be seen, in early twentieth-century images of women constructed by men in films, photography and elsewhere: the pin-up; the sight of the mass ranks of the female typing pool (shared or watery?); the public dispersal of images of the singular secretary and the mass of secretaries; the expansion of the possibilities of fantasy about women by men. Men's hetero-sexuality was from now on about women unknown, and outside state organisations, in New York and Hollywood, as well as women known. The historical period 1870–1920 provided both the materials and the means for the mass, popular and near permanent portrayal by men of both pre-established archetypes and new images of women. These new forms of elements, together in various combinations, were usable in the production of masculinities.

In state and other organisations the agency of men, both organisational and sexual, ie men's sexuality/men's apparent organisational asexuality, was and is at work in the production of images of women for other men as a currency between men, and involving certain women in limited, specific, organisational ways. These images are produced by real material processes, including the degradation of women, yet once produced they are clearly not real bodies; they are speech: women become speech of/for men. 'Woman' portrayed is the speaking of the unspeakable, ie our/ men's sexuality, by men acting apparently 'asexually', organisa-tionally, for other men. This particular historical pinning-up of women is a huge diversion both from the production of these images by and between men and their currency between men as 'consumers'. This sexualisation of women is part of the homo-sexual subtext of modern organisations, dominated by men.

While men's control of sexuality may well be the central dynamic of patriarchy, the form this centrality takes has changed with the historical transition to public patriarchy. This shift involves not so much the loss of power of the individual patriarch as the creation through agency of novel organisational forms in the public domain in which women are used to speak that which we dare not say, our own sexuality – its hierarchic heterosexuality, homophobia and homosexual subtext. To change men's sexuality, including its heterosexisms, oppressions, violences, powers and arousals, is not just a matter of individual will; nor is it to be accomplished by 'sexual instruction'. To change men's sexuality requires change in and to organisations, for these have become a major force in the shape of our sexuality. This is an increasingly urgent matter in terms of current debates on AIDS and 'normal sex', Clause 28 and anti-'homosexual' politics, Page Three and current attempts to outlaw it, and the escalating interplay of increasing violence in pornography and increasing promotion of controls on television and other media.

NOTES

1. This chapter is a development of the Edinburgh Conference paper (Hearn, 1988). Related papers have also been given in the Sociology Departments of Birmingham Polytechnic (November 1987) and York University (January 1988). I am grateful to participants at these sessions, and to Helen Corr and Lynn Jamieson, for their critical and helpful comments.
2. Further details on the significance of early film for development of masculinities and male sexuality are given in the original Edinburgh Conference paper.
3. Comparison can be made between fears of women's sexuality in the First World War (Lewis, 1984, p. 185) and Second World War factories (Harrison, 1943; Hearn and Parkin, 1987, pp. 26–9).

REFERENCES

Anderson, G. L. (1976) *Victorian Clerks* (Manchester University Press).

Barker, D. (1983) 'How to Curb the Fertility of the Unfit: The Feeble-Minded in Edwardian Britain', *Oxford Review of Education*, Vol. 9, No. 3.

Bland, L. (1982) '"Guardians of the Race" or "Vampires Upon the Nation's Health"? Female Sexuality and its Regulation in Early Twentieth Century Britain', in E. Whitelegg *et al* (eds), *The Changing Experience of Women* (Milton Keynes: Open University Press).

Bland, L. (1986) 'Marriage Laid Bare. Middle Class Women and Marital Sex 1880–1914', in J. Lewis (ed.), *Labour and Love. Women's Experience of Home and Family 1850–1940* (Oxford: Basil Blackwell).

Bland, L., McCabe, T. and Mort, F. (1978) 'Sexuality and Reproduction: Three Official Instances', in M. Barrett, P. Corrigan, A. Kuhn, J. Wolff (eds), *Ideology and Cultural Production* (London: Croom Helm).

Brehony, K. (1985) 'Popular Control or Control by Experts? Schooling between 1880 and 1902', in M. Langan and B. Schwartz (eds), *Crises in the British State 1880–1930* (London: Hutchinson).

Brod, H. (1983) 'Work Clothes and Leisure Suits. The Class Basis and Bias of the Men's Movement', *M*. Vol. 11, Winter.

Brod, H. (1987) 'Introduction: Themes and Theses of Men's Studies', in H. Brod (ed.), *The Making of Masculinities. The New Men's Studies* (Boston: Allen & Unwin).

Brookes, B. (1986) 'Women and Reproduction 1880–1919', in J. Lewis (ed.), *Labour and Love. Women's Experience of Home and Family 1850–1940* (Oxford: Basil Blackwell).

Brophy, J. and Smart, C. (1982) 'From Disregard to Disrepute: The Position of Women in Family Law', in E. Whitelegg *et al.* (eds), *The Changing Experience of Women* (Milton Keynes: Open University Press).

Brown, C. (1981) 'Mothers, Fathers and Children: From Private to Public Patriarchy', in L. Sargent (ed.), *Women and Revolution* (Boston: South End).

Burrell, G. (1984) 'Sex and Organizational Analysis', *Organization Studies*, Vol. 5, No. 2.

Burstyn, V. (1983) 'Masculine Dominance and the State', in R. Miliband and J. Savile (eds), *The Socialist Register 1983* (London: Merlin).

Carrigan, T., Connell, R. W. and Lee, J. (1985) 'Toward a New Sociology of Masculinity', *Theory and Society*, Vol. 14, No. 5.

Cockburn, C. (1983) *Brothers. Male Dominance and Technological Change* (London: Pluto).

Cohen, E. (1965) *The Growth of the British Civil Service* (London: Cass).

Connell, R. W. (1985) 'Theorising Gender', *Sociology*, Vol. 19, No. 2.

Copelman, D. M. (1986) 'A New Comradeship between Men and Women: Family and Marriage and London's Women Teachers 1870–1914', in J. Lewis (ed.), *Labour and Love. Women's Experience of Home and Family 1850–1940* (Oxford: Basil Blackwell).

Delgado, A. (1979) *The Enormous File. A Social History of the Office* (London: John Murray).

D'Emilio, J. (1984) 'Capitalism and Gay Identity', in A. Snitow, C. Stansell, S. Thompson (eds), *Desire* (London: Virago).

Dubbert, J. (1979) *A Man's Place. Masculinity in Transition* (Englewood Cliffs, N J: Prentice-Hall).

Durham, M. (1985) 'Suffrage and After: Feminism in the Early Twentieth Century', in M. Langan and B. Schwartz (eds), *Crises in the British State 1880–1930* (London: Hutchinson).

Ferguson, H. (1989) 'Rethinking Child Protection Practices: A Case for History', in Violence Against Children Study Group, *Taking Child Abuse Seriously* (London: Unwin Hyman).

Filene, P. G. (1986) *Him/Her/Self. Sex Roles in Modern America* (2nd edn) (Baltimore: Johns Hopkins University Press).

Harrison, B. (1982) *The Peaceable Kingdom. Stability and Change in Modern Britain* (Oxford: Clarendon).

Harrison, R. and Mort, R. (1980) 'Patriarchal Aspects of Nineteenth-Century State Formation: Property Relations, Marriage and Divorce, and Sexuality', in P. Corrigan (ed.), *Capitalism, State Formation and Marxist Theory* (London: Quartet).

Harrison, T. (ed.) (1943) *War Factory: A Report* (London: Victor Gollancz).

Hartmann, H. (1979) 'The Unhappy Marriage of Marxism and Feminism: Towards a More Progressive Union', *Capital and Class*, No. 8.

Haug, F. (ed.) (1987) *Female Sexualization* (London: Verso) (1st publication 1983).

Hearn, J. (1987) *The Gender of Oppression. Men, Masculinity, and the Critique of Marxism* (Brighton: Wheatsheaf).

Hearn, J. (1988), 'Speaking the Unspeakable: The Historical Development of Organisations and Men's Sexuality in the Public Domain', British Sociological Association Conference, 'Sociology and History', University of Edinburgh (Mimeo. University of Bradford, March).

Hearn, J. and Parkin, P. W. (1987) *'Sex' at 'Work'. The Power and Paradox of Organisation Sexuality* (Brighton: Wheatsheaf).

Hearn, J. and Parkin, P. W. (1988) 'Women, Men and Leadership: A Critical Review of Assumptions, Practices and Change in the Industrialized Nations' in N. J. Adler and D. N. Izraeli (eds), *Women in Management Worldwide* (New York: M. E. Sharpe).

Kimmel, M. S. (1987) 'The Contemporary "Crisis" of Masculinity in Historical Perspective', in H. Brod (ed.), *The Making of Masculinities. The New Men's Studies* (Boston: Allen & Unwin).

Kroker, A. and Cook, D. (1988) *The Post-Modern Scene. Excremental Culture and Hyper-Aesthetics* (London: Macmillan).

Lewis, J. (1980) *The Politics of Motherhood: Child and Maternal Welfare in England 1900–1939* (London: Croom Helm).

Lewis, J. (1984) *Women in England 1870–1950. Sexual Divisions and Social Change* (Brighton: Wheatsheaf).

Lewis, J. (1986) 'The Working Class Wife and Mother and State Intervention', in J. Lewis (ed.), *Labour and Love. Women's Experience of Home and Family 1850–1940* (Oxford: Basil Blackwell).

Lunn, E. (1985) *Marxism and Modernism* (London: Verso).

MacKinnon, C. A. (1979) *The Sexual Harassment of Working Women* (New Haven: Yale University Press).

MacKinnon, C. A. (1982) 'Feminism, Marxism, Method and the State: An Agenda for Theory', *Signs*, Vol. 7, No. 3.

MacKinnon, C. A. (1983) 'Feminism, Marxism, Method and the State: Toward Feminist Jurisprudence', *Signs*, Vol. 8, No. 4.

Mort, F. (1985) 'Purity, Feminism and the State: Sexuality and Moral Politics 1880–1914', in M. Langan and B. Schwartz (eds), *Crises in the British State 1880–1930* (London: Hutchinson).

Mort, F. (1987) *Dangerous Sexualities. Medico-Moral Politics in England Since 1830* (London: Routledge & Kegan Paul).

O'Brien, M. (1981) *The Politics of Reproduction* (London: Routledge & Kegan Paul).

Pankhurst, C. (1913) *The Hidden Scourge and How to End it* (London: E. Pankhurst).

Pleck, J. and Pleck, E. (eds) (1980) *The American Man* (Englewood Cliffs, N J: Prentice-Hall).

Rowan, C. (1985) 'Child Welfare and the Working-Class Family' in M. Langan and B. Schwartz (eds), *Crises in the British State 1880–1930* (London: Hutchinson).

Simmons, H. G. (1978) 'Explaining Social Policy: The English Mental Deficiency Act of 1913', *Journal of Social History*, Vol. 11, No. 3.

Stacey, M. (1988) *The Sociology of Health and Healing* (London: Unwin Hyman).

Walby, S. (1986) *Patriarchy at Work* (Cambridge: Polity).

Weeks, J. (1977a) *Coming Out: Homosexual Politics in Britain from the Nineteenth Century to the Present* (London: Quartet).

Weeks, J. (1977b) 'Havelock Ellis and the Politics of Sex Reform', in S. Rowbotham and J. Weeks, *Socialism and the New Life* (London: Pluto).

Wood, R. (1987) 'Raging Bull: The Homosexual Subtext in Film', in M. Kaufman (ed.), *Beyond Patriarchy*, (Toronto: Oxford University Press).

Part II
The Development of the Welfare State Revisited

4 The Second World War and the Welfare State in Britain: Sociological Interpretations of Historical Development

Graham Fennell

INTRODUCTION

'Almost certainly the importance of evacuation has been exaggerated, but . . .' (Marwick, 1968, p. 268)
'Modern war has had – at least in Britain – a profound influence on social policy' (Titmuss, 1958, p. 86)
'The decisive event in the evolution of the welfare state was the Second World War' (Bruce, 1961, p. 326)

In sociology we are often studying contemporary events and situations, trying to make sense of and often demystify features of society to which we are physically, socially and chronologically close. By training, professional routine and disciplined 'thought experiment' we try to give ourselves sufficient *distance* to increase our objectivity. When we operate in less familiar historical time, the problem is simultaneously to get *closer*, while still preserving distance. In getting closer, we run the risk of being captured by the mythology. This is especially so of the Second World War, aspects of which have a romantic, almost legendary, appeal for the British.

I do not remember the Second World War but my life was affected by it. My parents lived in East London, their kinship network extending over East Ham, Ilford, Wanstead. My sister, born before the war, was evacuated with my grandmother to escape the Blitz. A second child was postponed because of it. By 1942 all seemed to be over bar the shouting. My parents moved to Orpington and I was born in 1943, just in time for the crump of the V1s and V2s falling on South London to rock my infant cradle: I spent much of my first two years (so I am told) asleep on my mother's breast in the air raid shelter.

The fact that my parents' lives were profoundly affected by the war both at the time and subsequently (my grandmother's nerves were too upset to live alone again, so she became a member of our household for the next twenty years) did not mean that they talked about it: quite the reverse. In the domestic context I would hardly have known it had happened. My mother recently commented: 'If you've lived through it, it's not something you ever want to remember or to talk about. If you'd heard babies crying after the raids, mewing like kittens in the ruins, you'd not want to talk about it'. This contrasts with authors quoted later, like Jonathan Miller or Peter Townsend, who saw no death or destruction at first hand and who describe the period as one which alternated between peaks of excitement and troughs of boredom.

Invited in the 1960s to teach about the Welfare State in Britain to mixed classes of history and sociology students, I discovered a tacit agreement that a crucial period in its history – the 1940s – existed in a sort of no man's land. It was slightly too modern for historians to feel comfortable about and slightly too ancient for sociologists to pretend it was contemporary. However, since historians seemed to regard the Welfare State as the natural habitat of sociologists; and since they regarded it as originating in the 1940s, they tended to cede the 1940s to sociology: we had entered the period of mass observation, which was more akin to sociology than to history. Moreover there was a sociological literature on the war and its relationship to social policy. This chapter addresses itself to this relationship.

THE WELFARE STATE: DEFINING IT, OR DEFINING ITS NATURE

Is a definition of the Welfare State needed? Most people seem to know what they mean by the Welfare State and an ostensive definition, simply pointing at it, saying, 'That's what it is', will suffice for them. A typical example is Fraser's: 'That synthesis of social security, universal health and welfare services, education, housing and full employment which came to be called the British welfare state' (1973, p. 1). While this may do for some historical purposes, it does not sufficiently identify the principles or elements involved either to permit international comparisons (welfare states in different places) or assess changes over time. We cannot, with an ostensive definition, answer questions of the type, 'Is there a Welfare State any more, or is there more or less welfare in the Welfare State?'

If Fraser's approach to defining the Welfare State has the limitation of over-specificity, Gough's more theoretical one suffers from the drawback of over-generality and also defines out of frame the question of similarities and differences between capitalist societies and others: 'The use of state power to modify the reproduction of labour power and to maintain the working population in capitalist societies' (1979, p. 44).

A more comprehensive and analytically detailed approach was provided by Briggs (1961, p. 222). Briggs identified two necessary conditions which had to be established in advance: some system of 'guaranteeing individuals and families a minimum income irrespective of the market value of their work or property' and some provision of, for instance, hospitals, old people's homes, child-care and welfare counselling to 'narrow the extent of insecurity by enabling individuals and families to meet certain social contingencies'. If these were met, the key feature of a welfare state would be to superimpose the goal of *optimum* standards in respect of at least some welfare services on a *universalistic* basis as opposed to the guarantee of certain minimum standards on a principle of selectivity.

Briggs captures many of the particular and generalisable features of the Welfare State but leaves out both the commitment to full employment which Fraser mentions and another feature which I would regard as crucial: the association between welfare rights, democracy and civil liberties in the British context. It is important to retain this element to understand some issues of relevance to us today: reformers of the 1940s would sympathise with debates about whether or not the powers of police, local government or trade unions should be extended or curbed, whether racism (or other 'isms' identified as deleterious) should be attacked or ignored and whether or not a society should have open access to a civil service, mass media and statistical apparatus which are protected from political manipulation.

The campaign in Britain for a welfare state was part of the struggle to create what Popper (1945) termed 'the open society' and emerged out of *antithesis*, as an oppositional idea to the Nazi state or power state, in the context of a war which came to be defined in ideological terms as concerning freedom and democracy versus dictatorship and totalitarianism. As Thoenes writes: 'The Welfare State was brought into being after a world crisis and a world war, in a period of scarcity in which it was patently obvious to everybody what it was they did *not* want, and that was: danger, thirst or cold, unemployment, dictatorships and squandering of either food or talents' (1966, p. 133). The term is thought to have entered the language in Archbishop Temple's *Citizen and Churchman* (1941):

> The state exists to serve the common man . . . In place of the conception of the power state we are led to that of the welfare state . . . The state . . . is a servant and instrument of God for the preservation of justice and for the promotion of human welfare so far as this can be done by universal enactment or through opportunities created by universal enactment. (Derived from Schottland, 1967, pp. 21, 24)

Temple was clarifying his thoughts at the same time as the Allied war aims were being defined in terms of the four freedoms of the Atlantic Charter:

> Freedom of speech
> Freedom of religion
> Freedom from want
> Freedom from fear

Hence, given the close association between the British concept of the Welfare State and what the war was thought to be about (democracy versus totalitarianism), any full definition should include reference to concepts of universality, optimality and freedom from domestic or external oppression.

As Temple noted, such concepts are inherently dynamic: when faced with external aggression or violence on the streets, these are the factors we find immediately oppressive and in need of check. However, 'as personal immunity from attack is secured', we can turn to identify – and try to remedy – other sources of oppression. These might include class, ethnic, gender and age inequalities; the vulnerability of the individual in the face or organised power (the client versus the welfare bureaucracy, the patient versus the hospital, the child versus the education system); or, for instance, the ecologically conscious individual or community in the face of powerful and organised environmental polluters. Although such campaigns may appear fragmented or even in competition with one another, they share a unity of concern in attempting to enlarge the life-chances of the individual or enhance the general quality of life in what Barrington Moore Jr (1972) has called the 'decent' society.

THE WELFARE STATE: DEFINING ITS NATURE

There has to be some agreement about the nature of what it is we are to explain in order to set about explaining it. However, ideas about the nature of the Welfare State seem entangled with hypotheses about how it came about. Seven partially different and overlapping ideas about the nature of the new order can be identified, the first four of which all assume there was a new order to explain, the last three tending to suggest that the 'Welfare State' was a myth.

(1) It involved a reduction in social inequality, flattening the stratification pyramid.
(2) It was a ransom, paid by capital to labour, to preserve inequality.
(3) A complex new system of horizontal redistribution arose within identifiable social categories (from those in work to those not in work, from the currently healthy to the currently ill, from men to women, adults to children), but vertical class redistribution was limited and sometimes inverse.
(4) It embodied a new spirit of altruism, reflected a new sense of social integration, a new answer to the question, 'who is my stranger?' (Titmuss, 1970)
(5) It reflected and reinforced a patriarchal division of labour, debarring or disadvantaging women as consumers or beneficiaries of welfare, creating or reinforcing women as paid or underpaid providers of welfare.

(6) It involved centralization and modernization of the state, but no new principle of social organisation.

(7) It was an accelerated maturation of trends inherent in the development of industrial societies within the old world (hence, apart from the 'forced growth' effect, the Second World War was largely irrelevant).

In deciding *what* the Welfare State was, there are three main types of difficulty. One is that 'what it was' might depend upon 'who you are'. Lloyd George, for instance, said that 'the best policeman for the syndicalist is the socialist', in other words that tactical or even cosmetic concessions would ensure that more radical paths would not be followed. This machiavellian approach to statescraft was said to underlie some of Bismarck's welfare reforms in Germany; and the same idea is captured by Campbell-Bannerman when he spoke of social reform as a 'sop for Labour'. Here he was undoubtedly thinking classically of the sop for Cerberus: the image is of a fierce and terrifying animal the destructive powers of which must not be unleashed. In the 1940s Quintin Hogg (on the basis of contact with the troops) argued for a pre-emptive reform strike: 'social reform or else social revolution' (Addison, 1977, p. 232).

However, while some members of the élite might concede tactical reforms (and others be deluded by their own rhetoric to think they had reformed more than they supposed), others – lower down the pyramid – might perceive real benefits and not worry about the motivations or power-struggles of the reformers. (The distinction being made here is akin to that sometimes made between 'high' and 'low' politics [Bentley and Stevenson, 1983].) The problem, then, is whose definition of the situation carries most weight? Consider this story by Lena Jeger:

> I can remember nothing less dignified than when my mother used to sit in a misery of embarrassment on the edge of a chair in the consulting room on the rare and desperate days when one of us had to be taken to the doctor – opening and shutting her purse, waiting for the right moment to extract the careful, unspareable half-crown . . . Sometimes we dropped the money and that was the least dignified of all, especially if the fat doctor let my mother pick it up.
>   Sometimes he would shout at my mother for not having come

before, like the time we had to wait for my sister's sore throat to turn unmistakably into diptheria before she was pushed off in a pram to his surgery. 'Good God woman, why didn't you bring this child days ago?' And then even he read the silence as the half-crown came out. 'Damn the money', he said, as he slipped it in his pocket. (Quoted in Forsyth 1966, pp. 26–7)

A second difficulty has helped to give rise in sociology to the distinction between manifest and latent functions. This is one way of coping with the problem that almost everybody might be wrong in their perceptions *at the time*. In other words, socialists might hail their victory; capitalists might lick their wounds in their funk-holes (Orwell's image); A. J. P. Taylor might write that 'there was nothing left to reform', and yet, as Benn has suggested, beneath the political clamour they might all be wrong:

> Hailed or condemned at the time as the beginning of a process which would lead to the transformation of Britain into a fully-fledged socialist state, it now can be seen, in retrospect, as having been nothing of the kind. When [Attlee's administration] was finally replaced by Tory governments . . . the transition was so smooth as to make us wonder just exactly what had changed, in either the political or the economic system . . .
> Looking back on it all now, it is clear that its policies were based on the political consensus which had arisen during the years of Churchill's wartime coalition, that it was able to use the framework of planning which had been developed to win the war, and that, in its turn, it actually laid the foundation of an even more durable consensus – which lasted until the mid-1970s. (Benn, 1987)

Another intellectual tool used by some to cope with this problem is that of contradiction (Gough, 1979): the Welfare State was *both* one thing *and also* another; not so much a ransom paid by capital to labour as a redrawing of the frontier of institutionalised class conflict; not simply a triumph for those (notably women) who had campaigned for family allowances and for the entitlement of women to education, health care and other benefits such as maternity grants and maternity allowance but a paradoxical achievement which reinforced associations between women and maternity, domesticity and care-work (Wilson, 1977; Ungerson, 1985).

However, the third type of difficulty is that writers may implicitly assess the Welfare State in terms of its perceived potential rather than the reality. We might liken the Welfare State to a growing runner bean. Different outcomes can be envisaged: the bean can quickly find support, climb upwards, strengthen, flower and thrive, reaching full maturity; but it may equally drift in the wrong direction, fail to find support, exhaust its resources in the struggle to grow and never attain its full potential; alternatively, the growing point of the bean may be nipped off by slugs and be permanently retarded.

At least some of the writers on the Welfare State implicitly assess its nature in the seedling stage from a judgement of what it *might have been*, if only it had grown to look like the picture on the packet. These are the gardeners. But slugs have a different outlook. Even if we are sympathetic to the *weltanschauung* of the gardeners and unsympathetic to that of the slugs, we should perhaps be cautious about regarding the gardeners' world view as superior (more true), simply because in this context they are the *herrenvolk*.

Personally my assessment is that the Welfare State did involve an important departure of principle in definable areas and the beanstalk analogy is helpful. From similar roots, welfare states could thrive and transform society (as in Sweden); but in the United Kingdom the advances at the time were not great and slug damage in years to come inhibited dynamic growth. The achievement in Britain might have been greater, particularly if the political system were better able to deliver outcomes which reflected majority support for the Welfare State.

HYPOTHESES CONCERNING THE POSSIBLE WAR/WELFARE STATE CONNECTION

If there is a connection between the Second World War and the emergence of the Welfare State, an abundance of sociological hypotheses to 'explain' the connection can be listed. Some of them are illustrated below:

(1)   *external aggression* increases social solidarity (deviance in-

dicators go down, social participation increases). This is a classic Durkheimian hypothesis – a group under threat values its own members more and this might take the form in this case, for instance, of improving school meals or raising pensions;

(2) as the *military participation ratio* increases (Andreski, 1954), the stratification pyramid flattens. In other words, as more people are involved in the war effort (not just a warrior class with its special privileges, but all citizens in one way or another) so they come to enjoy rights normally reserved for warriors. As an example, the distinction between 'civil' and 'military' hospitals began to be eroded during the Second World War and the better medical care began to be extended to civilian bomb casualties and to those injured in industrial accidents;

(3) *cutting of local ties* and allegiances opens minds to new ideas while *fraternisation* with different sorts of people under conditions of shared hardship and common threat fosters feelings of altruism. To give a simple example, Britain was 'on the move' and complete strangers would talk to one another on trains, in the shelters and in the forced social mixing which arises from conscription of men and women into the armed services or the civil labour force;

(4) increased *visibility* to middle classes of poverty/urban deprivation prompts reforming consciences: the government is more receptive (for different reasons) than at other times. Evacuation of young children with their mothers from slum areas would be an example, prompting awareness of poverty and lack of education. The government was in some ways more likely to respond to reformist lobbying, because of the next hypothesis;

(5) *radicalism in the ranks*: heightened political interest and general volatility create a threat of revolution. Men under arms could be an unstable political force, particularly after years of mass unemployment and in a struggle where the enemy was able for the first time in history to fight a propaganda war over the air-waves. The government had to be seen to care for women and children and fight its own internal propaganda war to maintain morale (hence 'demo-strategy' under (9) below;

(6) the so-called *inspection, concentration and displacement effects* of

wartime are elaborated later. Briefly, war imposes a stock-taking requirement (inspection) and, having taken stock, the government is likely to take powers (concentration) to act. Once new levels of government intervention are accepted, expectations about the appropriate level of intervention are permanently changed to a new level (displacement). Having taken stock of the hospitals, for instance, and found them inadequate, having taken powers to improve the situation and injected state capital into the health system – then it was unlikely that health care would revert to the previous piecemeal provision;

(7) *system mobilisation*, the need to cut through local bureaucracy and speed things up. This follows on from the previous idea but, in this case the government takes stock of and reforms its own apparatus;

(8) *catalytic effect* ('war is the locomotive of history' – Marx). Here the basic proposition is that change is always resisted, even when long overdue. The imperatives of war alter the balance of forces: old arguments for inactivity are brushed aside, the need for new measures is apparent to all, the 'old guard' is likely to be swept away;

(9) a *'demostrategy'* is forced on the government which creates hostages to fortune which can be cashed later as political promises. Here the hypothesis is that the government has to have a civil plan as well as a military one. The war was one of industrial production as well as a war of munitions. The government had to develop a propaganda machine to explain why the war was worth fighting, what the Allies had to offer, what the brave new world of post-war reconstruction would be like: subsequently, the government would have to deliver at least some of these promises, because of factors such as (5) and (10);

(10) *incorporation* into the political machine of groups necessary to successful prosecution of the war leads to strategic concessions for participants then (or later) and increases their political skill. This hypothesis, associated particularly with the work of Abrams (1963), is a qualification to the military participation ratio hypothesis. Abrams argues that it is not so much general participation in the war effort as strategic incorporation into the political machine of particular groups able to exploit their openings which explains why certain reforms occur and not others.

MODES OF EXPLANATION

'The momentum of war spread and quickened a trend towards social altruism, and crystallised within the nation demands for social justice' (Titmuss, 1950, p. 54). In sociology, it is commonly said, there are two major modes of approach to explanation. One is system-centred and structural/functional, taking little interest in human actors and their motivations but constantly running the risk of reification. The other is more person-centred, actionist, is concerned with meaning and strives to avoid reification – but probably has more difficulty in demonstrating how the links work between human agents and system changes except in obvious ways (for example, through 'great reformers').

These two styles of explanation can be seen clearly if we contrast the above quotation from Titmuss with the dry function-alism of Marshall or with Townsend's exuberant actionist approach. Marshall writes:

A modern total war has certain predictable effects on the social problems of the warring nations. It absorbs the unemployed, it stimulates health services in both their technical and their organizational aspects, and it creates a housing shortage, either by destroying houses or preventing them from being built, or both. In a more general sense total war obliges governments to assume new and heavier responsibilities for the welfare of their peoples, especially by controlling the production and distribu-tion of scarce necessities . . . and by looking after those who have been made homeless by invasion, evacuation, or aerial bombardment . . .

The nature of the effect (of war on social policy) will depend to a considerable extent on the fortunes of war – on whether a country is invaded or not, on whether it is victorious or defeated, and on the amount of physical destruction and social disorganization it suffers. (1967, p. 75)

Townsend is less interested in the system properties of war and more in what ordinary people were doing and thinking:

In the early part of the war the upheavals of evacuation caused many people to understand for the first time how the other half lived, and what the years of unemployment had wrought. Here were two nations confronted. The rich were chastened by this sudden revelation of social misery and the young wanted to put an end to it. Involvement in the problems of others, and a respect for them, as well as mere patriotism, made people prepared to accept sacrifices . . .

There was an attitude of trust, tolerance, generosity, good-will – call it what you like – towards others; a pervasive faith in human nature. Then there was a prevailing mood of self-denial, a readiness to share the good things in life and to see that others got the same privileges as oneself; an urge to give everyone, including the poor, the sick, the old and the handicapped, the chance of having certain elementary rights or freedoms so that they could achieve individual self-respect. (1958, pp. 93–5)

Townsend writes that 'progress was little short of breathtaking' by 1948 and yet by 1951: 'Those who had discussed the plans for a new society so ardently during and immediately after the war found their hopes sadly deflated. They were completely dis-illusioned' (1958, p. 97).

MAKING CONNECTIONS: SOME EXAMPLES

We do not necessarily have to choose between different modes of explaining what was happening, but we might like to know how they interconnect and the literature abounds with illustrative examples. For instance, the 'inspection effect' occurred at institutional and personal levels: the government had to conduct stock-taking exercises and individuals also took stock. Some of these were 'influentials' like Chamberlain who had been Minister of Health and who wrote privately in the wake of evacuation: 'I never knew such conditions existed, and I feel ashamed of having been so ignorant of my neighbours. For the rest of my life I mean to try to make amends by helping people to live cleaner and healthier lives' (Addison, 1977, p. 72).

At the institutional level, the government had to survey the housing stock in 1939 to discover where evacuees could be placed: 100 000 visitors inspected five million houses occupied by 18 million people. To organise a national hospital service, the Ministry of Health had to find out what sort of hospitals it had to work with and the Director General of the Emergency Medical Service wrote in 1939: 'Prior to the repeated surveys which have been made by the Ministry of Health during the past 18 months, there was little appreciation of the low standard of hospital accommodation in the country as a whole' (Quoted in Titmuss, 1950, p. 64). According to Titmuss the surveys revealed that when war broke out the civilian population was short of hospital beds by one-third, or 'roughly 98,000 beds for acute general, maternity, tuberculosis, infectious disease and chronic sick needs. It was on top of this "normal" shortage that the abnormal wartime shortage . . . would be imposed' (1950, p. 72).

Titmuss also illustrates how inspection, concentration and displacement effects – I am generalising the terminology used by Peacock and Wiseman (1967) in their discussion of the impact of war on taxation – go together:

Nearly 1,000 new operating theatres were installed by October 1939. Some 48 million bandages, dressings and fitments had been ordered. Close on 1 million surgical instruments were said to be wanted. The estimated number of artery forceps required represented over 30 years' demand for the whole country. . . . 100,000 blankets were hurriedly cut from stocks of men's overcoating. (1950, pp. 83,86)

Another way in which inspection occurred was by dispersing decision-makers and administrators from the vulnerable centre. Titmuss reports that the Assistance Board opened 605 new offices, and transferred 2400 staff to them. Iron rations for four million evacuees were distributed and stockpiled. As well as decentralising top medical teams to safer hospitals:

The Ministry of Health had to set up a small replica of itself in each region, composed of administrators, doctors, architects and specialists in housing, accountancy, water supplies and other matters. A large number of civil servants were now to be sent out of their offices and into the field to acquire personal experience of local conditions, to meet and talk to local government officers, and to see hospitals, maternity homes, welfare clinics and other social services in action. (1950, p. 89.)

The war undoubtedly involved tremendous personal and institutional upheaval, a mixing of social groups and, through removing the parameters of normal life, permitted more radical attitude change than would otherwise occur, a 'forced-learning' effect. Ferguson and Fitzgerald, for instance, report: 'Unprecedented population movements: 60 million changes of address in a population of only 38 million were recorded in a five year period, to say nothing of unrecorded temporary moves' (1954, p. 4). What this felt like in practice is vividly described by Jonathan Miller – to whom evacuation, conscription into the armed services and mobilisation of women's labour made it seem as if the whole country was on the move:

> There was a huge convection current and nothing seemed to be anchored any more, but drifted instead in slow perpetual motion. The trains were crowded with troops who seemed to have been en route for ever. They snoozed in the corners of our compartment and the corridors were jammed with their helmeted kitbags. Whenever the trains pulled into grimy midland junctions, they'd be waiting there too, propped up against each other, assembling for some obscure connection but without any real prospects of a final destination. It was called total mobilization. And that's just what it was. The cutting of everyone's local attachments so that everything and everyone became chronically mobile – as if the whole of English society had turned into plankton. (1968, p. 201)

There seems good reason for linking this 'plankton effect' with receptivity to new ideas: Addison concludes that: 'However cautiously interpreted, the evidence suggests that by the autumn of 1942 a major upheaval in public opinion had taken place' (1977, p. 15).

Thoenes argues that the war acted as a catalyst, both changing ideas and permitting them to be implemented. Without this extraordinary period, new ideas would not have permeated the society so extensively and the political will to drive them through would not have been sufficiently concentrated:

> How were [employers] to be won over to the notion of the much greater governmental interference required by this [Keynesian] New Deal? And how was it going to be possible for the government itself to solve this problem in a country where the principle of non-interference had always been held in such high regard?

The Second World War gave the unmistakeable answer to these questions. National requirements compelled the government to intervene in civil life through rationing, evacuation, school meals, rebuilding and active mobilization of all labour resources . . . The Beveridge Plan of 1942 obviously fitted very well into this political climate. It was a plan for social welfare that was economically viable, and was moreover desirable and in keeping with a standard of ethical values which had long been ripe for just such a system. (1966, p. 139)

REFORMULATING THE QUESTIONS

No one disputes that the Second World War occurred and that during and after it legislation was passed and administrative practices changed to such an extent that there was general agreement that a 'welfare state' had come into being. However, contentious questions on the history/sociology interface include:

(a) If these reforms were of a certain nature, why did they occur after the war and not, say, before?
(b) If the Second World War had these effects, why did not the First World War?
(c) If the Second World War had these effects, why were they not more extensive?
(d) If causal mechanisms existed, can the machinery be displayed, so that the connections can be traced through?
(e) How should 'deviant cases' – of the type discussed in Grafton (1981) – be evaluated?

We might briefly sketch an answer to these questions. An answer to question (a) would depend upon presuppositions about the nature of the reforms. Suppose that the Welfare State reforms were 'radical': that these reforms were either designed to change the stratification system or to reflect stratification changes which had occurred during the war. With this assumption, the role of the war is central. Stratification systems otherwise have a massive inertia: 'piecemeal' social reform would never have accomplished so much. On this assumption, hypotheses 1-5 (external aggression/increased military participation ratio/cutting of local attachments/heightened visibility/radicalism in the ranks) become plausible.

Suppose the reforms were not radical with respect to social stratification, but only with respect to centralisation and extension of government powers, then the role of the war in permitting or necessitating such changes again becomes central, as in hypotheses 6–8 (inspection/concentration effect/system mobilisation/catalytic effect).

Suppose the reforms were *not* radical, not even the culmination of a long process of piecemeal extension of welfare legislation, but simply a part of a periodic stock-taking and rationalisation, then the role of the war becomes relatively peripheral and argument turns more on the 'profit and loss account', considered shortly.

Turning to question (b), comparing the effects of the First World War and the Second World War, a few comments may suffice. The wars were different in their scope and nature. The First World War was fought more by men overseas than the Second World War in which, as Titmuss notes: 'Not until over three years had passed was it possible to say that the enemy had killed more soldiers than women and children' (1950, p. 335). As numerous commentators point out, the Second World War was more than ever before a 'people's war' (Calder, 1971), a war of civilian as well as military casualties, a war of civil production as well as military operation, an ideological war of words as well as a war of munitions. Following this line of reasoning, hypothesis 9 (demostrategy – the idea that the government had a plan to raise civilian morale by making promises which it subsequently had to implement) is plausible.

Also, hypothesis 10 (political incorporation), coupled with Middlemass's argument (1979, pp. 266–77) that the Labour leadership was so incorporated during the Second World War, makes it more likely that political gains were made by the Labour movement in this time. Similarly, Abrams (1963) suggests that the only tangible beneficiaries of the First World War were propertied married women who, because of previous political incorporation, gained the vote. Both wars brought women into the labour force and permanently displaced expectations about the role of women although, as Braybon and Summerfield (1987) argue, the tangible benefits to women perhaps smacked of tokenism and there were strong moves to push women back 'in the cage' of domesticity after both the First World War (Braybon, 1981) and the Second (Summerfield, 1984).

As to question (c), why the changes were not more extensive, the Second World War did not involve invasion and occupation by a hostile power – if it had done, the social dislocation of that occupation, the destruction of traditional institutions and the development of a resistance movement might well have led to more radical political changes subsequently (had the hostile power been defeated). Labour was incorporated into the ruling élite, but the élite did not change *fundamentally* in its composition. In this way, a blend of hypothesis 9 about demostrategy and Abrams' hypothesis 10 about incorporation would seem relevant here also.

Question (d) is an underlying theme in the whole chapter and will not be specifically addressed here, but question (e) about deviant cases does need to be tackled.

DEVIANT CASES

There are two types. There are the 'men and women out of step with World War II', as Grafton (1981) calls them. Calder in his Foreward to Grafton's book writes:

It shows us so many things that have been forgotten because they 'don't fit in'. Neither the heroics of *Angels One-Five*, nor the delightful comedy of *Dad's Army*, represent the dominant strains in British life during the war years. Boredom, frustration, fear, anger, class, class and again class were at least as often to the fore.

In Grafton's tape-recorded interviews we find fresh evidence that there are many different perceptions of events and that people experienced different wars: perhaps the intelligentsia and literati, particularly those who were young at the time, have made their own contribution to its mythology. Those who survived may have experienced a heightened sense of excitement, solidarity, altruism and political promise. They could put it into words and thus set the agenda for discussion.

Then there are the contrary examples, not so much of people out of step as of events out of step. If the war was so efficacious in cutting through red tape and improving efficiency, how does one explain the cautiousness of the moves in this direction, the resistance of the Treasury, the hospitals paid to keep beds empty for casualties who never came, and so on? If there was a demostrategy, why was Churchill (apparently) so inept as to try to suppress discussion within the Army Bureau of Current Affairs (ABCA) of the Beveridge Report or let his displeasure at 'visions of Eldorado' be made known?

Two sorts of answer can be made. With regard to public opinion we cannot nowadays suppose it is a unitary animal always moving in a consistent direction. More, our impression might be of a fickle creature, perhaps a multi-headed one, swaying this way and that. Had it not been for the euphoria of El Alamein, for instance, perhaps the Beveridge Report would not have been hailed with the popular enthusiasm it received (to quote one notable example). We should not be surprised by Grafton's people out of step: in a stratified mass society, we surely always expect to find people 'out of tune' with the times: the sinking of the Argentine warship *Belgrano* during the Falklands War would display similar divergencies in public opinion.

As to the deviant institutional examples (as compared with deviant people), the policies and practices which did not 'fit in' with the time, one answer is that this highlights the problem with 'conspiracy theories' of history. There *may* be conspirators, who understand events and seek to control them, but they will not usually be numerous enough to have their hands on all the levers of power; and they may be outnumbered by other people who do not share their understanding of the trend of the times, or who are actively trying to hold back the tide rather than open the floodgates to it. Hence, for example, some highly placed persons may have perceived the need for a 'demostrategy' and attempted to advance it; but others, equally highly placed, may not have perceived the need, may therefore not have advanced it, or may positively have hindered it.

To sum up this discussion, then, to expect a unified message to come from the political élite is an unreasonably high demand: even subsections of the élite would be capable of pursuing non-aligned political goals. Second, in a highly stratified society, even during a time of heightened social solidarity, the messages transmitted by the élite would be imperfectly relayed and variously interpreted.

THE PROFIT AND LOSS ACCOUNT

The relationship between the Second World War and the Welfare

State seems a paradoxical subject of intellectual curiosity: what is the underlying motif? One motif seems to be, 'it was good to be alive, in England, during the Second World War'; or alternatively, 'out of corruption came forth sweetness: the war was horrible, but at least it brought about the Welfare State – what an interesting combination'. If these are the lessons, later generations are unlikely to find them appealing: nostalgia for the 1940s is as uninviting as nostalgia for the 1960s – if one was born subsequently. Also, if progressive incorporation of the population into the war effort was thought to involve progressive gains in social integration and altruism, we can hardly carry this line forward into the thermo-nuclear age and suppose there would be paradoxical benefits to a more extensive 'total war'.

In prosaic arithmetic it may be noted on the debit side that, if the war brought about the Welfare State, it did so in an economic climate which was highly disadvantageous to its future prospects. The National Health Service might have been created, but it was immediately dogged with financial crises, and no new hospital construction occurred for more than a decade. The new pension and benefit levels under the national insurance system were set (again more for economic than political reasons) at levels guaranteed not to eliminate poverty and the stigma of means-testing but to maintain them. If the Attlee governments owed their origin to the Second World War, so their demise and disarray (and, arguably, all hopes of a radical consolidation of the Welfare State) might be attributed to other wars – the Korean War, the Cold War and the rearmament programme.

A parallel might be drawn with Sweden: while non-belligerent in the Second World War, Swedish society was affected socially and politically by the armed conflict all around it. A social democratic coalition came to power which presided over the transformation of that society from impoverished Sweden to prosperous welfare state (från fattig-Sverige till välfärdsstaten – Elmér, 1963): but Sweden did not lose 400 000 citizens as war casualties, nor have four million houses destroyed or damaged, quite apart from the destruction of factories, hospitals, schools and other plant which Britain experienced.

The United Kingdom had sold overseas capital assets to a total of over £1000 million and incurred an overseas debt of well over £3000 million; more than half the nation's shipping tonnage had been lost and only 2 per cent of the population were producing goods for export at the end of the war (Gregg, 1967, p. 39). These sparse figures indicate what a two-edged sword the war was. It may have brought to power a government which eventually thought it had 'nothing left to reform', but it simultaneously deprived it of the resources to implement the reforms in a way which might have established the Welfare State on a firmer foundation. The war did not achieve a world safe for democracy but, even before it was over, gave way to a new Cold War between the Eastern and Western blocs in which defence expenditure continued to compete with welfare allocations.

The post-war atmosphere of crisis at home and abroad did not foster participatory democracy or help ordinary people to feel the Welfare State belonged to them: there was too wide a gap between their aspirations and the day-to-day outcome of 'top-down' reforms, like those traceable to the Beveridge Report. Women were not consulted about being pushed back into the home to make way for demobilised men and the neglect of the consumer was to be highlighted by Barbara Wootton in 'Daddy Knows Best' (1959), a trenchant criticism of Eileen Younghusband's *Report on Social Workers* (1959). Wootton's article can be seen in retrospect to be the first of numerous critiques of the Welfare State from a variety of perspectives, critiques which left its defenders false-footed when attacked from a different flank in the 1980s by the radical right.

REFERENCES

Abrams, P. (1963) 'The Failure of Social Reform 1918–20', *Past and Present*, No. 24, pp. 43–64.

Addison, P. (1977) *The Road to 1945* (London: Quartet).

Andreski, S. (1954) *Military Organisation and Society* (London: Routledge & Kegan Paul).

Benn, A. (1987) 'The Consensus Behind a 'Socialist' Triumph', *Guardian*, 19 January.

Bentley, M. and Stevenson, J. (eds) (1983) *High and Low Politics in Modern Britain, Ten Studies* (Oxford University Press).

Braybon, G. (1981) *Women Workers in the First World War* (London: Croom Helm).

Braybon, G. and Summerfield, P. (1987) *Out of the Cage, Women's Experiences in Two World Wars* (London: Pandora).

Briggs, A. (1961) 'The Welfare State in Historical Perspective', *European Journal of Sociology*, Vol. 2 (2), pp. 221–58.

Bruce, M. (1961) *The Coming of the Welfare State* (London: Batsford).

Calder, A. (1971) *The People's War* (London: Panther).

Elmér, Å. (1963) *Från Fattigsverige till Välfärdsstaten* (Stockholm: Gleerups).

Ferguson, S. and Fitzgerald, H. (1954) *History of the Second World War: Studies in the Social Services* (London: HMSO and Longmans Green & Co).

Forsyth, G. (1966) *Doctors and State Medicine, A Study of the British Health Service* (London: Pitman).

Fraser, D. (1973) *The Evolution of the British Welfare State* (London: Macmillan).

Gough, I. (1979) *Political Economy of the Welfare State* (London: Macmillan).

Grafton, P. (1981) *You, You and You: The People Out of Step with World War II* (London: Pluto).

Gregg, P. (1967) *The Welfare State* (London: Harrap).

Marshall, T. H. (1967) *Social Policy* (2nd edn) (London: Hutchinson).

Marwick, A. (1968) *Britain in the Century of Total War: War, Peace and Social Change 1900–1967* (Harmondsworth: Penguin).

Middlemass, K. (1979) *Politics in Industrial Society, The British Experience since 1911* (London: André Deutsch).

Miller, J. (1968) in B. S. Johnson (ed), *The Evacuees* (London: Victor Gollancz).

Moore, B. Jr (1972) *Reflections on the Causes of Human Misery and upon Certain Proposals to Eliminate Them* (London: Allen Lane).

Peacock, A. T. and Wiseman, J. (1967) *The Growth of Public Expenditure in the UK* (2nd edn) (London: Allen & Unwin).

Popper, K. R. (1945) *The Open Society and Its Enemies* (London: Routledge & Kegan Paul).

Schottland, C. I. (ed) (1967) *The Welfare State* (New York: Harper & Row).

Summerfield, P. (1984) *Women Workers in the Second World War* (London: Croom Helm).

Temple, W. (1941) 'The State', in *Citizen and Churchman* (London: Eyre & Spottiswoode). [Extracts reprinted in Schottland (ed).]

Thoenes, P. (1966) *The Elite in the Welfare State* (London: Faber & Faber).

Titmuss, R. (1950) *Problems of Social Policy* (London: HMSO and Longmans Green & Co.)

Titmuss, R. (1958) *Essays on 'the Welfare State'* (London: Allen & Unwin).

Titmuss, R. (1970) *The Gift Relationship* (London: Allen & Unwin).

Townsend, P. (1958) 'A Society for People', in N. Mackenzie (ed), *Conviction* (London: MacGibbon & Kee).

Ungerson, C. (ed) (1985) *Women and Social Policy: A Reader* (Basingstoke: Macmillan).

Wilson, E. (1977) *Women and the Welfare State* (London: Tavistock).

Wootton, B. (1959) 'Daddy Knows Best', *Twentieth Century*, No. 166, pp. 248–61.

Younghusband, E. (1959) *Report of the Working Party on Social Workers in the Local Authority Health and Welfare Services* (London: HMSO).

5 Wartime Designs for a Welfare State: Australia and Britain in 1942

Sheila Shaver

Australia entered the Second World War with only fragmentary welfare provision: by the end of the war it had laid the foundations of its present-day Welfare State. Australian war-time leaders assigned social security a new significance, presaging a post-war future worthy of sacrifice. During the war the Joint Parliamentary Committee on Social Security, set up to symbolise that commitment, travelled the country taking evidence on appropriate welfare provision for Australia and making recommendations for new forms of social provision. It covered the full spectrum of social security: pensions and benefits, housing, social planning, health and recreation. Over five years it issued nine official reports and saw most of its recommendations followed by legislation.

Something very similar happened in Britain, notwithstanding its already more developed welfare apparatuses and a prime minister chary of post-war promises. In 1942 Sir William Beveridge produced a comprehensive scheme for the 'abolition of want' through universal social insurance. Sketched into his plan were further programmes for family allowances, a national health service and an economic policy commitment to full employment. The Beveridge Report supplied the outline for Britain's post-war 'Welfare State'.

These war-time exercises in social planning make a revealing study of the processes by which certain common-sense propositions for welfare reform were translated into institutional machinery of the Welfare State. Titmuss (1950), Wilson (1977) and Roe (1976, pp. 220-22), among others, have remarked on the multiple connections between war, nationalism and social security. The class content has been argued more contentiously. Crosland (1958) and Cairns (1957), for example, have presented the Welfare State as won through working-class struggle, whereas O'Connor (1973), Gough (1979) and Higgins (1978) have shown it as refurbishing the state to suit monopoly capitalism. Offe (1984) and Watts (1980) have better caught the ambiguities of the Welfare State for class relations, accounting for strong political continuities in social policy between the parties of opposed classes. Feminist critiques have shown a politics of gender in the structures of the Welfare State: Summers (1973), McIntosh (1978) and others have maintained that women's citizenship in the Welfare State is undercut by the family unit basis of social security provision. Finally, Wilson (1977) and Wheeler (1985) have suggested a relation between war, nationalism and gender relations in the genesis of the Welfare State.

In Australia conflict over class interests in social security had blocked the development of welfare for a generation. During its first nine months of work the Committee issued three reports (1941, 1942a, 1942b) dealing with income security. The war-time conjuncture enabled the Joint Parliamentary Committee to resolve this deadlock temporarily and the Australian Labor Party (ALP) to legislate a range of new welfare measures. Though the argument had been about class, the politics of social security also had consequences for gender and race. The distinctive character of the Australian Welfare State is a product of this temporary resolution.[1]

The Committee's work on income security has sometimes been called 'Australia's Beveridge Report', and it is interesting to compare it with its better remembered British counterpart (Inter-departmental Committee on Social Insurance and Allied Services, 1942). These two exercises in post-war planning took place at almost exactly the same time, during the period of acute war emergency in each country.[2] They arose in similar ideological contexts, and they covered common policy ground. Yet they reached radically different conclusions about the fundamental principles of income security, with consequences for class, gender and community in the two national systems.

Made up of Government and Opposition members of both houses, the Joint Parliamentary Committee on Social Security was established in June 1941. This was the same month in which the UK's Inter-departmental Committee on Social Insurance and Allied Services was appointed with William Beveridge as its chairman. Both enterprises had their origins in the pragmatic politics of war-time government and the ideological impulse to make war serve progressive ends. But their larger political contexts were somewhat different. Since 1940 Britain had had a coalition government with Churchill at its head and Labour Party ministers in its ranks. The Beveridge Committee was instituted to placate a restive Trade Union Congress (TUC), solidify the Coalition and, despite Churchill's sharp displeasure, symbolise the worthier aims of war effort (Addison, 1975, pp. 120–2, 167–8; Harris, 1977, p. 381). In Australia conventional party government was maintained throughout the war. The 1940 elections had produced a near stalemate, but Prime Minister Robert Menzies' anti-Labor coalition governed with support from two independents. He set up the Joint Parliamentary Committee on Social Security (and four other joint committees) in a ploy to shore up this government. The anti-Labor government fell in October 1941, shortly after the Committee's first report, and because of the war emergency Labor took office without new elections. The Committee carried on, now with an ALP chairman but otherwise only minor changes to its membership. For most of its life the Australian Committee reported to a Labor government.

No one expected much of either body. The Beveridge Committee was supposed to conduct a routine administrative review of existing social insurance schemes, though it was soon clear that Beveridge himself intended more. One of the attractions of the exercise, for Ernest Bevin at least, was the opportunity to sideline Beveridge out of his Ministry of Labour. Except for the chairman its members were middle-level bureaucrats, technically competent but lacking authority to make policy. When Beveridge foreshadowed contentious recommendations their roles were rapidly downgraded, and he was left to sign the report alone (Harris, 1977, pp. 386–8). The Australian Committee was a means of keeping some backbenchers busy, and its terms of reference were appropriately vague: it was to review the state of social provision in Australia and recommend a broad range of new measures. The Committee consisted of six, later seven, undistinguished backbenchers, none of whom brought to the task either experience or indeed any demonstrated interest. In its first months of operation the anti-Labor Minister of Social Services tried to get the Committee to endorse his own plans for contributory social insurance. When Labor came to government it openly snubbed the Committee, establishing its own body of experts in Treasury.

Both exercises nevertheless had far-reaching consequences for the shape and content of the post-war Welfare State, the first outlines of which appeared in their reports. The Beveridge Report proposed a unified, comprehensive system of social insurance in which subsistence benefits were financed through contributions by workers, employees and the state. Benefits and contributions would be universal and flat-rate. The social insurance scheme was in turn predicated on three 'assumptions' about post-war social policy, presuming further and far-reaching policy commitments to family allowances, the maintenance of full (male) employment and a comprehensive national health service. Addison pays tribute to its significance:

> The historian of social administration finds in the Beveridge Report a blueprint of the postwar welfare state in Britain. The political historian finds it also as a brilliant coup by one man, which at once synthesised the pressures for a more progressive capitalism, and jolted all three parties into accepting the resulting formula as the basis of a new postwar consensus. (1975, p. 211)

At first sight the reports of the Australian Joint Parliamentary Committee on Social Security compare badly. Their work had neither the imagination of the Beveridge synthesis nor its political acuity. But like the Beveridge group the Joint Parliamentary Committee sifted through propositions for welfare reform and identified the basis of a practicable war-time consensus. Defining welfare as a national responsibility in Australia's federal system, it recommended the immediate establishment of Commonwealth widows' pensions and unemployment benefits. These were to be financed not by contributions but from a progressive income tax.

The nub of the nationalist, class and gender character of British national insurance and Australian social security can be found in these reports. In both countries war-time designs identified income security with the unity of the nation. Social rights of citizenship (Marshall, 1963) were to be national, expressing the community of the people as a whole. Moreover in Australia the social boundaries of the nation itself were to be widened to include Aboriginal and immigrant peoples racially excluded from social security in the past. The reports differed, however, in the way they defined class and gender relations in income security. The Australian Committee defined class equity in terms of income: it opposed a contributory levy on workers in favour of a graduated tax on the incomes of all but the lowest income earners. Tax finance represented Labor's long-standing commitment to social security as redistributive social justice for the working class. The Beveridge Report was prepared for a nation already accustomed to contributory finance. It recommended that all classes join in a single social insurance scheme with uniform rates of benefit and contribution. Equity now meant liberal equality among individuals.

These different financial principles had consequences for the treatment of gender relations in British and Australian income security. The reports of both countries affirmed the principle that social security should be based on the family unit of one or both parents and dependent children. This gave the notion of redistributive social justice a twofold character, adding a second axis of family and life cycle to income and class. Beveridge's plan also built conventional assumptions about women's dependence into the contributory framework in a way that Australian income security did not have to. In the result the sexual division of labour was less deeply entrenched in the Australian than the British Welfare State.

The central principles of the Beveridge Report sprang almost fully formed from the mind of Beveridge. Liberalism and long years of experience with unemployment insurance had already shaped his views (Beveridge, 1955, p. 298). His initial memoranda set out his scheme in all but fine detail, and its early presentation doubtless pre-empted much debate. As lone signatory he had little cause to concede strongly held views to his advisers, though in the end he would have liked more endorsement than they were prepared to grant (Beveridge, 1955, p. 310; Harris, 1977, p. 388). The Australian Committee, in contrast, reached consensus only through laborious processes of travel, hearing evidence and negotiating the political commitments of their parties. Agreement on the divisive financial question came only as the war neared Australia.

WAR AND NATIONAL UNITY

In June 1941 the war in Europe was going disastrously for Britain and the Empire. London continued under air siege. Empire forces in the Middle East, including the Second Australian Infantry

Force, were being steadily forced back. In the Pacific German raiders harassed shipping off the coasts of Australia, and Japanese forces were on the Indo-Chinese mainland. The critical war situation had given impetus to the formation of the two committees and its atmosphere suffused their deliberations.

In Britain the long-term shift of responsibility for social security from local to national government had been largely completed by the end of the 1930s. The result was a plethora of diverse and inconsistent schemes, which it was the Beveridge Committee's task to rationalise. The war crisis of 1940 had resolved Beveridge's own ambivalence about centralised social planning (Addison, 1975, pp. 117–18) and he now proposed that the national government have sole responsibility for income security. The various schemes were to be integrated in a single unified framework of universal contributions and entitlements, with only workmen's compensation excepted from its subsistence principle. The whole was to be administered by a single Ministry of Social Security, which would replace the approved societies previously responsible for cash benefits and also take over the remaining vestiges of social assistance from local authorities. These were not new proposals. They were continuous with and rounded off developments over a long period (Bruce, 1966, p. 274; Harris, 1977, pp. 416–17). War-time gave their symbolism new appeal.

The Australian Committee had to argue for welfare reform in war-time. In 1939 declaration of war had provided a convenient pretext for the conservative United Australia Party to set aside proposals for contributory social insurance: it would be irresponsible for a nation at war to commit scarce resources to expensive innovations at home. By 1941 the war was an immediate reality, and welfare advocates now claimed that social services would enhance the nation's effort. The Committee embraced this idea in its *(First) Interim Report*. This began with a stocktaking, reporting that 'a considerable proportion of Australia's citizens are poorly housed, ill-clothed or ill-nourished – living in conditions which reflect no credit on a country such as ours'. The Report maintained that social services would not necessarily impede the war effort. They would contribute directly, investing in the productivity of war workers, and also indirectly, 'by improving the morale and willingness to work of the employees, who will feel that a regime which is prepared, even at this time of emergency, to improve their conditions is worth working and fighting for' (JCSS, 1941, paras 1–3). In its *First Report* (1941) the Committee called for an 'Australian outlook', a 'national policy', and a unified Commonwealth Social Security Act but stopped short of recommending total transfer of responsibility for income security from State to Commonwealth government until its *Second Report* (1942a).

The Committee also considered the limits of membership in the Australian nation. Aborigines and 'Asiatics' had been ineligible for age and invalid pensions since their introduction at the turn of the century. Then child endowment, introduced in early 1941, treated Aborigines in the same way as other Australians, provided that they were not nomadic and not wholly supported by the Commonwealth or a state government (i.e. living on a reserve). The Committee recommended that age and invalid pensions and maternity allowance also be available to 'aboriginals who prove to the satisfaction of the Commissioner [of Pensions] that they are making a genuine endeavour to live approximately in conformity with accepted European standards' (JCSS, 1941, para 21). The new child endowment legislation had marked a major social policy transition from a theory of absorption based on genetic notions of blood mixture to one of assimilation based on social concepts of acculturation (Rowley, 1971, p. 38). The Committee's recommendation confirmed and generalised this policy transition.

Aborigines were not then political citizens of Australia. Naturalised Asian immigrants were. The injustice of denying them pensions and benefits was especially obvious in war-time. The Committee had not intended to consider this anomaly until ethnic organisations brought it to their attention. One letter in particular, from the Australian Syrian-Lebanese Association, pointed to war service by members of their community in both 1914–18 and the present conflict. Australian troops were in Syria at that moment. The Committee took the point: 'It is considered illogical and unfair to refuse pension and maternity allowance benefits to aliens who become naturalised British subjects, provided they are otherwise entitled to these benefits' (1941, para 22).

CLASS AND FINANCIAL EQUITY

By the time Labor took office in October 1941 the war had come much closer to Australia. By the following March, when the Committee was drafting its second and third reports, Japan was in Singapore and New Guinea. Darwin had been briefly under air attack. The war situation made its work on unemployment urgent, for a relief payment would make it easier to transfer workers from civilian to war production. Plans had to be made, too, for possible enemy action in Australia. The Committee decided to issue two reports, one dealing with the immediate war emergency and the other with post-war measures.

In these reports the Committee broke the long-standing political stasis over what was called the 'contributory question' to endorse financing income security from an income tax. Since early in the century the anti-Labor parties had been committed to replacing Australia's 'free' but means-tested pensions with contributory social insurance. They considered that contributory pensions would both encourage thrift and give entitlement by right. Moreover the working class would pay for its social security protection. Labor was bitterly opposed to contributory finance. Since 1936 the ALP had argued that if social security were financed from a progressive income tax, capital could be made to pay.

During the period of its *First Report* the Committee had been unable to agree. Expert witnesses differed on the merits of contributory finance. Most favoured the social insurance concept, criticising means-testing and upholding the virtues of individual responsibility. They frequently cited British arrangements as the modern practice. The most articulate opposition to social insurance came from the Fabian left, represented by a group of young academic economists who preferred the concept of the 'national minimum of real income'. The key to social security lay in continuous full employment, but this should be underpinned with a minimum standard below which no citizen need fall. Central to their proposition was a commitment that the national minimum would be redistributive.

Soon after Labor had assumed government, a Treasury economist submitted a plan turning the general case for a 'national minimum of real income' after the war into a limited scheme for a 'guaranteed minimum income' now. He proposed widows' pensions and unemployment benefits bringing income to subsistence level, subject to both a means-test and, except for widows with children, a work test. Rates were to be based on existing old age and invalid pensions plus supplements for dependants. The proposal again rejected contributory finance in favour of finance through taxation. Meanwhile the Committee's research officer was also working on technical aspects of the question. He wrote a lengthy report on the finance of social security in which he noted the incapacity of a financial system based on contributions to provide benefits to farmers and small shopkeepers, and described the types of machinery possible to enable them to be covered in a taxation-financed scheme. This argument was aimed at Opposition members wanting coverage for the self-employed.

The *Second Interim Report* was tabled on 6 March 1942. It recommended payments to all unemployed workers, subject to a work test. Strengthened National Security Regulations, promulgated in February 1942, placed 'the whole community virtually under Government direction' (Hasluck, 1970, pp. 115–25). The ethos of the war-time moment stressed mutual obligation between citizen and state. This atmosphere found military imagery in the *Second Interim Report*: 'If 'A', being unemployed, is to hold himself in readiness to answer the Government's call, he should be maintained while he remains so ready. He should be paid on the same principle as the soldier is paid whether he is fighting, training or resting' (1942a, para 11). Social security now symbolised the unity of the nation in war-time, and it followed logically that progressive income taxation was the appropriate financial basis for unemployment protection (paras 11–12). The immediacy of the war emergency led Opposition members of the Committee to agree to set aside their commitment to contributory finance and recommend funding from taxation.

Three weeks later the *Third Interim Report* (1942b), dealing with post-war unemployment, put this temporary agreement on a permanent basis. It proclaimed a central ideal that the nation should provide 'work or maintenance for every unemployed person in the community as a right for the full period of unemployment, it being understood that compliance with a work test is a condition' (para 6). The scheme was to be financed by a progressive income tax on all but the lowest income levels. Neither report made any reference to the means-test.

In Britain the themes of war-time national unity and class justice took a different financial inflection. Class interest in redistributive social security was not an issue, but the means-test was. The insurance model had been established with Lloyd

George's National Insurance Bill of 1911, with finance from flat-rate contributions already accepted practice (Gilbert, 1966, p. 354). Beveridge gave only nominal consideration to more progressive forms of finance, through income taxation or income-related contributions, nor was he under any pressure to do so (Harris, 1977, p. 388). Class contention over the provisions of the scheme was largely confined to workmen's compensation and TUC opposition to replacing wage-related industrial compensation with flat-rate welfare benefits. Beveridge spent considerable time negotiating with the TUC, which 'had been largely responsible for securing establishment of the Committee' (Beveridge, 1955, p. 300). He proposed to compromise with higher rates for long-term industrial disability, a position he maintained even after the TUC had rejected it (Harris, 1977, p. 401).

In other respects class feeling focused less on financial relativities of contribution and benefit than the indignities of means-testing, which equally offended Beveridge's own liberal conscience. He was proposing,

first and foremost, a plan of insurance – of giving in return for contributions, benefits up to subsistence level, as of right and without means tests, so that individuals may build freely upon it . . . benefit in return for contributions, rather than free allowances from the State is what the people of Britain desire. (Inter-departmental Committee on Social Insurance and Allied Services, 1942, paras 10 and 21)

Beveridge's most significant innovation was to make social insurance universal, a single scheme covering the whole spectrum of income and class. The image of all social groups sharing the adversities of personal and working life symbolised the unity of the war-time nation. Administrative consolidation and central government control implied purpose and efficiency. These ideological symbols made tangible the implied contract between government and people that war sacrifice would be rewarded (Addison, 1975, pp. 213–15; Bruce, 1966, p. 262), and may have been responsible for the popularity of the recommendations even before they were published.

GENDER, FAMILY AND DEPENDENCY

Both reports defined and codified gender and family relations in income security, giving newly systematic character to the role of the state in personal life. The relations concerned were widowhood, female sole parenthood and wife and child dependency. Basic differences in the way in which they were treated in the reports followed from the different financial models adopted.

The Beveridge Report made children's allowances one of its three basic 'assumptions'. The purpose of children's allowances was to rationalise the contradiction between the wage and welfare systems. The allowance would redistribute resources towards families with children, and perhaps encourage parenthood. Paid whether or not he was employed, it would also redress the situation where the father of a large family could be better off out of work than in it (Land and Parker, 1978, pp. 345–6). This 'assumption' cleared the way for social insurance.

Beveridge's scheme defined the insurance principles of risk, contribution and entitlement in terms of employment status. Its provisions distinguished between employees, an interruption of whose earnings could be treated as an insurable risk, and others, for whom a loss of current income could not be defined so satisfactorily. All would be covered for pension on retirement, medical treatment and funeral expenses, but only employees would be covered against unemployment and short-term disability. Flat-rate benefits would provide subsistence income, and would include a joint rate for a man and his dependent wife. While children's allowances did not normally cover the first child in a family, that child was covered while the reponsible parent was on benefit.

Expectations about the sexual division of labour were clearly inscribed in Beveridge's framework for social insurance, with the result that insurance principles were inconsistently applied in the treatment of women under the scheme. The Report assumed that husbands and wives were one, sharing income and expenditure (Wilson, 1977, p. 150). All men were assumed to be breadwinners and treated uniformly, whereas women were codified by martital as well as labour market status. There was to be a special insurance status for housewives, whose benefits were to be financed from the contributions of their husbands. This contradicted the basic insurance principle requiring that circumstances on which benefits are based be outside the control of the claimant. Beveridge saw it as recognising that housewives do work of national importance (Harris, 1977, p. 404). In consequence there would be a general differential in rates of contribution and benefit for men and women, and a further differential between single and married women. The lesser benefits of married women contradicted normal actuarial principles, constructing a pattern of gender redistribution primarily at their expense (Land, 1976; see also Wilson, 1977, p. 151). At the same time the scheme excluded other groups of women because their circumstances could not be defined in conformity with insurance principles. 'Domestic spinsters' could not be provided for because they had no husbands to finance their benefits. Separated or deserted mothers could not be included because they had legal recourse to maintenance from their husbands. These groups were to continue to be provided for through national assistance (Harris, 1977, pp. 403–7).

In Australia children's allowances, called child endowment, had been introduced just before the Committee was set up. The proposal had originated with the Labor Party in the 1940 elections and been taken over by the government in 1941 when its timing was used to influence the Arbitration Court against granting a wage rise (Kewley, 1973, pp. 190–1; Cass, 1983). Child endowment was paid on behalf of each child except the first, who was considered to be covered by the family wage.

A widow's pension was the first item on the agenda of the Joint Parliamentary Committee. Widows had been the group most severely affected by the long stalemate over the contributory question. War widows were supported by Repatriation Department services, but pensions were available to civilian widows only in New South Wales and, more penuriously, in Victoria. Witnesses unanimously favoured immediate Commonwealth action. The otherwise thorny question of contributory finance caused little difficulty, for even its strongest advocates preferred provision from general revenue to any delay. The Committee recommended immediate introduction of a means-tested payment similar to existing age and invalid pensions.

The Committee considered that in caring for their children widows were performing a 'national service' entitling them to community support. It sought to relieve pressure on them to take paid employment and 'deprive their children of essential parental care and supervision'. It was probably the pragmatic orientation to immediate relief of distress which prompted the Committee to broaden the conventional understanding of widow. Although the *First Report* did not draw attention to the point, its recommendations for the widow's pension included deserted wives and women whose husbands were inmates of mental hospitals (JCSS, 1941, paras 26 and 46).

The Committee also considered the support of dependent wives and children of age and invalid pensioners. The inadequacy of the pension for more than the individual pensioner was obvious and the remedy, allowances for the dependants of the incapacitated breadwinner, had been suggested in previous legislative proposals and established practice overseas. The Committee recommended allowances for the dependent wife and for the first, unendowed child of age and invalid and widow pensioners. These recommendations extended the family principle of Australian wage determination through the Arbitration Court to income security, enabling pensioner 'breadwinners' to fulfil their roles as heads of households (Bryson, 1983). The military metaphor of the *Second Report* defined the nation's obligation as properly 'related to [the citizen's] domestic obligations and his family needs' (1942a, para 11), and the family structure of breadwinner and dependants was repeated in its recommendations for unemployment insurance.

The complex codification of women's circumstances of the Beveridge plan for social insurance was largely absent in Australian provisions, where the rejection of the insurance model made many such distinctions unnecessary. Women were to qualify for age and invalid pensions and unemployment benefits on more or less equal terms with men. Widows and deserted wives qualified according to their circumstances, unmediated by the contributory status of their husbands. Rates of benefit were equal for men and women, though only women were eligible for allowances as dependants.

But while gender was not very salient in the Committee's recommendations the tacit acceptance of means-testing gave the family a central place in income security. Age and invalid pensions had since Federation been subject to a means-test on the joint income and property of husband and wife, and this framework was carried over without question into the Committee's recommendations for widow's pensions and unemployment benefit. The assumption was that husband and wife pooled their income, and the effect to make the access of either partner to social security contingent upon the circumstances of the other.

AFTER THE REPORTS

The substance of both the Beveridge and Joint Parliamentary Committee Reports was eventually written into the institutional structures of the British and Australian Welfare States, but not necessarily as a simple consequence of the Reports. Even before their publication both were caught up in complex political interplays which affected the outcome of their recommendations.

The Beveridge Report, while ostensibly the work of non-political public servants, was visibly political from its outset. The exercise had begun with Greenwood trying to make his low-ranked position in the Coalition cabinet into a vehicle for Labour (Addison, 1975, p. 167). Beveridge himself openly flouted public service conventions to lobby and even campaign publicly for his developing proposals. The main outlines of his thinking were so quickly known that by April 1942 a report on home intelligence said they already had widespread popular support. When the Report was released on 1 December Beveridge was given ambivalent, on-again-off-again support to publicise it (Harris, 1977, pp. 421–6; Addison, 1975, pp. 215–17). With rather less official blessing he spent much of the next two years campaigning for its adoption outside and then within Parliament.

The Report sold in prodigious numbers in Britain and in America. Popular audiences were enthusiastic, and Labour supporters such as G. D. H. Cole organised an active movement to promote its implementation. In contrast, official circles of both party and bureaucracy were cautious and divided. Liberal parliamentarians and some Conservative backbenchers supported the Plan. Though Labour generally favoured the Report, its ministers were reluctant to press a hostile Churchill on the point. Pressure for an immediate government commitment culminated in the Commons debate in February 1943, when Labour's front and back benches split. It was the largest anti-government vote of the war. The 1944 *White Paper on Social Security* followed.

The political conflicts set up by the Beveridge Report helped to bring on the 1945 election and the end of war-time coalition government. Conservative Party support for the Beveridge proposals during the war effectively precluded its opposition to them afterwards, and the enactment of family allowances (1945), national insurance and national health (1946), and revamped national assistance (1948) was uncontroversial. The Labour Party now associated Beveridge's proposals for social reform with its own policies for nationalisation, presenting that programme as similarly transcending the sectional divisions of class society (Attlee, 1954, pp. 132, 162–4). These too aroused little effective opposition (Attlee, 1954, p. 165; Wilson, 1977, p. 147).

The legislation establishing Labour's post-war 'Welfare State' followed the general principles of the Beveridge Report remarkably closely, though differing in some important points of substance. All three 'assumptions' of the Report were fulfilled at least to some degree, though children's allowances were far below the expectations of the Report. The plurality of separate insurance schemes was replaced by a single system of social insurance, using the basic framework of contributions and benefits recommended in the Report. This included the complex categorisation of women's statuses and gender differentials. The proposition of a benefit status for the housewife survived despite its inconsistency with insurance concepts, but some of her intended benefits did not. For the aged at least neither did the commitment to benefits eventually reaching subsistence levels. Finally national assistance was made an integrated central government function, but was not put under the Ministry of Social Security as Beveridge had recommended (Harris, 1977, pp. 448–9).

The Reports of the Joint Parliamentary Committee never aroused open political contention like that surrounding the Beveridge Report. Committee reports were tabled in Parliament, where they evoked congratulatory responses but no debate. Social policy experts discussed and publicised their recommendations, but the war, then at its most desperate point, crowded them off any wider political agenda. Nevertheless some of its proposals were acted on almost immediately, and virtually all had been implemented before the war was over. Committee recommendations were selectively embraced by a willing Labor government which, however, also used them to legitimate pragmatic manoeuvres in war-time administration. By the end of the war the Committee's key ideas had been made the foundations of a newly systematic framework for income security.

The war emergency of early 1942 gave new urgency to taxation reform. Central government was simply unable to command the war effort while the chief source of revenue was controlled by the states. In May 1942 Treasurer Ben Chifley pushed legislation through Parliament giving the Commonwealth power over the income tax. In a ploy much resented by state premiers, Chifley associated the nationalisation of income-taxing powers with a national widow's pension enacted in the same month. This new pension followed Committee recommendations very closely. At the same time, other changes were made in line with Committee recommendations: age, invalid and widow's pensions were extended to Aborigines, and racial exclusions also removed for naturalised Asiatics and Pacific Islanders ('Kanakas').

These measures contained all the essential elements of a national framework for income security. Coming at the crest of the war emergency, they gave institutional substance to a momentary spirit of national unity. Social security provided a fertile symbol for the nation as 'imagined community' (Anderson, 1983). The association of taxation with income security signified mutual obligation between citizen and state. Exclusions of non-white racial groups, which had previously seemed natural, were now obviously anomalous. Widowhood and war-caused adversity, first new charges on the nation-community, would no longer have to be borne as individual misfortunes.

Early in 1943 pragmatic politics of war finance were again linked with new income security measures. The quickening war economy was generating rapid growth in personal income threatening to create inflationary demand. Chifley relieved the pressure with a new National Welfare Fund withholding current resources to finance welfare protection. The measure enabled him to justify extending the income tax downwards to low and middle income groups (see Watts, 1980 for details). There would be small first instalments on the post-war future: allowances for the dependent wives and children of age and invalid pensioners, funeral benefits on behalf of deceased pensioners and increased, universal maternity allowances. Unemployment and sickness benefits were promised for the near future. Some of these benefits were Committee recommendations, but the National Welfare Fund itself owed little to the Joint Parliamentary Committee on Social Security. It was Chifley and the Treasury who translated the ALP's vague commitment to tax-financed social security into a politically astute budgetary device. The Committee's contribution had been to confer joint-party endorsement on Labor's financial principle for social security.

Chifley's association of uniform federal income tax with widow's pensions had established a symbolic connection between taxes and social security. The National Welfare Fund now institutionalised this linkage in the budgetary machinery of the state. The principles of national unity and financial equity were embodied in the fund itself and the family principle expressed in its first disbursements. The systemic basis was given full substantive content one year later with legislation for unemployment and sickness benefits (February 1944). These pursued the ideal expressed in the Committee's *Third Report*, in which tax financed benefits would provide for the full period of unemployment, subject to a work test. In September 1945 Treasurer Chifley moved to put the finance of social services on what Labor considered a proper 'contributory' basis. A separate graduated income tax levy labelled the 'social services contribution' was to be used exclusively for financing social services. This completed the basic outlines of Labor's tax/transfer system of income security, integrated and consolidated in the Social Services Consolidation Act of 1947.

Australia 'caught up' with Britain, and both nations entered the post-war period with newly modernised income security systems protecting their citizens against many of the contingencies of personal and economic life. In both countries the state was to provide flat-rate, subsistence income as a social right of membership in the nation community. But within these similarities were important differences. Australia had constructed a single-tier system attaching eligibility to citizenship and financial obligation to taxation. Liability for financial 'contribution' varied with income, while all citizens had the same right to benefits independently of employment status, work history and (imperfectly) of race and gender. Such right was, however, conditional upon a means-test of applicant and spouse. Unity and equality of the nation were symbolic rather than material. Social rights depended, too, on marital status, for the means-test on joint income made one partner's access to social security contingent on the income of the other. Britain, in contrast, had a two-tier system. National insurance funded flat-rate benefits from flat-rate contributions.[3] Unity and equality applied to the individuals, with benefits and contributory liability defined by personal history as employee or wife. Underpinning national insurance was national assistance, funded from general taxation and accessible through a means-test on married-couple income. National assistance was similar to Australian income security and like it provided benefits to people in circumstances not amenable to the insurance principles of the Beveridge legacy such as female sole parents, 'unmarried wives' and even 'domestic spinsters'. In principle these benefits also were rights of citizenship (Donnison, 1985). As a secondary tier, however, national assistance never conferred as strong a sense of rightful entitlement as the unitary Australian framework.

CONCLUSION

As soon as the Beveridge Report appeared the Australian Committee sent for a copy, but the archives do not show what they made of it. By that time their own labours on income security were complete and they had moved on to discussions of national health and a protracted battle with the Australian branch of the British Medical Association.

Both Reports were less original than timely. They were largely culminations of past historical development, rounding off established patterns of institutional evolution more significantly than they began new ones. Addison (1975, p. 213; also Harris, 1977, p. 449) describes the Beveridge Report as representing 'a conservative mode of advance': while it replaced pre-existing schemes with class limits in their ceilings with a single minimum for all, it retained insurance principles ensuring that everyone paid their own way and individual thrift might be rewarded. It implied only a mild redistribution between classes. He sees the three 'assumptions' of the Report as far more sweeping in their implications for the future than the social insurance scheme itself.

It is ironic then that the Beveridge proposals became so much more central an object of class politics than the Australian commitment to social security financed from progressive income taxation. The Australian principle allowed, at least in theory, greater scope for class redistribution and moreover made no individual connection between contribution and benefit. But all the Committee endorsed was a principle. Its actual class content, Labor's dream of redistributive social justice, depended on the actualities of taxation. In the exigencies of war finance the working class was newly incorporated into the income-tax base, and it had to pay much of the cost itself. The effect was not unlike contributory finance (Watts, 1980, pp. 247–9). Though its precise calculus has since depended on the total structure of direct and indirect taxation, it too has never been more than mildly redistributive between classes.

And as an embodiment of national unity, tax-financed social security now symbolised individual as much as class-based social justice. Social security conferred protection against individual misfortune, with the financial burden distributed according to individual incomes. Constructed as a system of individual rights and responsibilities, social security took on the liberal democratic character of political contract between citizen and state. The ground was laid for the discourse about wealth and class to give way to another about income groups and poverty lines.

Gender politics were also much more salient in the British case, where women's groups actively supported and contested the provisions for women, family and dependency outlined in the Beveridge Report (Wilson, 1977, pp. 153–4). The Beveridge proposals embodied internal contradictions between family and insurance principles. These were especially evident in the house-wife's benefit and Beveridge's personal advocacy of the proposal, finally abandoned, to 'insure' her against marital breakdown, which he (rightly) saw as a legitimate industrial risk. The two-fold patriarchal character of the Beveridge proposals is a logical outcome of this contradiction. Women's claim to the rights of insurance was to be mediated by the contributory status of their husbands, even in widowhood and old age. In circumstances not covered by insurance, such as unsupported single parenthood, they would fall to second-tier national assistance and the administration of the cohabitation rule.

Australian women's groups put forceful arguments to the Committee, including radical demands for gender equality, but there was little or no public discussion of the Committee's response in its Reports. Perhaps the long hiatus in the development of social security made any advance welcome. Child endowment had been introduced only shortly before, and a badly needed widow's pension was now proposed. More important, the Committee's recommendations for both widow's pensions and allowances for wives and children of pensioners gave to welfare provision the 'family wage' form long established in Arbitration Court determinations, where a male worker was presumed a breadwinner supporting wife and children and women workers presumed to be supported by a father or husband. Australian women were then contesting the family wage in claims for equal pay, but they were doing so in the more promising venue of an expanding war economy.

Australia's non-contributory framework gave women comparatively direct access to social security, for it did not make their claims contingent on a husband's insurance status. Like men they paid taxes in relation to their incomes,[4] and as citizens they had rights to claim benefits according to formal criteria of need and eligibility. Besides age and disability there were specific rights for women in the event of widowhood or desertion. In this limited sense the Australian income security was, while clearly patriarchal (Shaver, 1983), at least potentially less so than its British counterpart.

The underside of war-time advances in Australian social security was the continued reliance of the system on means-testing. Esping-Andersen (1987) has pointed to the central place of universalism in social democratic strategies for the Welfare State. Programmes which cater to narrow groups, what he calls the 'class-ghetto model', entrench status and other differentials within the working class. Universalism in welfare provision promotes solidarities of nation and class, though usually at the cost of redistributive possibilities. Perhaps means-testing was not so much hated in a country with no domestic experience of the poor laws. Perhaps the war-time atmosphere suppressed such a divisive issue. Whatever the reason, Australian war-time discussion of income security effectively ignored the question, and it did not arise again until after the war. On it depended the redistributive virtues claimed for Australia's distinctive form of welfare state, and these have been a central pivot of Australian welfare politics through the post-war period and beyond. Its effects on working class solidarity have been less openly acknowledged, but may in part explain weak working-class identification with welfare politics (see Castles, 1985).

Applied to the joint resources of husband and wife, the means-test was also central to its patriarchal character, for it made the social rights of all married individuals contingent upon the actions and resources of the other (see Shaver, 1984 and forthcoming). Structurally its married-couple basis converted the framework of class stratification in welfare entitlements from a ladder of individuals to a ladder of family units. Though less widely recognised, this too underlies contemporary welfare politics, where the social entitlements of sole parents especially are newly controversial.

NOTES

1. A detailed historical account of this phase of the Committee's life is published in Shaver (1987).
2. An American inquiry into social security and employment planning was also conducted at much the same time. See Marion Clawson, *New Deal Planning; The National Resources Planning Board*, Baltimore, Md, Johns Hopkins University Press, 1981.
3. Beveridge's flat-rate principle for contributions and benefits was not abandoned until the mid-1970s, since when contributions have been related to earnings and gender differences in benefits greatly reduced (see Land and Parker, 1978, pp. 339–40).
4. The Australian income tax applies to individuals, husbands and wives reporting as separate individuals.

REFERENCES

Addison, P. (1975) *The Road to 1945* (London: Jonathan Cape).

Anderson, B. (1983) *Imagined Community: The Origins of Nationalism* (London: Verso).

Attlee, C. R. (1954) *As It Happened* (London: William Heinemann).

Beveridge, Lord [Sir William] (1955) *Power and Influence* (New York: The Beechhurst Press).

Bruce, M. (1966) *The Coming of the Welfare State* (rev. edn) (New York: Schocken).

Bryson, L. (1983) 'Women as Welfare Recipients: Women, Poverty and the State', in C. V. Baldock and B. Cass (eds), *Women, Social Welfare and the State in Australia* (Sydney: Allen & Unwin).

Cairns, J. F. (1957) 'The Welfare State in Australia', unpublished Ph.D. Thesis, University of Melbourne, Australia.

Cass, B. (1983) 'Redistribution to Children and to Mothers: A History of Child Endowment and Family Allowances', in C. V. Baldock and B. Cass (eds), *Women, Social Welfare and the State* (Sydney: Allen & Unwin).

Castles, F. (1985) *The Working Class and Welfare* (Sydney: Allen & Unwin).

Clawson, M. (1981) *New Deal Planning: The National Resources Planning Board* (Baltimore, Md: Johns Hopkins University Press).

Crosland, A. (1958) *The Future of Socialism* (London: Jonathan Cape).

Dickey, B. (1980) *No Charity There* (Melbourne: Nelson).

Donnison, D. (1985), 'The Cohabitation Rule', in C. Ungerson (ed.), *Women and Social Policy* (London: Macmillan).

Esping-Andersen, G. (1987) 'Citizenship and Socialism: De-Commodification and Solidarity in the Welfare State', in M. Rein, G. Esping-Andersen and L. Rainwater (eds), *Stagnation and Renewal in Social Policy* (Armonk, New York: M. E. Sharpe).

Gilbert, B. B. (1966) *The Evolution of National Insurance in Great Britain* (London: Michael Joseph).

Gough, I. (1979) *The Political Economy of the Welfare State* (London: Macmillan).

Harris, J. (1977) *William Beveridge, A Biography* (Oxford: Clarendon Press).

Hasluck, P. (1952) *The Government and the People 1939–41* (Canberra: Australian War Memorial).

Hasluck, P. (1970) *The Government and the People 1942–1945* (Canberra: Australian War Memorial).

Higgins, W. (1978) 'State Welfare and Class Warfare', in G. Duncan (ed) *Critical Essays in Australian Politics* (Melbourne: Edward Arnold Australia).

Inter-departmental Committee on Social Insurance and Allied Services (1942) *Social Insurance and Allied Services*, Report by Sir William Beveridge (London: HMSO).

Joint [Parliamentary] Committee on Social Security (JCSS) (1941) *[First] Interim Report*, 24 September; (1942a) *Second Interim Report*, 6 March; (1942b) *Third Interim Report*, 25 March (Commonwealth of Australia, Parliamentary Papers, 1940–41–42–43, Vol. 2).

Kewley, T. H. (1973) *Social Security in Australia 1900-1972* (rev. edn) (Sydney University Press).

Land H. (1976) 'Women: Supporters or Supported?', in D. Barker and S. Allen (eds), *Sexual Divisions and Society: Process and Change* (London: Tavistock).

Land, H. and Parker, R. (1978) 'United Kingdom', in S. B. Kamerman and A. J. Kahn (eds), *Family Policy, Government and Families in Fourteen Countries* (New York: Columbia University Press).

McIntosh, M. C. (1978) 'The State and the Oppression of Women', in A. Kuhn and A. M. Wolpe (eds), *Feminism and Materialism* (London: Routledge & Kegan Paul).

Marshall, T. H. (1963) 'Citizenship and Social Class', in *Sociology at the Crossroads* (London: Heinemann).

O'Connor, J. (1973) *The Fiscal Crisis of the State* (New York: St. Martin's).

Offe, C. (1984) *Contradictions of the Welfare State* (Cambridge, Mass.: MIT Press).

Roe, J. (ed) (1976) *Social Policy in Australia* (Sydney: Cassels).

Rowley, C. D. (1971) *Outcasts in White Australia* (Canberra: Australian National University Press).

Shaver, S. (1983) 'Sex and Money in the Welfare State', in C. V. Baldock and B. Cass (eds), *Women, Social Welfare and the State* (Sydney: Allen & Unwin).

Shaver, S. (1984), 'The Assets Test and the Politics of Means Testing', *Australian Journal of Social Issues*, Vol. 19, No. 4, pp. 300–6.

Shaver, S. (1987) 'Design for a Welfare State: The Joint Parliamentary Committee on Social Security', *Historical Studies*, Vol. 22, No. 88, April pp. 411–31.

Shaver, S. (1989) 'Sex and Money in the Fiscal Crisis', in R. Kennedy (ed.), *Australian Welfare: Historical Sociology* (Melbourne: Macmillan).

Summers, A. (1973) *Damned Whores and God's Police* (Melbourne: Penguin).

Titmuss, R. M. (1950) *Problems of Social Policy, UK (Cabinet Office) History of the Second World War* (London: HMSO).

Watts, R. (1980) 'Origins of the Australian Welfare State', *Historical Studies*, Vol. 19, pp. 175–98.

Wheeler, L. (1985) 'War and Welfare', unpublished Ph.D. thesis, University of New South Wales, Australia.

Wilson, E. (1977) *Women and the Welfare State* (London: Tavistock).

6 The Politics of Caring: The Case of Municipal Homemaking in Finland

Leila Simonen

There are several feminist views of the rise of the Welfare State: a shift in the primary site of male dominance from the family to the state (Hernes, 1984); a burgeoning of ways to reorganise women's everyday lives in the interests of the state (Wilson, 1977; Liljeström and Dahlström, 1981); or, less negatively, the articulation of women's own interests. My intent is to analyse the kind of interests women as political actors have had when struggling to establish caring reforms and thus to found Welfare State services.

The focus of my chapter is to analyse the emergence and development of one social service system in Finland – 'municipal homemaking'. In many ways, Finland seems to be a 'deviant case' among Western countries and, as such, it forces rethinking of feminist accounts of relations between women and the Welfare State services. How is it that Finland has a system of municipal homemakers which serves women's interests much better than their equivalent in other countries with developed welfare states? In order to understand the system of municipal homemaking I turned to its historical grounding. Who campaigned for paid homemakers in Finland and why? What role did women play in campaigning for this reform? What are the implications of this 'relative success story' of the Finnish municipal homemaker for feminist theorising about women and the Welfare State?

THE POSITION OF WOMEN IN FINLAND

The political position of women has been exceptional in Finland. Already in 1917 10 per cent of the first Parliament of independent Finland consisted of female Members of Parliament. Women have also been important in economic life. From the beginning of the century, Finnish women have comprised at least 44 per cent of the labour force. In 1982 women in Finland represented 47.7 per cent of the labour force. Both the relative and absolute labour force participation of women has increased during the last 25 years (*The Position of Women in Finland*, 1985, pp. 74 and 84).

The *high percentage of economically active women* partly relates to the late industrialisation of Finland and to the rapid development of Welfare State services providing employment in paid caring. In the 1950s, when other Western sisters were suffering from the 'problem with no name' (Friedan, 1963), as suburban married women were confined in their homes as housewives, Finland was still predominantly agrarian. Until 1950 half the population earned their livelihood from agriculture and typically lived on family farms or small-holdings, although there was an increasing growth in waged labour: temporary labouring and lumbering for men, and domestic service and increasing factory work for women.

During the Second World War it was up to women to carry on with normal life and its tasks. And after Finland lost the war, the Finns had to pay a heavy war indemnity with the products of heavy industry. Heavy industry therefore increased drastically in those post-war years. There was a *shortage of labour power* because 200 000 men were dead or badly wounded (out of a population of under four million). Although heavy industry remained a man's area, labour shortages ensured that women were needed in other industries. Women were also needed to organise the resettling of 400 000 Finns moving into Finland from Karelia and other areas (former Finnish territories) which belonged from then on to the Soviet Union. Unlike other Western countries, women were also of great importance in political and economic life *after* the war. They were not pushed back into the home in the same way as in other Western countries (see for instance, Pierson, 1986).

A number of factors contributed to a positive attitude to women's labour force participation. Since the Second World War, the education of girls has been more common than that of boys in the Finnish countryside. The female population started to leave the Finnish countryside earlier than men. Educating girls gave them a better opportunity for an occupation. The population in Finland belonging to the upper class or upper middle class was quite small in number. The bourgeois model of women as potential wives who would not work outside the home was not commonly rooted in Finnish culture. Already, as early as 1959, only 23 per cent of working-age women were exclusively house-wives. In 1982, the percentage staying at home was no more than 8.6 per cent.

Currently, working mothers with small children are much more common in Finland than in any other capitalist country in the world: 77 per cent of Finnish mothers with children under school age are economically active. Unlike women in other Nordic countries with a high labour force participation, Finnish women most often work *full time*: in 1982, only 11.6 per cent of economically active women worked part time (*The Position of Women in Finland*, 1985, pp. 93, 94, 96, 111–12).

Women actively participating in the labour force when their children are small indicates two things. First, a long chain of female generations has already experienced the dual role of performing waged work and running the home. Moreover, the importance of 'own' job and own salary is always emphasised by Finnish women who have been studied. The time spent at work is referred to as 'own' while the time spent at home is known as 'others' (Strandell, 1983). Second, there must be arrangements for high-quality caring organised by the state or on some other collective basis. The care of the elder generation must also be organised collectively.

MUNICIPAL HOMEMAKERS IN CONTEMPORARY FINLAND

Municipal homemakers work in the homes of old or handicapped people, or they work for families with children where there is sickness or a need for temporary care. Homemakers do not provide day care for children, except in the case of a sick child who cannot attend a day care centre. Municipal homemakers are not home helps, or workers in day care centres, or nurses. They are *qualified carers* with two and a half years of theoretical and practical training after at least nine years of comprehensive education.

Unlike other Nordic countries and some other Western countries where this kind of service is available, homemakers in Finland are monthly salaried public employees – in other words, full-time workers with total job security. They earn seniority benefits with accumulated service years; that is, higher salaries and longer holidays. Homemakers are public employees and thus, when nominated to a position, they can continue until retirement age. Municipal homemakers are, with few exceptions, all women. Although they are unionised (85 per cent), their fixed monthly 'salary is quite low as is common in all public caring occupations performed by women.

The number of full-time home help staff in Finland is 15 000 (the current population of Finland is under five million). In Finland, unlike most other Western societies, the 'crises of the Welfare State' have not yet become an actual threat for women. On the contrary, the number of public, full-time homemakers is going to double in a few years because of the growing need to care for the elderly, the handicapped and sick day care children.

In Finland, there are homemakers in every municipality, both in cities and in rural communities. Home help in Finland is almost totally state organised and financed by taxation. Receivers of home help pay only 4 per cent of the costs, and the rest is financed by the state and by municipalities. If somebody with a low income is in need of care, he or she can receive home help free of charge.

Although the ideology of universality (the right to social services for all residents of a municipality) still exists in Finland, not everybody in need of care or housework is able to receive home help. The best situation is in small municipalities and the worst is in the capital area where there is a shortage of home help personnel (because of expensive housing and the most intensive workload for homemakers). Thus, there are still priority ranks for those in need: single mothers, families with children in need of educational support or students are the first to receive help among families with children. Elderly or handicapped people living alone and willing to stay in their own home, instead of institutional or semi-institutional care, are also entitled to home help.

PIONEERS IN VISITING HOMEMAKING

The General Mannerheim League for Child Welfare

During the first decades of the century, the need to improve the social situation of children and women of the rural proletariat was articulated by (among others) Sophie Mannerheim, a sister of General Mannerheim (the military leader of the 'white' bourgeois troops in the Finnish Civil War of 1918). She received nursing training in England and had a strong interest in improving living conditions for children of less fortunate classes. General Mannerheim saw a national task in founding a civic organisation which would unify society and lessen class contradictions. The General Mannerheim League for Child Welfare[1] was thus founded in 1920. The aim of the League was 'To build a new society where citizens are both physically and morally healthy, where a greater understanding prevails between the classes, and where the prospects for positive development are better' (Kenraali Mannerheimin Lastensuojeluliitto, Toimintakertomus 1920–21 – The Mannerheim League for Child Welfare, Annual Report 1920–21, p. 14, in Finnish). Educating and advising women in domestic duties, and having them introduce values of middle-class family life at home, were inexpensive ways to try to avoid the re-emergence of socialism among the rural proletariat. Mothers and wives were identified by male medical professionals as core figures in the family. The underlying aim of helping mothers was actually to 'save the *children*' (Heydemann, 1980) and thus improve the quality of Finnish stock.

The desired reform in the everyday lives of rural, working-class women was initiated through advice from a 'lady visitor' (lady here referring to a woman). In the 1930s, the Mannerheim League for Child Welfare proposed establishing an occupation of visiting homemakers. Visiting homemakers could replace the mother in cases of illness or physical or mental overwork (Kenraali Mannerheimin Lastensuojeluliitto, 1922). The task of the homemaker was defined as follows:

> Homemakers are not maids, or servants, or nurses. They are warm-hearted women who are capable of performing household duties and whose sole concern is to maintain the welfare of our homes. The spur for their work lies in the truth that the success of the nation depends on the state and welfare of our homes. (Kodinhoitajattaren johtosääntö, 1931 – The Ethical Code for Visiting Homemakers, 1931, p. 1, in Finnish).

Visiting homemakers in Finland, in the early stages of their history, were not introduced as a replacement for a housewife, an urban mother or a wage-earner's wife, but as a replacement for a rural, small farmer's wife. Homemakers performed not only housework but also the whole range of domestic work. Domestic work done by small-holders' wives covered a large area: everything from knitting socks for children to milking cows and working in the fields. The 'productive' domestic work done by small-holders' wives (Delphy, 1984, pp. 85–6) was the whole family's cornerstone for survival. Husbands were often away engaged in temporary, waged work in lumbering or employed as seasonal workers in the fields of big farms (Siiskonen, 1984, p. 71). Women were core figures in the small-holding. The mother was of crucial importance for the family, and when she fell ill, the well-being and survival of the whole family was in danger.

The Population Federation and Homesister Training

In the 1930s the Finnish population political movement expressed concern about insufficient population growth. As a response to growing concerns about *declining population* and rural depopulation, the Population Federation was founded in Finland in 1941 (Väestöliitto, 1942).[2] The Population Federation was an important pressure group. It gave top priority to maternity care and to raising the standard of living for families with children. A series of Acts relating to maternity benefits, maternity leave and subsidised loans for all newly-weds was passed in the 1940s.

The ideology behind homesister training was partly influenced by quantitative and qualitative population policy (Hietala, 1987): homesisters represented a pool of qualified women able to work in families with several children. The training of homesisters was intended to help to relieve the *shortage of domestics* and replace 'poorly qualified' maids. Homesisters were also 'model housewives' providing information, advice and new enthusiasm for women in the household sector.

The main objective of the homesister training was to establish a permanent female occupation and to give hard-working women the chance to make a career in the household sector. However, the calling of the homesister occupation was quite soon outdated, and homesisters were willing to take positions as municipal homemakers as soon as the positions originated in the 1950s.

FIRST ACTS ON MUNICIPAL HOMEMAKING

'State Feminism' and the Struggle for Municipal Homemaking

The first efforts to make homemaker work a statutory and public form of caring were made as early as the 1940s. The contribution of female MPs was vital in these efforts. In this context it is possible to talk of 'state feminism' as women in politically powerful positions have struggled for better everyday lives for women. The first proposal to establish posts for visiting homemakers as municipal workers came from the Social Democratic Party (SDP). Among the most ardent proponents of this idea was Miina Sillanpää, a female SDP MP who not only worked hard for improvements in the position of domestic servants, but who was also active in the preparation of the Municipal Homemaking Act.

In Parliament, *gender blocks* were established across political party lines: Miina Sillanpää worked in close co-operation with Elsa Bonsdorff, a female MP of the Swedish People's Party. They both wanted to improve the situation of over-worked mothers in the countryside (Simonen, 1985).

In 1940 Miina Sillanpää suggested that over-worked small-holders' wives, those who had a seven-day-a-week responsibility for farm, livestock and kitchen, should have holidays without their children and husbands. This could be organised with the help of trained and reliable homemakers (Simonen, 1985, pp. 79–81). These kinds of holidays were actually organised in Finland in the 1940s and 1950s, often with the help of worker's organisations or of various women's co-operatives.

Throughout the 1940s the need for a municipal home help system was a regular bone of contention in Parliament. Plans were drawn up to make the homemakers' job a public, municipal occupation for women in both urban and rural municipalities. The selected targets for charity work of civic organisations had now been expanded to cover all residents of a municipality. This is why Liberal Party MPs were strictly opposed to the reform; they regarded municipal home help as one step towards socialism. Home help, in becoming a state organised caring reform, received its support from the political left and from part of the Agrarian Party (Simonen, 1985).

The first Act on municipal homemaking was passed in 1950 in

Finland (L 272/50). The municipal homemaker system was established to help rural, poor families with several children. The Act was passed within the framework of larger social reform to support underprivileged families, and homemakers were introduced as a new group of trained, female public employees in the field of social policy.

When homemaker occupations were established in Finland in 1950, there was a long discussion in Parliament about sufficient salary. Homemakers were presumed to be unmarried women. The homemaker's salary was commensurate with that of another female occupation – nursing. The salary, as the discussion went, should be a little bit less but enough to support a woman living alone, bearing in mind that the municipality was supposed to provide housing (Simonen, 1985). Thus, although in Finland as elsewhere, it was often assumed that women were not the main earners of households, from the beginning homemakers were envisaged as needing to support themselves.

The first homemakers in the 1950s were pioneers in the field; they did all kinds of work depending upon the needs of the family in question. The pioneering work of homemakers was simply in sharing the everyday compulsory work with another woman: there was no mistress–domestic hierachy in the house. The salary of the homemaker was paid by the municipality and thus she was not dependent upon the family. On the other hand, the family mother was not obliged to be grateful to the homemaker for her help because, in the mother's eyes, 'she was just doing her paid job'.

Homemakers' help was generally needed in rural Finnish families with several children in order to replace the 'mothering necessary for the care of children and the household'. In addition, homemakers provided a release for mothers in case of sickness and thus avoided bigger societal investments. If a large family could have a homemaker for two weeks, it would certainly be less costly than placing the mother in hospital and the children in a children's home when the mother fell ill because of too much work or too many pregnancies.

Mobile Carers: Municipal Home Help and Care for the Elderly

The Act concerning municipal home help was renewed in 1966 (L

270/66). New kinds of workers were introduced in the area of home help. Caring for the elderly had become a problem to be solved by the Welfare State, not by a caring arrangement within kinship relations. Home helps became a new group of workers acting as municipal home help providers. Home helps were often middle-aged women willing to earn their own money and do 'something practical within the household' after their own children had grown up. Home helps were trained for five weeks, but their training was very short compared with homemaker training. They were employed by municipalities and typically worked full time. For instance, in 1980 only 28 per cent of Finnish municipal home helps worked part time (Home Help 1980, 1981).

Another new group of workers introduced as administrative personnel in 1966 were supervisory homemakers. A supervisory homemaker received five months' training and was available for each municipality with at least ten homemakers.

Homemakers and home helps have become mobile carers, moving from one family in need to the next one. In the 1950s, homemakers stayed with one family for one or two weeks, but in the 1970s it became more typical that a homemaker would stay with one family for only a couple of days or even less (Simonen, 1982). Within the contemporary model of homemaker work, a sort of 'assembly line' model is unsatisfactory for workers and clients. If homemakers have less time for a family or an elderly client, they feel that they cannot fully do their 'real' work.

The last Act designating home help as a municipal social service was passed in 1982 (L 710/82). Home help services are a form of care available for everybody in need. The number of homemakers is going to be doubled in a few years.

WOMEN'S TWO-FOLD INTEREST IN COLLECTIVISED CARING

Working-class and peasant women's interests were shaped by the changes brought to the traditional peasant society by rising capitalism. Women's identities were based on the collective agricultural identity of community-based solidarity and rooted later on, with the ascendancy of capitalism, in the solidarity of the working-class movement. For instance, Miina Sillanpää, the female MP and working-class movement activist mentioned earlier, is a symbol of the main ideology among women's interests. Her action to change women's burdens was embedded in the fact that there was no clear distinction between private and public. Her work of involvement in networks and understanding herself as part of the working-class movement was based on collective solidarity (Sulkunen, 1987).

Second, upper middle-class women's societal awakening was based on the liberal idea of making a distinction between private and public. Their own experiences as 'lights of the home' were made available to the public in the form of philanthropic activity. Nevertheless women's positions were strictly embedded in the private sphere, but what is worth noticing is that middle-class women were also expected to become involved in community affairs, to help the poor, and so on. In Finland, at the beginning of this century, a woman's main aim was to strengthen the role of women as housewives and farmers' wives (see also, Tuominen, 1987). At that time, as Irma Sulkunen argues, all emancipational interests were of secondary importance to the ideology of motherhood (Sulkunen, 1987). The position of women was to be mothers in the home and mothers of the nation.

In the early decades of this century. Finnish women's interests were focused on class. Middle-class women wanted the same rights as men but, at the same time, they wanted to introduce middle-class values to the homes of working-class women. By valuing the concepts of motherhood and childhood (Key, 1909 and Key, 1970 [originally in 1914]), their activity made working-class women guilty of 'neglecting their duties'. Working-class wives were told to be responsible for stopping their husbands from drinking, and they were told to create a good home for their children. The actual material circumstances of working-class families were not always taken into consideration.

Working-class women's interests were constituted differently. They wanted to get more respect for motherhood (mothering as work), and they struggled for maternity allowances from a different angle than that of middle-class mothers. Working-class women's experiences of dependence upon their husbands resulted in their demanding a work place of their own and thus their own money. Working-class women and mothers wanted to become waged labourers in their own right; being dependent upon the state was less trouble than being dependent upon a private breadwinner.

MUNICIPAL HOME HELP AS A CARING RE-ARRANGEMENT

Anglo-American and Nordic feminist discussion has argued that the nature of the Welfare State has had its firm grounding in the nuclear, heterosexual family with a full-time caring wife. When homemaking in Finland became state-organised caring through social reform in 1950, the goal of the service was 'to replace the work at home that a housewife or a farmer's wife did' (L 272/50). The idea embodied in the Act was to provide temporary help for households in sickness, for the delivery of a new baby or for an overburdened housewife. Clearly enough there seemed to be a gender division of labour in mind when the Act was passed. However, there are two points which deserve further consideration. First, to provide trained women to work in a family when the mother, wife or housewife was not able is radical. The Finnish homemaker was not only an advisor who made suggestions and provided help with the problems of everyday life, but she also performed manual and mental labour right from the beginning of the homemaker occupation.

Finnish visiting homemakers came from the rural working-class or from farming backgrounds themselves, and they did all the work which the mother usually did at home under difficult circumstances. New demands from semi-public power and later from the state were mediated by a female homemaker: ignorance, poor mothering and the out-dated skills of a housewife could be changed by advice and example. A visiting homemaker gave not only her friendship and advice, but she also did the same tasks as the mother. A crucial difference between the Anglo-Saxon model of friendly visitors and the Finnish visiting homemaker was that less charity and *more practical work* were involved in the work of Finnish visiting homemakers.

British feminist critiques of social policy have exposed the taken-for-granted assumption that married women will be full-time carers of their families and accused government policy of colluding in the 'naturalness' of women's altruism. Land and Rose (1985) criticise the way social benefits based on waged work (and the assumption that a labourer is a man) were structured to confirm the priority that *all* married women should do their 'duties' in the home. Unlike men whose rights to benefits were determined by their relationship to the labour market, women were defined entirely in terms of their marital status. Losing a job gave a man a claim to maintenance from the state, whereas losing a husband gave a woman similar claims.

Showstack Sasson writes that the assumption in the creation of the Welfare State is that the family (= women) will provide primary services (Showstack Sassoon, 1982, p. 10). This analysis is shown to be unsatisfactory by the Finnish case. From the women's point of view, it is of crucial importance how caring is shared within a society.

Unlike the British case, class and gender struggles of Nordic welfare states have taken the individual as the unit rather than advocating the model of 'family wage'. The Nordic system has empowered women socially. The creation of Welfare State services in Finland has provided women with new potentials for caring networks. Female support networks of caring were rooted in the society – first as part of civil society and later as part of a state organised *caring infrastructure*. In Finland there is no pool of women able to do voluntary work and take full-time care of dependent relatives without pay. Although as Waerness (1978; also, Simonen, 1982) has pointed out, even in most developed Western societies, there is an invisible welfare state, where women still do the bulk of caring.

CONCLUSION

Women's particular interests can be seen in the creation of welfare services. Women's dependence on the family has decreased, but their dependence on the Welfare State has increased. And the crucial issue is, *what kind* of welfare state they are dependent on? As Finnish women say, they would rather be dependent on the state than on the private family (= husband), because women themselves are inside the state and can thus transform it accordingly (through union politics, decision-making as public employees or decision-making as politicians). The struggle for the Welfare State reinforces gender relations in a way which improves women's position: women would be much better off with an advanced welfare state than with a private patriarchal family (Julkunen, 1987).

History suggests that women have had a two-fold relationship or double interest in social policy. First, women's *reproductive interests* have influenced social policy (Rantalaiho, 1986). In other words, women have demanded that they be valued as women and mothers, and thus they wanted maternity rights in the form of maternity benefits. Second, women have also demanded *civil rights* similar to those of men. Together these interests have dominated and also intertwined throughout the history of social policy.

Women's reproductive interests seem to be embedded in the relational understanding of the political nature of everyday life. Women's interests are intertwined with the continuity of the needs of everyday life: consequently, women's historically specific experiences have often been struggling with the necessities of caring for the elderly, children and handicapped people. The context of every day life has to be taken as important, meaningful and problematic. That way the history of women acting as *political agents* in the creation of a caring infrastructure becomes visible. As pointed out in many feminist studies the Nordic model of the Welfare State has inherited its caring nature from women.

Thus far, the bulk of androcentric social policy analysis has focused mainly on the social insurance system and issues related to wage labour. Caring and how it is shared seems to become the core of feminist social policy analysis. Finnish experience shows that it is of crucial importance for women's emancipation to concentrate on everyday life, and how women act as political subjects can articulate the reproductive interests of women in the formation of the Welfare State.

NOTES

1. The Mannerheim League for Child Welfare is still an active organisation but its profile has drastically changed. At the moment it runs some quite radical programmes (for example, a telephone service for children in distress, intensified family help for families in crises, health education programmes, housing projects).
2. The Population Federations as a voluntary organisation, still exists. Its updated profile is now to provide information on family planning and sex education.

REFERENCES

Delphy, C. (1984) *Close to Home. A Materialist Analysis of Women's Oppression* (London: The Explorations in Feminism Collective, Hutchinson).

Friedan, B. (1963) *The Feminine Mystique* (New York: Dell).

Hernes, H. M. (1984) 'Women and the Welfare State. The Transition from Private to Public Dependence', in H. Holter (ed.), *Patriarchy in a Welfare Society* (Oslo, Bergen, Stavanger, Tromsø: Universitetsforlaget) pp. 26–45.

Heydemann, I. (ed.) (1980) 'Suomen lapsen pitkä marssi', (The Long March of the Finnish Child, in Finnish) *Mannerheimin Lastensuojeluliiton vaiheita ja Arvo Ylpön muistelmaa* (Porvoo, Helsinki, Juva: WSOY).

Hietala, M. (1987) 'Väestöliiton kotisisaret – auttajia koteihin', (Homesisters of the Population Federation – Helpers for Homes, in Finnish) *Tulen kesyttäjät. Suomalaista naistutkimusta* (Helsingin Akateemisten Naisten 60-vuotisjuhlakirja. Porvoo, Helsinki, Juva: WSOY) pp. 175–203.

Home Help 1980. Official Statistics of Finland XXI A:30 (1981) (National Board of Social Welfare, Bureau for Planning and Statistics: Helsinki).

Julkunen, R. (1987) 'Miesten vai naisten hyvinvointivaltio', (A Welfare State for Men or for Women, in Finnish) *Sosiaalinen Aikakauskirja*, Nr 2. pp. 31–6.

Kenraali Mannerheimin Lastensuojeluliitto. Toimintakertomus 1920–21 (1922) (The Mannerheim League for Child Welfare. Annual Report 1920–21, in Finnish) (Helsinki: Suomalaisen kirjallisuuden seuran kirjapainon osakeyhtö).

Key, E. (1909) *The Century of the Child* (New York: G. P. Putnam) (first published in Swedish).

Key, E. (1970) *The Renaissance of Motherhood* (New York: Source Book Press) (first published in Swedish).

Kodinhoitajattaren johtosääntö perusteluineen 1931 (The Ethical Code for Visiting Homemakers, in Finnish). Mannerheimin Lastensuojeluliiton arkisto, 1931.

L 272/50. Laki kunnallisista kodinhoitajista (Act Relating to Municipal Homemakers in 1950, in Finnish and Swedish) (Helsinki: Suomen Asetuskokoelma).

L 270/66. Laki kunnallisesta kodinhoitoavusta (Act Relating to Municipal Home Help in 1966, in Finnish and Swedish) (Helsinki: Suomen Asetuskokoelma).

L 710/82. Sosiaalihuoltolaki (Social Welfare Act in 1982, in Finnish and Swedish) (Helsinki: Suomen Asetuskokoelma).

Land, H. and H. Rose (1985) 'Compulsory Altruism for Some or an Altruistic Society for All?', in P. Bean, J. Ferris and D. Whynes (eds), *In Defense of Welfare* (London and New York: Tavistock) pp. 74–96.

Liljeström, R. and Dahlström, E. (1981) *Arbetarkvinnor i hem'arbete och samhällsliv* (Working Women at Home, at Work and in Society, in Swedish) (Stockholm: Tidens Förlag).

Pierson, R. R. (1986) *They're Still Women After All': The Second World War and Canadian Womanhood* (Toronto: McClelland & Stewart).

The Position of Women in Finland. Statistical Information on the Situation of Finnish Women (1985) in Finnish, Swedish and English. The Statistical Central Bureau (Helsinki: Valtion Painatuskeskus).

Rantalaiho, L. (1986) 'Reproduktion maisema', (The Landscape of Reproduction, in Finnish), in L. Rantalaiho (ed.), *Miesten tiede – naisten puuhat. Yhteiskuntatieteen kritiikkiä naisten työn näkökulmasta* (Jyväskylä: Vastapaino/ Tampere) pp. 19–56.

Showstack Sasson, A. (1982) 'Dual Role: Women and Britain's Crisis', *Marxism Today* (December), pp. 6–11.

Siiskonen, P. (1984) 'Talonpoikaisnaisen aseman histriallinen kehitys Suomessa', (The Historical Development of Finnish Peasant Woman, in Finnish) in L. Husu and M. Honkasalo (eds), *Työ, nainen ja tutkimus*. Valtioneuvoston kanslian monisteita 2. Helsinki. pp. 70–6.

Simonen, L. (1982) *Kunnallinen kodinhoitoapu lapsiperheiden tukijana* (Municipal Home Help Supporting Families with Children, in Finnish). Sosiaalihallituksen julkaisuja 7. Helsinki.

Simonen, L. (1985) *Kunnallinen kodinhoitaja – palkattua huolenpitotyötä tekevä hyvinvointiäiti* (The Municipal Homemaker in Finland – A Mother of the Welfare State in Waged Caring, in Finnish. Unpublished Licentiate's thesis) (Tampere: University of Tampere, Department of Social Policy).

Strandell, H. (1983) *Kvinnosocialisation och lönearbetets betydelse. Kvinnor i fabriks-, kontors- och omsorgsyrken* (The Socialization of Women and the Significance of Waged Work, in Swedish). Unpublished Licentiate's thesis (Helsinki: University of Helsinki, Department of Sociology).

Sulkunen, I. (1987) 'Naisten järjestäytyminen ja kaksijakoinen kansalaisus', (Women's Organisation and the Two-fold Citizenship, in Finnish) in R. Alapuro *et al.* (eds), *Kansa liikkeessä* (Helsinki: Kirjayhtymä) pp. 157–72.

Tuominen, K.-M. (1987) *Marttayhdistyksen Emäntälehti 1902–1906: kodin ja yhteiskunnan suojelija* (The Agrarian Housewife –: Journal 1902–06: The Protector of Home and Society, in Finnish). Unpublished thesis. (Tampere: University of Tampere, Department of Finnish History).

Väestöliitto 1941. ohjelma – säännöt (1942) (The Population Federation 1941, The Program and Rules, in Finnish). Väestöliiton julkaisuja no 2. (Helsinki: Forssan Kirjapaino Oy).

Waerness, K. (1978) 'The Invisible Welfare State: Women's Work at Home, *Acta Sociologica. Supplement*. (Special Congress Issue: The Nordic Welfare States) pp. 193–225.

Wilson, E. (1977) *Women and the Welfare State* (London: Tavistock).

Part III
Nineteenth-Century Intervention and Reform

7 Women in the Factory: The State and Factory Legislation in Nineteenth-Century Britain

Barbara Harrison and Helen Mockett

INTRODUCTION

The relationship between the state and women has long been a neglected and historically under-informed area of research. In part this is accounted for by a theoretical insistence that the state chiefly functions in relation to the struggles between capital and labour. It has been feminists who have insisted that the state also acts to secure the conditions that continue to define the subordination of women, and that political struggle also concerns gender as well as class relations. However, much feminist analysis has also remained at the level of theoretical debate that has tended to result in an either/or dichotomy of state interests in relation to capitalism and patriarchy. Other work (Hartmann, 1979; Barrett, 1980; Walby, 1986) has argued such a dichotomy is unproductive, even though there are differences between authors on how that duality is to be conceptualised. Further, theoretical resolution is problematic if attention is not paid to empirical data that seeks to demonstrate state action in relation to women in a number of different spheres.

This chapter is an initial attempt, using primary historical sources, to examine state intervention in one particular field – that of women's industrial work in the period from 1830 to the early 1900s. It focuses on two main strands of state action and regulation in the field of women's employment: hours of work legislation and intervention with respect to industrial ill-health from the 'dangerous trades'. Hours of work legislation was the dominant form of state action initially and remained prominent while other concerns arose. One of these, sanitation, essentially became a matter for local government, while more specific threats to health from poisoning, machinery and dusts became a focus for action from the 1880s onwards. Indeed it can be argued, as one contemporary commentator did, that 'the control of the dangerous and injurious trades is in complete contrast to the stagnant conditions of legislation for hours' (Anderson, 1922; p. 148).

These two areas provide us with insights into the contradictions and paradoxes of state intervention in relation to the interests of patriarchy and capitalism, since if we only use hours of work legislation as Walby (1986) has done for this period, or examine specific, and to some extent exceptional, industries such as mining (Humphries, 1981; John, 1980; Mark-Lawson and Witz, 1988) alternative interpretations of state action can be obscured. The 'dangerous trades' brings some of these contradictions into sharper focus. In examining these interests it is also imperative that an attempt is made to redress the neglect of the issue of state action for women themselves. Although historical study presents some difficulties in ascertaining women's subjective perceptions and experiences, it is still possible to shift the analysis so that the centrality of gender relations enables women's interests to be interpreted.

We are going to side-step the issue of what is meant by the state, although we do not see it as either monolithic or autonomous. We realise that a clear theoretical formulation remains necessary. For our purposes we refer to the state as essentially comprising the officials of central government, political and elected office holders; and those who occupied positions within the state apparatus such as factory inspectors, or served the state in some official capacity as did some members of the medical profession.

There are essentially two main strands of state action and intervention that we consider here: first, investigation which occurred mainly through Commissions, Committees of Inquiry, and official regulatory agencies; and second, various forms of regulation such as legislation. These forms of action can elucidate assumptions about the 'need' to act and about how particular problems should be tackled, and as such the political strategies and processes of state action in relation to women's employment[1] in the nineteenth century can only be understood by reference to broader ideological concerns and social relations. In this regard there are some difficulties, however. Stated intentions cannot easily be disentangled from assumptions, implicit and explicit, which provide a basis for these intentions, and they do not always coincide. In the same way there can be a disjuncture between 'intention' and the consequences of legislation in practice. The 'intentionality' of state action is therefore difficult to establish, as are the effects of pressures upon the state from outside, which we are unable to discuss here.

In the sections that follow we will examine the 'problem' of women's work as defined by the state in both spheres of legislation; and consider the extent to which there were shared assumptions underlying the interference with women's labour. Some assessment will then be made of the adequacy of this intervention from a number of perspectives. This will enable us to explore the problematic concept of intentionality with respect to state action. Intervention that is at one level ideological can be seen as firmly rooted in economic and social relations, and the articulation between these has particular significance for women.

'Protectionism' as a rationale for regulation rested on explicitly stated concerns about women's vulnerability or weakness, physically, psychologically and politically. This ideology of 'protection', we will argue, was in fact an attempt to regulate domestic life and to maintain patriarchal relations at home and work, so long as the means adopted did not significantly undermine capitalist interests. It is in this context that sex-specific legislation with its exclusionary tenor and demands can be understood.

'EXPOSING THE EVIL ... CASTING ABOUT FOR A CURE' [2]

Women were employed in a wide range of occupations in the nineteenth century (Alexander, 1976; Hewitt, 1958; John, 1986) and whatever the employment they were commonly paid the lowest wages. Women's labour always offered the possibility of a cheaper alternative for employers anxious to realise high profits, if not because women were regarded as a more compliant group of workers (Pinchbeck, 1930). The payment of low wages and the difficulties for women to enter struggles around working conditions were because they were women. State intervention in the nineteenth century with respect to women's employment was almost entirely restricted to forms of industrial work (the exception being some concern with shop work). Although this was not the largest form of employment (this was domestic service) it was the mines and the factories that presented society and the state with the clearest dilemmas. It was not just that the work was arduous and/or a threat to the health or moral character of women, but because the nature of and changes in the division of labour – by skill, by gender and by family units – enabled the confinement of women to domestic labour to be considered. While some feminists have argued that a sexual division of labour was a consequence of state intervention and exclusionary practices pursued by some male workers (Walby, 1986; Rose, 1988), it seems that in many cases such a strategy could be pursued because the labour market was already highly segregated along gender lines. In particular a strategy of exclusion can only be followed if men do, or can be seen as available for, that work.

Despite the scale of exploitation evident, and the seriousness of the perceived problems affecting women, the scale of state intervention was in fact minimal in the earlier decades of the century and, although by the end of the century it had increased considerably, even here there was more investigation than attempts to interfere directly with conditions of labour. Investigation, as numerous commissions testify, was not always a precursor to legislation. As Harold Tennant, Chair of the Dangerous Trades Committee, commented on this example, the recommendations of the committee would 'at this rate take thirty-four years to put the whole into force' (Hansard, 1900, lxxxv; 1495). There was not, in any case, a consensus about the need for state intervention, and in fact there were strong lobbies arguing against any interference in this area as in the economy generally, and the state concurred with this view (Hall and Schwartz, 1985).

In their contemporary account of factory legislation, Hutchins and Harrison (1903) argued that essentially state intervention was cautious and slow, viewed only as an exceptional remedy for particular problems. These particular problems came to be seen as particular classes of employee, ie children and women, rather than working conditions generally. In fact the whole area of protective legislation for women was coloured by the premise that it was not just factory work *per se*, but women in factory work that constituted the real problem. Various aspects of this problem were identified and different groups emphasised specific aspects, but throughout the history of the legislation this was to be the basic premise upon which the state acted.

In this context three major assumptions underpinned state activity in relation to both hours of work and 'dangerous trades' legislation, although the relative importance of the three varied in different time periods and between the two spheres of intervention. First, it was assumed that the work threatened women's health in ways which did not apply to men; second, that there were particular social problems resulting from women's work; and third, that for various reasons women were more susceptible to the adverse consequences of their employment and were in need of special 'protection'. While it would be misleading to suggest that the state at any time presented a unanimous voice on any of these aspects, these were the arguments most consistently and successfully utilised in debates surrounding the legislation.

The first of these was identified as early as 1832 when a Select Committee, set up to consider the viability of limitation on the labour of children and young persons, suggested that there were possible reasons to include women in any such legislation. A vast array of medical witnesses gave evidence to the effect that women were too weak to bear the excessive hours of factory labour and that it adversely affected their ability to bear children (PP 1831–32, XV; 524–93). However, the following year a Royal Commission repudiated these assertions, despite including similar 'evidence', and summed up the case for female factory labour thus:

> Whatever may be said about the delicacy of the female organisation, and the inability of the female operative to endure fatigue, the female, as a child, an adolescent, and an adult, bears factory labour better than the male, and in regard to her own peculiar constitution and health, sustains no appreciable injury from it. (PP. 1833, XXI; 6)

Clearly there was no unanimity on the issue, and in fact the early legislation concerning women (1844, 1847) rested but lightly on the health aspect. Where arguments to this effect were used, however, they tended to stress the particular case of expectant and recently confined mothers, and frequently the concern expressed was more for the child than the woman. In 1862 the Fourth Report of the Medical Officer of Health reiterated this concern

(PP 1862, XXII; 655) and in the Report to the Local Governments Board (PP 1873, LV) virtually all the medical practitioners lamented the short period of confinement taken by factory women. Debates in Parliament in the 1870s followed similar lines, and while there was clearly an assumption of women's peculiar physical vulnerability to long hours of labour, arguments concentrated on reproduction. In 1874 an unsuccessful proposal was made to exclude women from employment for twelve months following the birth of a child – 'not so much in the interests of the mothers as in the interests of the children' (Hansard 1874, CCXX; 326). Similar proposals continued to emanate from Parliament and from other branches of the state for many years, but it was not until 1891 that a clause prohibiting women from working for four weeks following confinement was passed. Until this point the most frequently identified source of ill-health to women was tackled only within the context of hours of work legislation.

In practice, far more important to this type of intervention were the perceived social and moral problems associated with women's work outside the home. Concern for the morality of factory women was expressed by all arms of the state from 1832 onwards, and although this concern covered various aspects (drunkenness, bad language and mode of dress, for example) the emphasis was undoubtedly placed on sexual behaviour. Essentially then, the fear for the moral consequences of women's work was a fear for the social repercussions of it.

The 'social' evils were vociferously brought to public attention for the first time in the 1830s, when numerous articles and pamphlets appeared from a variety of sources (see, for example, Kay, 1832; Greg, 1831) emphasising the neglect of women's 'proper sphere' wrought by factory work, and stressing the devastating effects of this on men, children and society: 'This disruption of all the ties of home is one of the most fatal consequences of the factory system. The social relations which should distinguish the members of the same family are destroyed. The domestic virtues, man's natural instincts, and the affections of the heart are deadened and lost' (Gaskell, 1836). It was this line of argument that was taken up by the state and pursued to the greatest effect by parliamentarians in the 1840s, and re-emphasised again and again in all subsequent intervention. In 1844 the first Act to restrict women's labour was passed, and members of the House of Commons drew heavily on the social aspect of the 'problem';

> You are poisoning the very sources of order and happiness and virtue; you are tearing up root and branch, all relations of families to each other; you are annulling, as it were, the institution of domestic life, decreed by Providence himself, the wisest and kindest of earthly ordinances, the main-stay of social peace and virtue, and therein of national security. (Hansard 1844, LXXIII; 1100)

The investigations of the 1860s and 1870s, and debates in Parliament reproduced these arguments, emphasising particularly the effect on infant mortality (although despite a growing 'professionalism' and increasing claims to scientific expertise there was no agreement among the medical practitioners on this issue). Nevertheless these arguments above all others advanced by the state with regard to hours of work legislation held the widest public currency and were by far the most difficult for opponents to counter.

In terms of translating these perceived social evils into a successful case for intervention, the state drew heavily on the notion of women's particular vulnerability and their special need for 'protection'. Notions of female susceptibility traversed health, social and moral objections to women's work, and although the issue gained the greatest prominence in terms of the 'dangerous trades' the concept was perhaps the main 'enabling' factor in hours of work legislation; that is, it successfully countered arguments against the principle of intervention *per se*, and allowed the state to interfere in women's work in a way that was always considered unacceptable for men.

Several aspects arose here. Concern for women's health was clearly linked with the susceptibility argument and rested on a notion of the inherent biological differences between men and women. But in this sphere of intervention it was women's psychological, moral and political weaknesses that were particularly important. The Home Secretary, Sir James Graham, advanced the basis for the legislation in 1844: 'The law held that they were under such control that they could not decide and judge for themselves, and to the female sex generally many of the rights of freedom are denied' (Hansard 1844, LXXVIV; 630). Thus the right to interfere with the labour of women was justified in terms of their established political weakness, but in other ways too, women were seen as susceptible and in need of legal protection:

> With regard to women, however independent they might be, there was that in their character which gave them more endurance under pain, more fortitude under suffering, than men had, and which made them willing to undergo far more than men for the sake of those who were near and dear to them. They would wear themselves down by fatigue, quite reckless of the future consequences to themselves or to their offspring. It was for these reasons that he said they could not deal with women as absolutely free agents. (Hansard 1874, CCXIX; 1469)

Clearly the concept of susceptibility was firmly grounded in a social construction of women that established their unfitness for the public sphere of work and emphasised their political vulnerability. Thus women were seen as susceptible to ill-health and exploitation because of their social role and were 'encouraged' to reassume their 'proper' social role because they were susceptible.

In all senses then women were defined as a special group, unable to protect themselves and therefore in need of the special protection afforded by the state. And this factor was crucial to the rationale behind the strategy of the state in relation to the 'dangerous trades'.

Concern with the actual health of women was ostensibly more prominent in the spate of intervention at the end of the nineteenth century which can be differentiated from hours of work legislation in that it was directed at the specific dangers of work itself. It is interesting to note that the notion that work itself might constitute a danger to health had appeared much earlier in the century. Lack of proper ventilation in particular was identified as early as 1844, and the Medical Officers of Health raised the profile of industrial diseases in the 1860s, noting that 'no existing law is more than very imperfectly applicable to procure the mitigation of unwholesome industrial conditions' (PP 1862, XXII; 493). However, the specific problems of industrial ill-health were not raised again to any effect until the passing of the White Lead Act in 1883, and the 'dangerous trades' only received formal recognition and definition in 1892 under Schedule 8 of the 1891 Factory Act.

The concept of the 'dangerous trades' specifically referred to work where there was a threat to health from exposure to dusts, substances, fumes or organisms that essentially poisoned those working with or in proximity to them. In defining the trades for the purposes of applying special rules that would regulate aspects of work, they were to be included if they were 'dangerous or injurious to health, or dangerous to life and limb either generally or in the case of women, children or any other class of persons'. The number of trades that met this official notion of danger to health was large in the late nineteenth century but not all received official regulation. In the case of women workers two received the greatest attention; work with white phosphorous in lucifer match making, and work with lead in white lead manufacture, the potteries and enamelling. These were among the first trades to be scheduled under the 1891 Act. While all workers could be subject to special rules, the emphasis was put on particular classes of person, reinforcing the already established 'need' to protect women and children. As a consequence, in many dangerous trades where women and men were both employed and often in the same processes, the special rules were applied differentially. In all the scheduled trades where women worked there were some restrictions aimed specifically at them.

The basis of this approach by the state, as in hours of work legislation, was again one which stressed the peculiar suscepti- bility of women. In the case of the 'dangerous trades', investiga- tions increasingly drew on scientific and medical 'expertise' and numerous conditions of ill-health were identified. Some clearly related to women – lead, for instance, was implicated in miscar- riages, still-births and the deaths of children within days of birth from convulsions, and the Potteries Committee of 1893 indeed recommended the exclusion of married women on the grounds of the effect on pregnancy. In this sense the intervention was clearly part of the wider concern for reproductive health in the late nineteenth century, and probably had more to do with the health of children than with that of women.

In terms of the more general effects of lead poisoning, while noting that both men and women suffered, inquiries also observed that women suffered disproportionately. Towards the end of the century it became clear that this was in fact the case; in the potteries in the same processes the attack rate for women was higher than that for men, but the early legislation was passed on impressionistic evidence at best, and the notion that there was any differential biological disposition to lead poisoning was certainly questionable. The Chief Inspector of Factories, Sir Alexander Redgrave, had argued in his investigations in the 1880s that different rates were a consequence of conditions of labour, and had concluded that if dangers could be reduced to a minimum there would be no need to restrict women. However, the concept of women's greater susceptibility had already been placed on the agenda and remained so. In 1893 the White Lead Committee recommended that as women and young persons were more susceptible they should no longer be employed in certain processes, and in 1898 this became law.

In phosphorous poisoning the outcome was phosphorous necrosis or 'phossy jaw', a particularly painful and disfiguring disease which could have a fatal outcome. Again, as in lead, it was noted that there was a higher incidence of necrosis among women and girls, although this was probably due to the fact that many more of them were employed in the industry. Certainly there was more equivocation in this case over whether women were more susceptible. Dr Cunningham of the London Hospital reported to the Home Department on the use of phosphorous in the manufacture of lucifer matches in 1899:

> no statistics exist which enable us to determine with certainty the relative susceptibility of men and women to phosphorous necrosis. On the whole my contention is that the teeth of women are in a worse condition to those of men of corresponding ages employed in match factories . . . It would therefore appear that women are more liable to disease than men. (PP 1899, XII; 700–1)

However, he argued against the exclusion of women on the grounds that it would not alter the problem, but simply transfer it to other workers. Nevertheless, as in lead, intervention in this industry continued to differentiate between men and women.

While questions of susceptibility were frequently attributed to women's biological constitution, in the 'dangerous trades', as in earlier intervention, they also drew heavily on social and moral factors. Concern for the morality of both the women themselves and the working environment pervaded the inquiries. The Royal Commission on Labour in 1893 was required to comment specifically on the effects of industrial employment on morals and such concerns were evident in the reports of the Women's Factory Inspectorate.[3] Sometimes immorality was narrowly defined, as in the case of verbal or physical behaviour of a sexual nature, ranging from the possibility that women themselves were engaged in morally dubious activities, through to sexual assault on women by male supervisors and managers (Lambertz, 1985). But reports also made it clear that certain classes of women were thought to be morally suspect. Throughout the literature on working women and working conditions distinctions were made between those 'well brought up' and 'respectable' and those who were 'rough'. While these distinctions did in some cases reflect differences in the material and family circumstances of working-class women, they were just as likely to be a consequence of Victorian notions of respectability in terms of dress, appearance and behaviour.

The state, however, did clearly recognise that the social circumstances of many women workers predisposed them to the dangers of ill-health. Dr Olliver, physician at Newcastle Infirmary testified in 1893:

> there is a class of women too easily affected by lead but what that type is is impossible to say. Generally the class from which these people are taken are young girls who are practically without the comforts of a good home, many of them lead a questionable life, they expose themselves to cold, and are frequently in a state of chronic starvation before going to the lead works, and are therefore in a fit state for rapidly breaking down under the influence of lead. (PRO HO45/9848/B12393A)

In 1897 the Women's Inspectorate conducted a special inquiry into lucifer match works and drew attention to the impossibility of attaining the health so necessary for dangerous processes when wages were so low that 'sufficient food and clothing are impossible unless some of the necessities of life are supplied by relatives and friends' (PP 1898, XIV; 162).

It was generally accepted that there was a particular labour market for the 'dangerous trades', and it was suggested that because of the conditions and dangers only those very desperate for work 'chose' to work in them, and this desperation was clearly linked to women's domestic circumstances. It was thus difficult to distinguish between the effects of the occupations themselves and the consequences of poverty that characterised the lives of those involved in the work. Yet despite this acknowledgement on the part of state officials and others, the problem was never addressed in the legislation and the state continued to pursue a policy based on assumptions of individual risk.

The focus on the effects of the 'dangerous trades' on women was thus very much part of the 'moral panic' over women workers that dominated earlier legislation and which became increasingly important in concerns over the 'health of the nation' at the turn of the century. In this sphere, the 'problems' identified by the state were merely seen as more specific examples of how women's work led to social disintegration and how work, in turn, was affected by this.

The concept of susceptibility in the 'dangerous trades' consisted then both of the idea that there were actual biological or constitutional differences between sexes, and that circumstances predisposed women especially to the effects of exposure in particular working conditions. The discussion of female susceptibility was consistent with a general ideology of women's weakness and vulnerability, and the importance of the reproductive cycle to that, which applied in many spheres at this time (Duffin, 1979; Turner, 1987). The documented toll on women's health of industrial work, the continuing high infant mortality rates, and at least one industry where they were more liable to attack, all lent support to the ascription of susceptibility. In the case of the 'dangerous trades', the idea of susceptibility was clearly more important than the acceptability of substances and processes in the workplace, and this had particular consequences for women. First, it allowed questions of an essentially moral and social nature to intrude into the discussion. Second, it allowed the state to make increasing use of medical practitioners in regulation, by extending the role of certifying surgeons to the regular surveillance of women, with powers of exclusion, and this allowed physicians to use their increasing prestige on these matters to speak on non-medical matters also. Finally, it enabled the state to pursue a strategy based on 'protection' and inevitably this became the 'protection' only of those seen at risk, namely women. This remained the orientation of the day for the state in all its dealings with the 'dangerous trades'.

'DILATORY, MISTAKEN, AND ABOVE ALL INADEQUATE':[4] THE STATE'S RESPONSE

It is quite clear that even in terms of its own analysis, the state's response to the problem of women's work was both inadequate in extent and inappropriate in content. In both spheres of intervention, despite considerable legislative restriction, the state resorted frequently to inquiry in what seems to have been an attempt to forestall action. In part this was because state intervention was inconsistent with mainstream Victorian values, particularly in relation to *laissez-faire* in economic and labour matters, and indeed the sanctity of the private sphere; but it was also because the state had competing pressures and demands upon it and these conflicts had to be mediated. On the ideological level, however, there was some consensus reflected in state action and in assessments of its effectiveness.

In terms of the state's strategy in the face of the dangers to women's health then, almost without exception its solutions failed to match the nature and extent of the problems identified. Hours of work legislation consistently remained inappropriate to the evils accorded to women's work by the state. Indeed it was only in the perceived inability of women to withstand factory labour that the legislation was at all appropriate, and even here, given the number of exceptions and exemptions granted to many industries,[5] not to mention those which were always to remain outside the restrictions, the response was clearly inadequate. Moreover, of all the problems identified this was arguably the most understated aspect of the state's policy to limit women's hours. The issue of maternity, by far the more prominent of the arguments regarding women's health in this sphere, was in no sense mitigated by the legislation, and was not dealt with directly, and even then ineffectually, for almost fifty years after it was first noted. Hours of work legislation thus effected only minor improvements in terms of women's health, and left virtually untouched the main cause of work-related ill-health in both men and women: the actual conditions of production.

The state's response to the problem of ill-health in respect to the 'dangerous trades' suffered similar inadequacies. Given the enormous number of dangers identified, restriction and exclusion were inevitably going to be prominent in the discourse around this sphere of work, but the evidence produced on the subject provided few real reasons why only women should be the object of this. In practice, exclusion actually occurred rarely and only from some work processes rather than the workplace itself. But where exclusion was adopted, as in the case of white lead mills, the level of poisoning did not decline – there was simply a direct transfer of previous female rates to males (PP 1899, XII; Olliver, 1902).

Ostensibly both restriction and inspection did have some impact on working conditions and these measures would have contributed to the possibility of escaping poisoning, but these were essentially attempts to control a danger, not to eliminate it. The most effective way to have reduced two of the most important sources of poisoning, in lead processes and lucifer match making, would have been prohibition but, although raised, this was continually sidestepped as a solution. Thus the actual sources of danger were left unrestricted, and as in earlier legislation, many trades identified as a danger to health remained without effective regulation.

In both spheres of regulation, even more woefully inadequate and inappropriate was the state's response to its own evaluation of the social consequences of women's labour. Had the effect on children, men and society been anything approaching the magnitude claimed by the Commissions, the Inspectors, the Medical Officers of Health and the reformers in Parliament, the most logical response would have been a total exclusion of women, or at the very least of married women. However, given the economic and political pressures of the period, exclusion was clearly not an option generally available to the state and fortunately so, for there is little evidence to suggest that had women been excluded from these industries either the health of their families or themselves would have improved. Quite apart from the distress caused to many families through loss of essential income, there were many other factors that would mitigate against this being the case and there was little recognition that intervention along these lines might be more appropriate – maternal and income support, improved housing, children's work, environmental pollution, to name some. As it was, the restrictions adopted by the state in terms of regulating women's employment were unlikely to make much impact on the evils as identified, let alone the ones ignored.

Of course, there were other reasons why some of the measures adopted by the state can be judged to have failed. First, and particularly with respect to the 'dangerous trades', there was the state's relationship to employers. The 1891 Act had given employers arbitration rights with respect to special rules and these were used to contest them all along. There were constant demands to repeal such powers and these were lessened in 1905, while the state sought to counter employer objections that restrictions would affect their markets and make them vulnerable to foreign competition. Safe products, it was argued, were not what the customer wanted to buy. In the case of lucifer match making the state seemed sensitive to these concerns and it was no doubt important in delaying prohibition.

Second, the measures were not implemented or observed, although there was some dispute about where the responsibility for this lay. Employers would frequently claim that their best efforts were thwarted by workers who would not obey rules, were careless, or would not use the means provided for their own protection. This ideology of 'blaming the victim' (Crawford, 1977) was widespread and accepted as having some legitimacy. From 1844 onwards this apparent complicity of women workers in the violations that occurred was noted. And beyond suscepti- bility, biological or social, the idea that some women were by their own characteristics and habits responsible was used to explain the continued failure of preventive measures.

However, it was clear that many employers did evade the regulations. Continued inquiry into general conditions of work (Sweating Commission, 1889; Labour Commission, 1893) con- firmed that hours of work remained a persistent problem in enforcement and breaches of the restrictions were the largest single category of offences identified by the factory inspectors and the Women's Inspectorate. In the case of lucifer match making, there were a number of scandals in the 1890s involving Bryant and May, who were prosecuted for failing to disclose cases of necrosis in their works (Satre, 1982). In response the *Westminster Gazette* of 2 June 1898 noted, 'Here we have it proved to us that the most recent factory legislation can be evaded for five years . . . the whole machinery of detection and prevention completely baffled' (PRO HO45/B12393D).

At various points blame for the failure of enforcement was laid at the door of the Factory Inspectorate; one of the arguments for women inspectors had been the relative neglect of women's workplaces by male inspectors. But like their male colleagues, women inspectors were constantly to complain of the shortages of staff and their work overload, and they also claimed that their work was hampered by the lack of legislation and regulatory powers. Nevertheless, given the problems inherent in the state action and the assumptions which informed it, it is unlikely that more enforcement or more intervention could have effected any *significant* improvement in women's working conditions.

If the interference with women's labour was a failure from the perspective of the state's implicit intention to restore the value and the quality of working-class domestic life and the health of women and children, it must also be judged a failure in terms of recognising and meeting the real needs of women themselves. Of course, there was no political requirement to do so, since women were not political subjects, but others who were made it clear that the state had a duty to do so. Ultimately, however, a large part of the failure of the state to deal with the needs of the women lay in its identification of the 'problem'. Almost without exception the 'problem' of women's work was construed in terms of the effect on others – on men, children, the family and society – and while at certain points the interests of women might have coincided (Humphries, 1977) by and large the entire issue was placed firmly in a context of an image of women and women's sphere that in itself was highly discriminatory. The notion that women's interests, and indeed needs, might not 'fit' this image was certainly questioned, but with few exceptions this affected neither the direction of the legislation nor the continued premise on which state activity was based. Thus the rationale of susceptibility and the strategy of 'protection' by the state created a situation whereby one injustice (women's social and political vulnerability) was used to justify another (economic vulnerability) which in turn reinforced the first.

Nevertheless the legislation undoubtedly held paradoxes for the women concerned. Such paradoxes were highlighted by feminist involvement in the legislation from the 1870s onwards. The divisions within the feminist movement around protective legislation, characterised as essentially differences in class perspectives, reflected the contradictions between practical and ideological considerations, for working-class women. (Feurer, 1988). Thus, while the discriminatory ethos inherent in restrictions on women's right to work was deplored on the one hand, women activists, in their direct contact with working women and their conditions of labour, increasingly came to view legislation as a practical solution to the lack of power women had in the workplace and outside to change their situation. Freedom from the degrading conditions of work, they claimed, was more important than abstract notions of equality. Hence in so far as gender specific legislation was viewed as a necessary amelioration at a particular point (given the insuperable political objections to legislating for men) and not as a principle to be defended for ever, it constituted an essential weapon in the fight to improve the position of working women.

However, that there were important problems with the nature of the intervention cannot be denied. In the 'dangerous trades' women were constantly subjected to surveillance of their health status, as well as this being a precondition of their employment. With this, as women inspectors were successfully to argue, their privacy and sense of decency were frequently invaded by medical inspection, which in turn carried with it the threat of job loss and lost income. Many women did feel this to be a threat and attempted to avoid the consequences by concealing illness, or switching firms if this was possible.

The discrimination entailed in the legislation was thus one disadvantage, but it was the whole basis of the intervention that also contributed to its failure for women. In concentrating on the particular problem of women rather than the conditions of labour and the means of production, the legislation was entirely insufficient to address the many hazards facing women (and men) in many spheres of employment at that time. To interfere effectively, of course, required major challenges to cherished ideas about economic relations, but, more important, the state did not have to consider this option. It was not, we would argue, that employers exerted influence on the state to keep their interests uppermost; it was because there were other ideological forces which enabled the state to think that it was pursuing the right course. The need to protect the health of women and their offspring from the ravages of industrial employment was accepted. They evidently suffered (even if work was not responsible for their poor health); it was easy to argue that controls were necessary, especially as this was consistent with the separate spheres of men and women and the essential value of a male 'breadwinner'. Domestic ideology was supported by the supposed vulnerability of women and their susceptibility to poisons. The power of the susceptibility argument was precisely because it allowed the state to pursue a strategy in respect of women.

Finally the legislation clearly implied the rejection of employment for women as a right and, if in the short term women were only infrequently denied employment opportunities on the basis of the legislation,[6] the ideological repercussions of this were to be far more significant. For the legislation did remain gender specific, and the importance for working women of the long-term effects of the institutionalisation of their essential inferiority in employment terms should not be underestimated. The incorporation into legislation of the primacy of domestic labour over waged labour for women, for this is essentially what it constituted, consigned working women for ever to the 'double shift'.

CONCLUSION

At one level state intervention can be viewed as a recognition of the failure of capitalism to protect workers from the damage of the industrial system. By the time the 'dangerous trades' were a focus for that action the belief of the Victorian bourgeoisie in the enlightened and progressive nature of the factory system was severely undermined. In this respect reforms, which were also consistent with humanitarian values, could be accepted as an attempt to restore the benign image of capitalist industry. On the other hand, the state did not fundamentally challenge important aspects of capitalist production or its social relations in the legislation on working conditions.

Why it was women workers in particular who were to be the focus for that intervention was a consequence of the constraints of patriarchal social relations.[7] Fundamentally these made it unacceptable to interfere with the labour of men. It would have been unacceptable to capitalists too, and on this men's interests were one. For capitalism the reproduction of labour power vested in women, and the need for a healthy workforce in general, logically demanded restrictions on the labour of women and men, or the exclusion of women, but both would cause problems of labour supply. This paradox reveals the difficulties of reconciling the conflicting demands of patriarchy and capitalism, and not just for women's labour. Given these dilemmas 'protectionism' may be understood, especially in its earliest manifestations as a means to protect *all* workers, rather than simply the assertion of patriarchal control. Having established the means and the rationale for this by restrictions on women, it was a credible, if not a convenient, strategy to follow.

Despite the constraints of patriarchal social relations the state also drew on these and reinforced them. This is clear in the state's clear ideological commitment to the family. There was concern, if not fear, about the perceived moral and social disintegration of the working class and, since women were seen as crucial to this stability, female factory labour as an identifiable threat would come under attack. As evidence of women's working conditions mounted, the 'evils' were not just the corruption of both morality and domestic responsibilities, but the undermining of health to such an extent that the future health and survival of the nation were at stake. The broader concerns remained omnipresent, but in the latter period a significant shift in the 'need' to intervene occurred; the threat to reproduction became explicitly part of the rationale for state action. That the restriction on women would continue to be greater than for men was justifiable because biological reproduction, not just social reproduction, was women's work. In this way the discourse on the 'evils' of working conditions was constituted and then reconstituted these very relations.

But, to some extent, legislation was not just an attempt to regain some kind of control over the working-class family, or of working-class men over the labour market and their families. It resulted from compromises necessitated by humanitarian concerns with the significance of the income from factory work for many women and their dependants. Thus while exclusion certainly would have damaged capitalist interests, the state and working-class men were also unwilling to countenance the consequences of exclusion for these women at least. There were limits to the exercise of patriarchal control.

We argue, however, that over time the assertion of patriarchal interests became clearer and more vociferous. Increasingly working men called for exclusion, when there had been little evidence of this in relation to the 1840s legislation at least. But whether this was strategic, in terms of benefits for themselves, or a consequence of sex-antagonism, or a reassertion of control over the family and workplace, is difficult to disentangle, since for working men, too, these interests were not unambiguous in the short or long term. Furthermore each, and sometimes all, had validity in relation to specific industries. Certainly it is important to consider particular labour markets, skills required and dangers faced, since it is clear that sexual segregation, either as contributory to or a consequence of state action or male unionist policies, varied considerably. By the latter part of the century competition, exacerbated by economic and trade fluctuations, was for some a real fear; and the ideal of the male 'breadwinner' was by then a more potent force in male consciousness as struggles around the 'family wage' indicated (Seccombe, 1986).

Other men also had considerable powers to support the contention that factory work was not 'fit' for women, and many women not 'fit' to perform it. The use of medical expertise and practitioners directly in the policing activities of the state was an important extension of patriarchal control in the workplace. It was insidious, too, because of its ability to lay claim to a 'neutrality' of 'science'. In other respects medical practitioners were in an ambiguous position. Their role was often a mediating one between capitalists, the state and the community, all of which were sources of livelihood. As such, despite sharing bourgeoisie fears of women's sickness and working-class stability, industrial ill-health was compromised by individual 'professional' interests.

We also need to emphasise the extent to which women themselves had become publicly involved by the end of the century. There were certainly struggles between women over the whole question of state interference (Feurer, 1988) and between male and women unionists over discriminatory practices (Soldon, 1978); but working women had access to the state through their own sex for the first time. While women remained disenfranchised, and while their challenge to the patriarchal social order, which left the struggle confined to the public and not the private domain, tended to reinforce their position on the periphery, these changes were significant. There was greater visibility and recognition of their lives and working conditions as they viewed them; and women as servants of the state were here to stay.

However significant the increase in patriarchal interests over time, neither the legislation nor its effects achieved any of the changes hoped for in women's relationship to the paid labour market. Ideologically these interests were not threatened by this failure; to some extent they were strengthened, because the problem of women at work and the debates themselves reinforced these values and social relationships. This allowed discriminatory practices to continue and to be pursued elsewhere.

Thus the legislation constituted a confirmation and a continuation of the different relationship of the state to women from that of adult men; a relationship rooted in economic relations that confirmed men's primacy in the labour market and women's dependency on and service to others in the private domestic sphere.

NOTES

1. We stress that although we use the term working women to refer to women who are in the paid labour market, we do not imply that other women do not work. On the contrary not only was the 'double day' an important consequence of the sexual division of labour in both the workplace and the home; it constituted a further differentiation of work-related ill-health in men and women.

2. From an article on state action by Canon Scott Holland, Commonwealth, July 1896. Cited in Anderson, 1922.

3. The first two women inspectors were appointed in 1893 by Asquith after over a decade of campaigning. By 1895 they formed a separate branch under their own superintending inspector, and filed separate annual reports. Their number substantially increased in the early 1900s, but in 1921 they were disbanded and reorganised within the inspectorate. They were initially peripatetic, and had a wide brief to investigate as well as regulate. For fuller accounts of their work by women inspectors themselves, see Anderson, 1922; Squire, 1927; and Martindale, 1938, 1944; and by others (McFeeley, 1986 and Jones, 1988).

4. Harold Tennant describing state law with respect to poisoning, 1898, LXIII; p. 455.

5. Many industries remained outside the legislation due to exemptions (either partial or whole) granted for a variety of reasons. Other industries were not involved in the legislation at all. Laundry work, for example, was not subject to restriction until 1895, and even then the provisions were minimal.

6. Overall female participation rates actually increased in most of the employments covered in the period in question. There is little evidence of any substantial decline except in the white lead industry where legislation could be held entirely responsible. However, this is not to suggest that women were not denied employment opportunities by other means (see, for example, Walby, 1986; Rose, 1988)

7. We take patriarchy to mean a system of social relations between men and women, operating within a number of structures that are characterised by male domination and control through which women are exploited and denied equality.

REFERENCES

Alexander, S. (1976), 'Women's Work in Nineteenth-Century London', in

158   *Women in the Factory*

J. Mitchell and A. Oakley (eds), *The Rights and Wrongs of Women* (Harmondsworth: Penguin).

Anderson, A. (1922) *Women in the Factory: An Administrative Adventure* (London: John Murray).

Barrett, M. (1980) *Women's Oppression Today: Problems in Marxist Feminist Analysis* (London: Verso).

Crawford, R. (1977) "'You are Dangerous to Your Health": The Ideology and Politics of Victim Blaming', *International Journal of the Health Services*, Vol. 7.

Duffin, L. (1979) 'The Conspicuous Consumptive', in S. Delamont and L. Duffin (eds), *The Nineteenth-Century Woman* (London: Croom Helm).

Feurer, R. (1988) 'The Meaning of "Sisterhood": The British Women's Movement and Protective Labour Legislation, 1870–1900', *Victorian Studies*, Vol. 31, No. 2.

Figlio, K (1978) 'Chlorosis and Chronic Disease in Nineteenth-Century Britain: The Social Constitution of Somatic Illness in a Capitalist Society', *International Journal of the Health Services*, Vol. 8, No. 4.

Gaskell, P. (1836) *Artisans and Machinery: The Moral and Physical Condition of the Manufacturing Population Considered with Reference to Mechanical Substitutes for Human Labour* (J. W. Parker).

Greg, W. R. (1831) *An Enquiry into the State of the Manufacturing Population and the Causes and Cures of the Evils Therein Existing* (J. Ridgway).

Hall, S. and Schwartz, B. (1985) 'State and Society 1880–1930', in M. Langan and B. Schwartz (eds), *Crisis in the British State 1880–1930* (London: Hutchinson).

Hartmann, H. (1979) 'The Unhappy Marriage of Marxism and Feminism: Towards a More Progressive Union', *Capital and Class*, VIII (Summer).

Hewitt, M. (1958) *Wives and Mothers in Victorian Industry: A Study of the Effects of the Employment of Married Women in Victorian Industry* (London: Rockliffe).

Humphries, J. (1977) 'Protective Legislation, the Capitalist State and Working Class Men', *Feminist Review*, Vol. 7, pp. 1–33.

Hutchins, B. and Harrison, A. (1903) *A History of Factory Legislation* (London: P. S. King & Son).

John, A. V. (1980) *By the Sweat of their Brow: Women in Victorian Coalmining* (London: Croom Helm).

John, A. (ed) (1986) *Unequal Opportunities: Women's Employment in England 1800–1918* (Oxford: Basil Blackwell).

Jones, H. (1988) 'Women Health Workers: The Case of the First Women Factory Inspectors in Britain', *Social History of Medicine*, Vol. 1, No. 2.

Kay, J. P. (1832) *The Moral and Physical Condition of the Working Classes Employed in the Cotton Manufacture in Manchester* (J. Ridgway).

Lambertz, J. (1985) 'Sexual Harassment in the Nineteenth-Century English Cotton Industry', *History Workshop Journal*, 19, Spring.

McFeeley, M. D. (1986) 'The Lady Inspectors: Women at Work 1893–1921', *History Today*, Vol. 36, November.

Malcolmson, P. (1981) 'Laundresses and the Laundry Trade in Victorian England', *Victorian Studies*, Vol. 24.

Mark-Lawson, J. and Witz, A. (1988) 'From "Family Labour" to "Family Wage"? The Case of Women's Labour in Nineteenth-Century Coalmining', *Social History*, Vol. 13, No. 2.

Martindale, H. (1938) *Women Servants of the State 1870–1938* (London: George Allen & Unwin).

Martindale, H. (1944), *From One Generation to Another, 1893–1944* (London: Allen & Unwin).

Olliver, T. (ed) (1902) *Dangerous Trades: The History, Social and Legal Aspects of Industrial Occupations as afffecting Health by a Number of Experts* (London: John Murray).

Pinchbeck, I. (1930) *Women Workers and the Industrial Revolution 1750–1850* (Frank Cass).

Rose, S. O. (1988) 'Gender Antagonism and Class Conflict: Exclusionary Strategies of Male Trade Unionists in Nineteenth-Century Britain', *Social History*, Vol. 13, No. 2.

Satre, L. J. (1982) 'After the Match Girls Strike: Bryant and May in the 1890s', *Victorian Studies*, Vo. 25, Autumn.

Seccombe, W. (1986) 'Patriarchy Stablized: The Construction of the Male Breadwinner Wage Norm in Nineteenth-Century Britain', *Social History*, Vol. II, pp. 53–76.

Soldon, N. (1978) *Women in British Trade Unions 1874–1976* (Gill & MacMillan).

Squire, R. (1927) *Thirty Years in the Public Service: An Industrial Retrospect* (London: Nisbet).

Turner, B. (1987) *Medical Power and Social Knowledge* (London: Sage).

Walby, S. (1986) *Patriarchy at Work* (Cambridge: Polity Press).

Wohl, A. (1983) *Endangered Lives: Public Health in Victorian Britain* (London: J. M. Dent & Son).

PRIMARY SOURCES USED

Factory Acts and Bills, 1840–1900

Annual Reports of the Medical Inspector 1893–1914.

Annual Reports of Her/His Majesty's Chief Inspector of Factories and Workshops including the Annual Reports of Her/His Majesty's Women Inspectors.

Reports from the Select Committee on the Bill for the regulation of Factories. 1831–32, XV

First Report from Commissioners appointed to collect information in the manufacturing districts relative to the employment of children in Factories. 1833, XX

Second Report of Commissioners (Medical Evidence). 1833, XXI

Supplementary Reports of Commissioners. 1834, XIX, XX

Reports from the Select Committee on the Act for the regulation of Factories, together with Minutes of Evidence. 1840, X (Evidence); 1841, IX (Report)

First Report of the Commissioners for inquiring into the employment of children in Mines and Factories. (Mines) 1842, XV

Reports of Subcommissioners. 1842, XVI, XVII

Second Report of the Commissioners for inquiring into the employment of Children in Mines and Manufactories. (Trades and Manufactures) 1843, XIII

Reports of Subcommissioners. 1843, VIV, XV

Reports of M.O. of Privy Council
4th Report 1862, XXII Appendix V, p. 649 (Excessive mortality of young
    children in Manufacturing Population)
6th Report 1864, XXVIII Appendix XIV, p. 458 (Excessive mortality of young
    children in rural districts)

Employment of Women and Children in Agriculture 1867–68, XVII, 1868–69,
    XIII

Children's Employment Commission 5th Report 1866, XXIV, 6th Report 1867,
    XVI

Factory Acts Extension and Hours of Labour Regulation Bills Report with
    Proceedings 1867, IX 575

Factory and Workshop Act, Report and Special Report 1870, VIII 1

Report of the Select Committee on the Best Means of Protecting Infants put out
    to Nurse 1871, VII

Report to Local Government Board on Proposed Changes in Hours and Ages of
    Employees in Textile Factories (Bridge and Holmes) 1873, LV 803

Commissioners Report on Working of Factory and Workshop Acts – with a view
    to Consolidation and Amendment
Vol. 1 Report, Appendix and Index 1876, XXIX 1
Vol. 2 Minutes of Evidence 1876, XXX 1

Children's Employment Commission 1883, PPXX XXI

Report of Standing Committee on Trade with Proceedings 1890–91, XII 87
    (Similar Report, 1895, X 9)

Report of Alexander Redgrave Esq, Her Majesty's Chief Inspector of Factories
    upon the Precautions which can be enforced under the Factory Act, and as to
    the need for further powers for the protection of people employed in White
    Lead Works PP XVIII 1882

Copy of Communications addressed to the Secretary of State on the subject of
    White Lead Poisoning, with Report by Alexander Redgrave, Her Majesty's
    Chief Inspector of Factories upon the same subject PP XVIII 1883

Report to Her Majesty's Principal Secretary of State for the Home Department
    on the Conditions of Labour in the Potteries, the Injurious Effects upon the
    Health of the Workpeople and the Proposed Remedies: Also known as the
    Potteries Committee of Enquiry. PP XVII 1893–94

Royal Commission on Labour: Conditions of Work in Various Industries in
    England, Wales, Scotland and Ireland. Reports of the Conditions of Women
    and Girls. PP XXXVII 1893–94

Report of the Departmental Committee on the Various Lead Industries PP XVII 1893-94

Interim and Final Report of the Departmental Committee to Inquire and Report upon the Miscellaneous Dangerous Trades. PP XXX 1896; PP XVII 1897; PP XII 1899

Report of Her Majesty's Principal Secretary of State for the Home Department, on the Employment of Compounds of Lead in the Manufacture of Pottery, their influence upon the health of the workpeople, with suggestions as to the means which might be adopted to counter their evil effects. PP XII, 1899

Reports to the Secretary of State for the Home Department on the Use of Phosphorus in the Manufacture of Lucifer Matches. Reports by Professor T. Thorpe, Dr T. Olliver and Dr G. Cunningham. PP XII, 1899

Report of the Inter-departmental Committee on Physical Deterioration and Evidence. PP XXXII 1904

Report of the Departmental Committee Appointed to Inquire into the Dangers attendant on the use of lead, and the danger or injury to health arising from Dust and other causes in the manufacture of Earthenware and China and the Processes incidental thereto in the making of Lithographic Transfers. PP XXIX, 1910

A Report on Regulations in the Potteries by Inspectors Pendock and Werner. PP XXVI, 1912–13

Hansard
British Medical Journal
Lancet
Englishwoman's Journal
Englishwoman's Review
The Woman Worker
Nineteenth Century
Contemporary Review
Fortnightly Review
Women's Union Journal

J. M. Cobbett Collection. Factory Pamphlets, 1832–56 London University Library.
University of London Collection of Broadsides. Vol. VI, 1818–68
University of London Collection of Broadsides. Oastler and the Factory Movement, 1830–35 (2 Vols).
'White Slavery' Collection. 16 Vols. of pamphlets in the Goldsmiths' Library, London University.
'White Slavery' Oastler's Letters and Cuttings. London University Library.
The Ten Hours Movement in 1831 and 1832. Six pamphlets and one broadside. British Labour Series: Contemporary Pamphlets, 1727-1850.
The Battle for the Ten Hours Day Continues, 1837–1843. British Labour Series:

Contemporary Pamphlets, 1727–1850.
The Gertrude Tuckwell Collection: TUC Library, Congress House.

Public Records Office (PRO) Files Home Office.
HO45/9848 B 12393 A-F
9899 B 18946
B 1137 AF
9933 B 26610
9849 B 1293

8 Women and the Inebriate Reformatories

Geoffrey Hunt, Jenny Mellor and Janet Turner

INTRODUCTION

The increasing recognition of the importance of women's history has stimulated new work on state intervention in women's lives. An historical period which has attracted attention is around the late nineteenth and early twentieth centuries. Pertinent questions have been raised about state control of female sexuality. This is a period of moral panic about working-class women. State intervention was concerned to reclaim women as the future wives and mothers of a healthier imperial race. This chapter examines the response of the state to the question of 'women and alcohol'. State reformatories were viewed as the best means of controlling, isolating and reforming 'inebriate' women. It relates explanations of the day for the predominance of women in reformatories despite their lower rate of drunkenness to wider debates about national efficiency and the imperial race. A case study is also provided of Farmfield certified reformatory, which was set up in 1900 by the London County Council (LCC) taking the discussion beyond the intentions of the reformers to the consequences of their measures.

The habitual Drunkards Act of 1879 was the first step in the direction of establishing residential treatment as an alternative to prison for habitual drunkards. By 1898 the Inebriates Act empowered local authorities to build or purchase suitable buildings for certified inebriate reformatories to be administered by local authorities and financed jointly by central government, local authority and/or charitable donations (Mellor et al., 1986). These were to be supplemented by state inebriate reformatories funded directly by the government. In fact, only two of these were established: one for men at Warwick prison and the other for women at Aylesbury prison. These state reformatories were under the control of the prison commissioners and were used as institutions of last resort to which refractory or violent inmates from the certified reformatories could be sent.

The philosophy behind the certified reformatories reflected some of the same ideas which inspired the development of borstals or other such institutions whose mandate was on the borderline between reform and rehabilitation and punishment. They were to be in pleasant rural surroundings away from the temptations of city life which were often blamed for excessive drinking in the first place. The regime was designed to bring about long-term changes in behaviour and attitudes. This was to be done through a regular routine, hard work and a plain but sufficient diet, interspersed in most cases by Bible reading and religious services. Because the regime was designed to cure and rehabilitate the inmates, a long period of confinement was necessary if old habits were to be eradicated and new ones firmly established. Therefore sentences to the reformatories for treatment were between one and three years as against one to three months in prison.

The reformatory experiment was not popular and in fact lasted only from 1899 until the beginning of the First World War. Local authorities were not keen to incur the expense and only 14 reformatories dealing with 4590 inmates were established. Furthermore magistrates were often unwilling to use the legislation partly because it involved sending the case to the Crown Court and partly because they felt that such a lengthy sentence was an infringement of personal liberty.

In spite of an indifferent attitude towards the reformatories by the courts and many local authorities the Society for the Prevention of Inebriety represented an influential body of opinion which nonetheless continued to campaign to extend the powers of the Acts of 1879 and 1898. The Society wanted compulsory committal for non-criminal inebriates, an indefinite period of detention, especially for 'unimprovable cases', and the ability to deal with cases earlier before they had reached the 'intractable' stage. These draconian measures were justified on the grounds that they could not interfere with individual liberty as the inebriate had no liberty because he was entirely enslaved by alcohol. The campaigners succeeded in putting an Inebriates Bill before the House of Commons in 1912, which would have supported such measures but it failed to become law, and the demise of the institutions began not long afterwards.

Clearly the whole experiment was one which could be regarded from different points of view, both as a genuine attempt at treatment and rehabilitation and as an extension of social control. There is evidence of both these viewpoints in the writings of the time. For example, Lady Henry Somerset and Mrs Bramwell Booth who were in charge of institutions discuss the merits of their regimes in terms of the benefits they confer on the inmates. But it is clear from the accounts of the hard regular work expected, the use of diet as a form of reward and punishment and the frequent referrals of intractable inmates to state inebriate reformatories, often for attempting to run away (McLaughlin, 1987, p. 145), that the benefits of the institution were not equally appreciated by the inmates themselves. Discontent in fact appears to have been widespread. McLaughlin quotes an inmate from Girgenti Home, one of two certified reformatories in Scotland, as writing in a letter (never received) to her mother:

> I am keeping in very good health I am thankful to say, but I am very downhearted when I think of all I have to stand from day to day and from year to year and I have to say nothing whether I am right or wrong and for nothing I ought to be outside working and treated with kindness and respect and getting paid for my work, but to work hard from day to day and not even get a kind word I shall never forget this as long as I live . . . My one prayer is to have my health and I will put up with the rest for it is an awful place to have anything wrong with you. (McLaughlin, 1987, p. 145)

There were persistent complaints, particularly from R. W. Branthwaite, the Inspector of Reformatories that the Act was consistently under-used. In fact, as we have already noted, the total number of committals to the reformatories between 1899, when they were first opened, and 1913, when the records cease, was 4590 as against approximately 250 000 committals to prison *annually* for drunkenness in the UK. What is surprising, however, is that 81 per cent (3741) of those committed to reformatories were women. This predominance cannot be explained by differences in the number of drunken offences committed by females. In 1910, for example, out of a total of 143 708 offences 82 per cent (117 754) were committed by men. Furthermore the disproportionate and seemingly unjustified use of the reformatories for women was not merely the accidental outcome of the workings of the Act. As McLaughlin points out 'the reformatories catered for women almost to the exclusion of men' (McLaughlin, 1987, p. 145). Moreoever he adds:

> the near dearth of places for the reception of men would suggest the the 'women only' policy was not so much an unforeseen consequence of the operation of the Act, as a conscious decision on the part of those responsible for administering the reformatories and perhaps on the part of the government itself. (McLaughlin, 1987, p. 145)

Our aim in this chapter is to examine first, the kind of explanation given by contemporary writers for the predominance of women in inebriate reformatories, and second, to consider briefly some of the arguments put forward more recently in an attempt to explain the growing concern about working-class women at the turn of the century. Finally we shall examine the evidence we have been able to gather from the records from Farmfield, the certified reformatory set up by the London County Council (LCC), which tells us something of the kind of women who were sent there and the concerns of the staff at the time.

EARLY TWENTIETH-CENTURY VIEWS

Contemporary writers appear to have accepted the predominance of women in the reformatories as a natural phenomenon and make few references to the large number of places in the reformatories filled by women. What might seem today to be a curious form of bias in social policy does not appear to have troubled contemporaries greatly. They approached the whole question of women and alcohol within the context of nineteenth-century concerns about the use of alcohol. A concern which is easily underestimated today. As Kitson Clark notes, 'It would be hard to say why historians have not rated the effects of strong drink as the significant factor in nineteenth-century history it undoubtedly was – its importance stands out from every page of contemporary record' (Clark, 1975, p. 127). In the final volume of *Life and Labour of the People of London* (Booth, 1971) Charles Booth took up the concern with women drinkers. He argues that, while drunkenness in general has declined, there is nevertheless more drinking, and furthermore that 'the increase in drinking is to be laid namely to the account of the female sex' (Booth, 1971). This is partly due, Booth argues, to the emancipation of women who no longer seem ashamed to be seen in a pub, and partly to their greater sociability. As he says, 'One drunken women in a street will set all the women in it drinking. A woman is so often talking with her neighbours; if she drinks they go with her' (Booth, 1970). He quotes several informants, mainly policemen or officials who also claim that drinking has increased among married women who become 'regular soakers of gin and ale' when they get older. A school superintendent reported that poor women smell of beer when they bring their children to school in the morning. An Anglican sister argued that young married women who move out into the suburbs miss the companionship of shop work and drink because they are lonely. Opinion at the time seemed to be, however, that problems arose not so much from the harm done by drink itself as from the poverty that resulted from it. Booth concludes this section by suggesting that blame was attached to women not only for the increase in their own drinking but for their husbands' as well. He quotes an East End matron as saying that men go out drinking because their homes are so miserable and uncomfortable. As she says, 'the standard of cooking and domestic economy is lower than it was, due to the preference for factory life over domestic service' (Booth, 1971). Her opinion is supported by an East End headmaster who says, 'with such houses as they have, men must go out at night . . . if they earn more they are so accustomed to bad houses that the extra money goes not to the home, but to the pub' (Booth, 1971).

Women seem to be at fault because home life is so poor, yet as another rather perceptive church of England clergyman remarked they too need the comfort only to be found in drink. As he said, 'worry is what they suffer from, rest and hope what they want. Drunkenness dulls the sense of present evil and gives a rosiness to what is to come, that is why they drink (Booth, 1970).

These brief comments seem to indicate a genuine diversity of opinion about women's drinking. Alongside some perceptive social explanations there was also some evident resentment about the changing role of women. However, even if there was a perception that women were drinking more, we still need to ask why the insitutional solution was considered so suitable for women. Carswell (Carswell, 1901) writing in 1901 suggests that women were less able than men to pay the fines required for release after arrest. Therefore they were more easily pressured into accepting treatment as an alternative to a much shorter period in prison. Additionally Carswell makes the point also mentioned by Branthwaite (1927) that magistrates were unwilling to send men, supposedly the supporters of their families, away for long periods of time – leaving the family to become a charge on the Poor Law. On the other hand, the women arrested for habitual drunkenness had often cut loose from their family connections and were therefore not considered either as potential breadwinners or as 'real women' with family responsibilities.

Where the question of women in the reformatories is addressed seriously the suggestion emerges that although there may be fewer women than men who drink excessively those who do are somehow 'worse' than men. Worse in this case may simply mean more visible. Notorious offenders like Jane Cakebread, who were notable for the number of times they were sent to prison for drunkenness, are mentioned as examples. Radzinowicz and Hood, 1986) quote J. J. Pitcairn, assistant surgeon at Holloway and Newgate prisons, who suggests that 90 per cent of women in Holloway are there through drink. 'There are hundreds, nay thousands of Jane Cakebreads in existence', he says. 'They go in and out of prison with monotonous regularity, turning to drink on release until they are picked up again by the police. Prison as a treatment for drunken women therefore is highly ineffective' (Pitcairn, 1897, p. 6). The Inspector of Reformatories, Branthwaite, suggests that women may be committed more readily because 'excess alcohol' has a different effect on women. He reports that:

> It has been necessary to point out . . . that the most cogent of all reasons why more women than men find their way to Reformatories is the different effect of alcohol upon the two sexes. A drunken woman nearly always becomes hysterical, laughs or dances, or sits on the pavement and screams. She 'goes for' her drinking companion on the slightest provocation, and a policeman has an attraction for her which she cannot possibly resist. A drunken woman quietly wending her way homewards is a sight rarely to be seen . . . Hysterical frenzy is the exception rather than the rule in the case of the drunken

man; he usually plods and struggles homewards with dogged determination, sometimes morose and surly, but more often than not, inoffensive if left alone. It is best to draw the curtain over what happens when he does get home; but anyway he escapes arrest. A semi-drunken man will often make super-human and successful efforts to get a drunken friend quietly home; but it is a rare occurrence to see one women fulfilling the same office for another. (Parliamentary Papers, 1909)

So, he concludes, 'consequently drunken women get into trouble' (Branthwaite, Parliamentary Papers, 1910).

It is possible also that the numbers of women sent to the reformatories were influenced by the increasing interest at the time in the relationship between alcohol and defective mentality. These ideas were reinforced by concern for the degeneration of the 'imperial race' and a growing disquiet about the changing roles of women reflected specifically in inadequate standards of mother-hood among working-class women. There was certainly a power-ful academic lobby which attempted to prove that mental defect was a causal factor in the development of inebriety (Branthwaite, 1908; Barrington, Pearson and Heron, 1910). They argue that, while the reformatories kept women out of trouble during their confinement there, their pre-existing mental deficiencies result in return to their old way of life on release. Furthermore they are in danger of passing on their disabilities to their children who will then become a charge on the state.

The authors make it plain that it is not alcoholism itself which is inherited but the feeble-mindedness which caused it. Nonetheless the identification of lack of will-power with feeble-mindedness seems to have been accepted by other people concerned with the running of the reformatories. For example, the distinction be-tween the 'feeble-minded' and the 'normal' inebriate becomes somewhat blurred in Branthwaite's discussion of the relation between alcoholism and mental deficiency. In a lecture discussing the causes of inebriety he argues: 'Alcohol, far from being the chief cause of habitual inebriety is merely a medium which brings into prominence certain defects which might otherwise have remained hidden' (Branthwaite, 1908, p. 109). He goes on to say: 'amongst all the characteristics and peculiarities encountered during a study of inmates of inebriate reformatories, none are so definite as those ascribable to mental defect or disease' (Branthwaite, 1908,

p. 113). However, as further evidence of mental defect he also discusses the impaired development of moral sense which he finds in the inmates of reformatories. His major complaint is that they fail to submit to the routine of regular work, they are dishonest, filthy and do not care what others think of them. They cannot adhere to the ethical codes of society and are able to justify anything they want to do, including prostitution and drunkenness if it suits them. In the lecture, he only refers to women specifically at the end when he claims:

> I do not believe, during that period [the last 25 years], that habitual drunkenness has decreased and, so far as women are concerned, I am convinced it has materially increased. The reason seems to be plain enough: while temperance workers have succeeded in inducing the moderately strong minded healthy man to exercise restraint . . . they have been unable to do much towards obtaining the same result in regard to the very persons who need it most, those who cannot realise the fact or carry out the remedy. (Branthwaite, 1908, p. 127)

Here the unfortunate women who cannot exercise control is contrasted unfavourably with the 'healthy man' who is amenable to sensible influence. Although the discussion generally talks about 'the inebriate', the printed lecture in the journal contains three pages of photographs of reformatory inmates, and all of these are women. Reflecting on his work, long after the reformatories had closed in 1927, Branthwaite again addresses the problem of drunkenness and heredity. He remarks, 'Drunkeness in two or three successive generations is no evidence to my mind of the heredity of drunkenness, but strong evidence of the persistence of a psycho-neurotic strain that predisposes to drunkenness or some other manifestations of abnormality' (Branthwaite, 1927, p. 14). Most significantly, perhaps, the group of 'normal' institutionalised inebriates, roughly 50 per cent in his estimation, exhibited this pathological strain including the 'inability to undertake regular work or anything that savours of monotony' (Branthwaite, 1927, p. 15). As at least 80 per cent of the reformatory inhabitants were women, it is clear that significant people in powerful positions considered that women as reproducers were in danger of passing on their own unfortunate characteristics to their children, which might range from outright mental deficiency to the kind of psychological tendencies which predispose children to various degrees of moral weakness. Moreover it seems to have been quite easy to move from the perceived increase in female inebriety, and in particular from the few 'notorious' cases with over 200 convictions for drunkeness, to the general assumption that women were more susceptible to the impaired development of moral sense than men, and therefore more deserving of the kind of long-term institutional treatment which effectively removed them from social life and the possibilities of breeding, and which was designed to bring about a fundamental change in attitudes and habits.

THE 'PROBLEM' OF WORKING CLASS WOMEN

Like McLaughlin (1987, p. 145) we accept that a proper explanation of the use made of the reformatories requires a deeper understanding of the Victorian state's concern with controlling working-class women. It is not so much any one idea alone which brought about the willingness to 'put women away' to an extent which was clearly not acceptable for men, but rather a combination of ideas which coalesced among influential sections of the population. Overall the concerns about national efficiency focused attention on the apparent decline of 'standards' among working-class women, and thus of the working-class family at the heart of the Empire.

Some supporters of the campaign were influenced by Social Darwinism and *laissez-faire*; others, notably the liberal imperialists and the Fabians believed that efficiency required state intervention to improve the health and living conditions of the poor. For example, in 1902 Lord Rosebery, leader of the liberal imperialists claimed:

An Empire such as ours requires as its first condition an Imperial race, a race vigorous, industrious and intrepid . . . in the rookeries and slums which still survive an imperial race cannot be reared . . . remember that where you promote health and arrest disease, where you convert an unhealthy citizen into a healthy one . . . you, in doing your duty, are also working for the Empire. (Semmel, 1960, p. 63)

It is possible perhaps that some contemporaries regarded the inebriate reformatories as reflecting both strands of social imperialist thought. Without doubt they did serve to isolate and control women, but equally they also sought to reclaim them as the future wives and mothers of a healthier imperial race.

Richard Soloway remarks that ideas about the degeneration of the race were among 'the manifestations of pessimistic thought which affected Edwardian Britain' (Soloway, 1982, p. 137). Deterioration in health and living conditions of the casual poor, especially in the towns, he argues, was too easily confused with racial degeneration for which, in fact, there was no supporting evidence. However, the view was encouraged by the declining birth rate among the middle classes in comparison with the working class, the high rates of infant mortality at the beginning of the century and the unfit condition of recruits for the Boer War.

Furthermore the testimonies to the inter-departmental committee on physical deterioration set up in 1903 to examine the condition of the poor revealed considerable support among some witnesses for the view that, 'city life had altered the course of evolution and created a smaller, weaker labouring class whose diminished physical and mental capacity was being transmitted to an ever expanding number of unfit people' (Soloway, 1982, p. 149). Nevertheless, when the committee reported in July 1904 it found that 'the most reliable evidence indicated that most children were born healthy; whatever deterioration followed was the result of the improverished conditions in which they were raised' (Soloway, 1982, p. 149). The report went on to emphasise 'the unhealthy effects of ignorance, neglect, malnutrition, slum housing, fetid air, polluted water, minimal hygiene, excessive drinking and the absence of physical training' (Soloway, 1982, p. 149) as the important factors contributing to the poor condition of the working-class population. These were all factors, the committee concluded, which could be put right with a programme of state intervention on an unprecedented scale. The government would have to enforce building and sanitary regulations, control the distribution and production of food and milk, and educate women and girls in cooking and mothercraft. The Unionist government of the day was not anxious to implement a costly programme of state intervention, so it was left to the Liberal government that came to office in 1906 to begin to ameliorate the effects of dreadful conditions on poor children by providing medical inspection and school meals for the most needy.

The suggestion that was taken up at the time with enthusiasm was the idea that women, and in particular working-class women, were ignorant and neglectful of the skills of homemaking, and therefore lessons in mothercraft (though seldom the feeding of under-nourished expectant mothers) would reduce the infant mortality rate and improve the general standard of child-care. The belief that appalling social conditions could be improved by education both absolved the authorities from undertaking further and more expensive responsibilities and reflected the widely held disquiet about the nature and capabilities of working-class women. Education and the supervision of working-class lives also provided new kinds of work for middle-class women, particularly for those who were single (Wilson, 1977, p. 43).

In the tradition of their nineteenth-century forebears in the Charity Organisation Society, the middle-class educators were willing to address the problems of working-class women across the barriers of social distance. They aimed to improve their attitudes and habits, not to identify with them as sisters. This kind of social distance was, of course, class based but it may also be partly accounted for by Victorian attitudes to sexuality which demanded innocence and repression of sexual awareness from upper- and middle-class women which could only be maintained by continued vigilance from parents and chaperones. In a perceptive article Peter Cominos maintains that male attitudes towards women divided the Victorian female population into two antagonistic parts.

> Victorian society and the family spawned two kinds of women, the womanly woman and her negation the whorely whore, the pure and the impure . . . the respectable ideal of purity represented unadulterated femininity, her opposite represented the projection of those rejected and unacceptable desires that must be destroyed to keep women pure beings. (Cominos, 1973, p. 168)

Working-class women were considered to have lost their innocence and 'once innocence was lost chastity became vulnerable' (Cominos, 1973, p. 157). They were always therefore potentially lacking in respectability. It is interesting to note how often Branthwaite cites lack of chastity as one of the defining characteristics of the inebriate (Branthwaite, 1908)!

Furthermore middle-class women of the time who came into

increasing contact with the poor through new forms of 'social work' were critical of their management of food, their ignorance of proper health care and above all their seemingly fatalistic attitudes towards the death of their children. If, in addition to this general estimation of the failure of working-class women to take advantage of improved standards of living, we take account of specific claims that working-class women were drinking more, and that drink was a major factor influencing infant mortality, it becomes more understandable that the idea of re-educating the worst cases through institutional treatment aroused little concern among middle-class women at the time.

Inebriate women came to be regarded both as a symbol of working-class irresponsibility and a symptom of national decline. Not only, therefore, did drunken women need improving and training in sober habits and useful work, they also needed to be removed from public view. Furthermore, although men's civil liberties had to be protected, the institutionalisation of women was less likely to be opposed by public opinion.

It may be that drunken women merely confirmed the suspicion of their contemporaries that working-class women were failing in their duties as wives and mothers. They were the most obvious and visible example of a general trend which had to be confronted. Therefore draconian measures including lengthy periods of detention might well have been considered both acceptable and necessary. After all, women were not yet quite regarded as autonomous adults so other people could decide what was best for them. Furthermore the institutions were thought of as genuine 'reformatories' which offered the inmates not only moral re-education but also the opportunity to improve their wretched condition in a healthy environment. In order to explore the way in which the reformatories reflected these ideas we now turn to our records from Farmfield to examine both the nature of the regime and the data we have on the women who were sent there.

FARMFIELD INEBRIATE REFORMATORY

As our investigation depends on the extent and thoroughness of surviving records that were kept for other purposes, we cannot hope to find the kind of information we need to test hypotheses with any degree of accuracy. We can only make an impressionistic assessment from the records, letters and case notes that exist. Nonetheless the records provide some illuminating data both about the regime itself and about the attitudes of the staff writing the reports. They give us a clearer picture of the social and moral world within which both the reformatory and the women who were sent to it existed.

Farmfield which opened in 1900 was the certified reformatory set up by the London County Council. The building and land (374 acres) in Horley, Surrey, were purchased in 1899 for £15 000 and a special committee on the Inebriates Act 1898 was set up by the LCC to administer its funding and control its organisation.

The reformatory was originally intended for male inebriates. However, while the negotiations over the property were being carried out, there was an urgent request from a magistrate in a North London police court to the LCC arguing that the reformatory should be for women, not men.

It is a home to send the women who qualify in Police Courts that we want. These women are nearly all, 95% of them what may be termed prostitutes. If the younger of these can be treated under the Act I think it is likely that their drunkenness and their prostitution might in a fair proportion of cases be cured and the Act proved to be of practical use and good. I much regret to see that the L.C.C. propose to provide a home to which males only can be sent, and I wish the Council could see that provision for female inebriates is required far more than for males. There are so many more women than men who require treatment and I am inclined to think that more permanent good would be likely to result from the treatment of women than of men. (LCC, 1899–1914)

Another letter from Mr Thomas Holmes of the London Diocesan Branch, Police Court Mission, Church of England Temperance Society, to Dr W. J. Collins, Chairman of the Special Committee on the Inebriates Act, dated 26 October 1899, stated: 'Believe me no rescue or philanthropic society can hope to deal with these women i.e. women four times convicted in one year, few of them can be considered victims of drink. If these are to be left to private societies I feel sure the Act will remain a dead letter' (LCC, 1899). It is clear from this correspondence that women were considered not only in need of institutional care for their moral protection,

but also to be able to benefit from it in a way that men could not –
either because the men were seen as incorrigible or because
their responsibilities as earners would prevent them from being
sentenced.

The Special Committee on the Inebriates Act was obviously
persuaded by these arguments (these two letters are examples of
others written in the same vein) and, at a meeting of the
Committee on 9 March 1900 it was resolved that a 'reformatory
for female inebriates be established on the Farmfield estate
Charlwood, near Horley' (LCC, 1900). In the summer of that
year, the first female patient was admitted. Detailed case notes of
all patients were recorded and from the period August 1900 to
July 1914 932 women were admitted to Farmfield, most of whom
were sentenced for three years.

Kate Elisabeth Dutch was the first patient admitted on 28
August 1900. She was English, aged 38 and, although married,
was living alone prior to her sentence. She had been born in
Cambridge and was the youngest of fifteen children. Her parents
were 'temperate' in their 'habits' and their 'mental state' was
'good'. She had been educated at a private school in Cambridge
and could write fairly well. Her occupation was that of charwoman. Kate had had eight children, two of whom had died. She
had started drinking when she was 30 and she had blamed
quarrels with her husband and the fact that she 'no longer cared'
as reasons for her intemperance. She used to drink regularly
(mainly ale) and continuously and had had fifty-two previous
convictions and had committed four other 'misdemeanours'. This
had resulted in her having been to prison thirty-one times.

She was 5ft 2in tall, weighed 128lbs and had scars on her shin
and several on her face. Her mental condition was recorded as
'sane' and her general health 'fair'. It was noted that she had not
been in an insane or inebriate asylum, had not taken opium or
other drugs and had no history of delirium tremens or alcoholic
convulsions. Kate's condition on admission was recorded as
'wretched, hatless and miserably clad' although her behaviour
was noted as 'cheerful'. She had been sentenced for just 12 months
and during that time her general conduct was 'industrious and
very good'. She was not given any punishment. Unfortunately,
after her discharge on 28 August 1901, she relapsed immediately.

This account of Kate Elisabeth Dutch, Farmfield's first patient,
was fairly typical of the detailed records kept for each patient. Of

the 932 women who were admitteed to Farmfield we examined the records of a one in ten sample, starting with the first patient. This gave us 94 case records to examine.

The Regime

According to the general regulations which applied to all reformatories 'the inmate should be encouraged to exercise his faculties and employ his time as remuneratively as possible' (Parliamentary Papers, 1901a). For the women at Farmfield, their day began at 6 a.m. and ended with lights out at 9.30 p.m. They had prayers twice a day, two hours of recreation and eight and a half hours of work (Parliamentary Papers, 1901b).

During the first year after the opening of Farmfield, 'work' consisted mainly of housework, laundry work, sewing, work in the dairy and home farm work. Patients were rewarded for good work by being given 'marks'. There were strict guidelines regarding the patient's diet including the exact weight of margarine and cooked meat to be provided (Johnston, 1985). Although patients were allowed visits from relatives and friends, again there were strict regulations regarding the frequency of these visits. For example, a patient was allowed a visit from her friends and relatives not more than once a week and only on conditoin that the conduct of the patient had been satisfactory.

Analysis of the Sample

The Patients and Their Social Background

Although the Inspector's report of 1902 stated that 'no case is eligible for admission to Farmfield if over 45 years of age', our sample showed that this ruling was not strictly adhered to. The youngest patient was 20, the oldest 58 and the average was 36. Of the 94 cases, 46 of them were married, 30 single, 16 widowed and two did not have their marital status recorded. Although nearly half the women were married, only nine were living with their families or husbands at the time of their admission.

The case records provide us with very little information about the children of the Farmfield patients apart from their numbers. The general anxiety about the future of working-class mothers did not seem reflected in practical concern for the fate of existing children.

The occupations of the Farmfield women were varied although mainly unskilled. There were 23 different occupations recorded, the most common being that of laundress. However, in the appendix of the Inspector's report for the year 1900, a report of the Superintendent of Farmfield stated:

> Each patient has some occupation stated on her charge sheet (laundress as a rule). Predominancy in laundresses is not due to laundresses being more addicted to drink, but owing to the fact that they term themselves such on their charge sheet because it is the work they prefer when in prison. Our experience hitherto has been that they know hardly anything about work. (Parliamentary Papers, 1901b)

Other occupations recorded were charwoman, housewife, flower seller, domestic servant, cook/housekeeper, dress maker, machinist, milliner, prostitute, barmaid, vocalist and book-keeper. In addition to these varied occupations the majority of the women appear to have received elementary education which at least enabled them to read and write fairly well.

As regards the physical condition of the patients, the first few inmates were described by such phrases as 'very wretched and dirty' and 'clean but very miserable looking', but in many of the comments the same phrases were often repeatedly used and many of the women were described as 'clean and tidy'. During their sentences the majority of the women were reported to have 'good' health and in describing their mental condition a variety of expressions were used including: good, sound, normal, depressed, clear, sane, rational, rather morose, sound with a tendency to hysteria, good, strong-minded and obstinate and cheerful but not fond of company. Seven of the women were recorded as having symptoms of syphilis and one had gonorrhoea. Other disorders mentioned show that the women were obviously well examined on admission to Farmfield and such details as weight, height, the number of scars or wounds and whether or not the patient had been vaccinated were recorded in great detail. Finally out of the sample of 94 women, three died during their sentence. One of these was in fact transferred to the local asylum where she died. Her case notes read 'Very excitable, erratic, appears on intimate terms with the Royal Family . . . Transferred to Horton Asylum . . . died March 1912 – a raving lunatic' (LCC, 1902).

Intemperance, Convictions and Sentences

From the case notes, the most common reason given for the cause of the women's intemperance was 'bad company' followed by 'domestic trouble'. It was obvious that many of the women had led extremely unhappy domestic lives often exacerbated by poverty. An example was that of Ellen Fan aged 46. In her case notes it was recorded; 'Husband deserted her and was very unkind. She then had to knock about and do daily work. She eventually got work at a Public House and she got in the way of drinking freely' (LCC, 1910). In the patients' case notes both the present conviction and their criminal history were recorded. The majority of the inmates had been convicted of either riotous and disorderly behaviour, or being unlawfully drunk in a public place. As a result of these past convictions, more than three-quarters of the women (77) were sentenced to three years at Farmfield.

It is interesting to note that despite the urgent requests from the London magistrates for a female reformatory to deal with the large numbers of prostitutes, in our sample, over the 14-year period, less than a quarter (22) of the women had had previous convictions for prostitution and there was no 'present' conviction for prostitution recorded.

Conduct and Punishment

There were varying degrees of punishment given to offending women ranging from withholding of marks to imprisonment in Holloway or transfer to the state reformatory in Aylesbury. Cell punishment at Farmfield was commonly used. By 1903, however, there was some concern that although an attempt was being made by the Courts to select more reformable cases for Farmfield, this method of selection was proving to be defective.

As a different selection procedure was adopted the class of inmates did, however, improve. The Southern Counties Inebriate Reformatory at Lewes and the Eastern Counties Reformatory in Norfolk acted as receiving houses for all inebriate women. This proved to be a more successful method of selection of 'reformable cases' (Public Records HO45/19199). On the whole the Farmfield inmates were well behaved and only a few were given punishment. Some of the more detailed comments included: 'fairly good early part of the time, became very abusive, had to be transferred to Aylesbury'; and 'A rough woman inclined to be a bully. She threw a spoon at a Sister. Was very rude and insolent. Was sent to the State Reformatory at Aylesbury'.

Staff Care and After-care

From the case notes it appeared that the staff of Farmfield genuinely cared about the well-being of their patients despite the strict regime. They were especially concerned about the women's physical health. An example of this concern can be seen in the case of Ellen Fan who was transferred from the Eastern Counties Reformatory. 'This woman looked as if she would never be able to go out again from the Home when she came from Norfolk. She looked in such a bad state of health. With Cod Liver oil and good food she rapidly got better and is most grateful' (LCC, 1901). One patient was in fact so appreciative of the care she received that she did not want to leave. 'A quiet woman. Anxious to do better, but felt very unable to fight her way in life. She would have liked to have stayed at Farmfield for the rest of her life' (LCC, 1901).

The care that the staff extended to the patients at Farmfield continued after they had left. Extensive work was done in trying to follow up the patients – in some cases, up to eight years after they had left. Unfortunately their success rate seemed disappointingly low when considering the three years' effort put into the patients' reformation. Follow-up investigations were routinely carried out after three, six and 12 months after discharge, and it appeared that the reformatory staff tried to keep in contact with their ex-patients for as long as possible.

The Closing of Farmfield

The demise of the inebriate reformatories has been discussed elsewhere (Melor *et al.*, 1986 and Radzinowicz and Hood, 1986) but in the Inspector's report for 1912, Branthwaite tried to draw conclusions about both Sections 1 and 2 of the Inebriates Act. 'It can hardly be said that the committal of 565 cases under Section 1 during the 14 years represents its value or its application to the extent intended by the legislative' (Parliamentary Papers, 1913).

Later in the report he also suggests possible reasons to explain why the number committed under Section 2 was also relatively small. These included magistrates' ignorance of the Act, a disbelief 'in the reformatory value of detention as a remedial measure' (Parliamentary Papers, 1913) and various administrative procedures. He concluded by noting 'that further progress with the work is improbable unless these difficulties are removed' (Parliamentary Papers, 1913).

Farmfield was eventually closed (along with most of the other inebriate reformatories) not long after the outbreak of the First World War. On 20 February 1915, at a meeting of the Inebriates Committee, it was resolved 'That the After-Care Committee be informed of the decision of the Council to discontinue receiving after the end of July 1915, patients at Farmfield Reformatory (LCC, 1915). After the war, the building was re-opened again in November 1924 as a mental handicap hospital and still exists as a hospital today.

As so much concern was expressed about the type of inmate who was to be selected for Farmfield, and as it was reported that the type of inmate had improved as Farmfield became established, we cannot claim that Farmfield inmates represented reformatory women in general. It could only be said to represent women considered to be capable of improvement. Therefore it is probably not surprising to find that the majority were healthy, mentally sound and reasonably educated, and there is no sign in this sample that they were a population who were mentally defective either before or after they started drinking. However, if being sufficiently weak-willed to return to drink on release is taken as a sign of mental weakness, we might interpret the data differently.

The Farmfield staff were obviously concerned about the women and noted with pleasure the way that their health improved after a few weeks at Farmfield. Those who became ill were cared for, and great pains were taken to follow up and befriend women who had left. Nevertheless the regime was strict, based on moral improvement through hard work. The women were treated very much as children and given 'marks' for good conduct and attendance at religious services, a system later adopted in borstal training. While most inmates seemed to conform to the institution, those few who did not were punished severely. For example, being sent to a state reformatory for throwing a spoon at a sister might seem an excessive penalty today, but in fact it is doubtful if attitudes towards drunken women have really changed so significantly in the last 80 years. Women are still sent to prison for drunkenness (Carlen, 1983), they are still treated like children in prison and still punished quite harshly for petty offences. Furthermore habitual drinkers may be categorised as subject to a personality disorder not amenable to psychiatric treatment (Carlen, 1983). Elements of incorrigibility still lurk behind enlightened discourse.

From the evidence we have, the occupations of the women appear somewhat ambiguous; whether or not the unskilled casual jobs recorded are simply a cover for prostitution is difficult to assess. On the one hand, a report of 1914 of the After-Care Committee for London women from Farmfield suggested that most of the women were or had been prostitutes but, on the other hand, less than a quarter of the women had previous convictions for prostitution. Furthermore Booth notes that although, of course, prostitutes drink, they seldom drink to excess (Booth, 1970). What does seem clear, however, was that the women suffered from all the disadvantages of the casual poor at the turn of the century, and as far as we can tell the majority had no family either to support them or to demand their care and involvement. In most cases there would be neither husband nor employer to protest at their absence.

CONCLUSION

At the turn of the century there certainly was public concern about national efficiency, and drinking, especially among women, was regarded as a potentially debilitating factor. It was held responsible for producing neglected children, improvident house-keeping and an increase in vice. However, it is clear from the Farmfield records that it was not simply a question of using the reformatory programme to control women in a way considered unacceptable for men. It was rather that the women were seen to be in a miserable and wretched state which three years at Farmfield might do something to change. It is not unreasonable to assume that the staff thought improved health, better skills, newly acquired habits of work and even regular religious attendance would make women better able to fend for themselves in a difficult world (Booth, 1911; Somerset, 1912). Again from the data we cannot assess adequately whether this view was shared by the women themselves. One woman wanted to remain at Farmfield after her sentence was completed but others were sent to the state reformatory for running away. For us today the issue would be whether people should be held for 'training or rehabilitation' anywhere if they did not choose to stay – even if it was for their own good. But it must be remembered that individualism with its emphasis on freedom and equal citizenship was not yet completely extended to include women. Although the struggle for female suffrage was intensifying between 1900 and 1914, political equality had not yet been won and paternalistic attitudes towards women still prevailed. For example, as late as 1910 government actuaries discussing health insurance could still claim

> married women living with their husbands need not be included since where the unit is the family, it is the husband's and not the wife's health which is important to insure. So long as the husband is in good health and able to work adequate provision will be made for the needs of the family, irrespective of the wife's health, whereas when the husband's health fails there is no one to earn the wages. (Fraser, 1973, p. 155).

This quotation suggests that married women's health was of no importance in itself unless the woman was the bread winner. Farmfield therefore could be interpreted as a step towards improving both the health and the earning capacity of women regardless of their marital status, and therefore evidence that women's rights were being taken seriously.

The First World War was to bring about a further change in attitudes to women and to the employment of the casual poor. Women, for the first time, entered the labour force as equal partners with men, often replacing those at the front in jobs which had previously been considered an exclusive male preserve. Equally as Gareth Stedman Jones points out

> All 'surplus' labour was absorbed by the needs of the war time economy . . . the First World War showed that the existence of the casual poor had not been the effect of some deviant mutation induced by the degenerating influences of city life . . . once decent and regular employment was made available 'unemployables' were impossible to find. (Stedman Jones, 1984, p. 336).

It is perhaps not surprising therefore that the war brought about the demise of Farmfield as an inebriate reformatory too.

REFERENCES

Barrington, A., Pearson, K. and Heron, D. (1910) 'A Preliminary Study of Extreme Alcoholism in Adults', *Eugenics Laboratory Memoirs*, No. 14.

Booth, B. (1911) 'The Management of Inebriate Women', *British Journal of Inebriety*, Vol. IX, No. 2.

Booth, C. (1971) 'London – A Portrait of the Poor at the Turn of the Century', drawn from the *Life and Labour of the People of London* (Harmondsworth: Penguin).

Branthwaite, R. W. (1908) 'Inebriety: Its Causation and Control', *The British Journal of Inebriety*, Vol. 5, No. 3.

Branthwaite, R. W. (1927) 'The Inebriates Act, 1898', *The British Journal of Inebriety*, Vol. 25.

Carlen, P. (1983) *Women's Imprisonment: A Study in Social Control* (London: Routledge & Kegan Paul).

Carswell, J. (1901) 'The Working of the Inebriates Act', *Journal of Mental Science*, October, 1-14.

Clark, G. K. (1975) *The Making of Victorian England* (London: University Paperbacks).

Cominos, P. (1973) 'Innocent Femina Sensualis in Unconscious Conflict', in M. Vicinus (ed), *Suffer and be Still: Women in the Victorian Age* (London: Indiana University Press).

Fraser, D. (1973) *The Evolution of the British Welfare State* (London: Macmillan).

Johnston, V. (1985) 'Local Prison Diets, 1835–1878', in D. J. Oddy and D. S. Miller, *Diet and Health in Modern Britain* (London: Croom Helm).

London County Council (1899–1914) Presented Papers: Letter from G. Snow Fordham, Magistrate North London Police Court.

London County Council (1899) Presented Papers: Letter Thomas Holmes, 26 October.

London County Council (1900) Committee Minutes. 9 March.

London County Council (1900-1914) Case History Books Vols. 1–5.

London County Council (1901) Report of Lady Superintendent, Vol. 2.

London County Council (1915) Committee Minutes. 20 February.

McLaughlin, P. M. (1987) 'Inebriate Reformatories in Scotland, 1902-1921', in S. Barrows, R. Room and J. Gusfield (eds), *The Social History of Alcohol* (Berkeley: University of California Press).

Mellor, J., Hunt, G., Turner, J. and Rees, L. (1986) 'Prayers and Piecework: Inebriate Reformatories in England at the End of the Nineteenth Century, *Drogalkohol*, No. 3.

Parliamentary Papers (1899-1914) Regulation for State and Certified Reformatories. Appendix 1.

Parliamentary Papers (1899) *The Report of the Inspector under the Inebriates Act for the Year 1900*.

Parliamentary Papers (1910) *The Report of the Inspector under the Inebriates Act for the Year 1909.*

Parliamentary Papers (1913) *The Report of the Inspector under the Inebriates Act for the Year 1912.*

Pitcairn, J. (1897) 'The Prison Treatment of Inebriates', in *The Proceedings of the Society for the Study of Inebriety*, No. 51.

Public Records. *The National Institutions for Inebriates.* Public Records Office, HO45/19199.

Radzinowicz, L. and Hood, R. (1986) *A History of English Criminal Law and its Administration from 1750, Vol. 5. The Emergence of Penal Policy* (London: Stevens).

Semmel, B. (1960) *Imperialism and Social Reform* (London: Allen & Unwin).

Soloway, R. (1982) 'Counting the Degenerates: The Statistics of Race Deterioration in Edwardian England', *Journal of Contemporary History*, Vol. 17.

Somerset, H. (1912) 'The Duxhurst Industrial Farm Colony for Female Inebriates', *British Journal of Inebriety*, Vol. 10.

Stedman Jones, G. (1984) *Outcast London* (Harmondsworth: Penguin).

Wilson, E. (1977) *Women and the Welfare State* (London: Tavistock).

Part IV
Local Political Action and the Central State

Part IV
Local Political Action and
the Central State

9 A 'Social Danger': The Contested History of Teacher–State Relations

Jenny Ozga

INTRODUCTION

This chapter is primarily concerned with discussing the historical development of teacher–state relations in England and Wales, and attempts, through focusing on key periods in that development – the 1860s, the 1920s and the 1940s – to fix attention on the strategies adopted by the state in managing its problematic teaching workforce. The intention of the discussion is to make apparent the covert and overt constraints within which teachers operated in the past (and which increasingly affect their current situation) and thus to take issue with approaches to teacher–state relations which stress state patronage of the emergent teaching profession, and which infer a coincidence of interests between teachers and the state (Tropp, 1957; Shipman, 1984).

The view of teachers as unproblematically incorporated into the state can be found in many sources, perhaps most obviously in some of the 'new' sociology of education of the early 1970s, which argued that schooling should be understood primarily in terms of social control and social reproduction (for example, Althusser, 1971; Bourdieu, 1973; Bowles and Gintis, 1976). Riseborough has attacked these structural marxists for ignoring 'the complexities of everyday life within capitalistic social formations which vitiate notions of the simple functional fit of humankind, underpinned by a straightforward socialization process. Teachers are erroneously conceived of as automatons, reproduced reproducers simply and easily subjugating children because teachers are state functionaries, "high priests of the ruling ideology" (Althusser, 1971, p. 246) and, as such, thoroughly pickled in it themselves.' (Riseborough, 1985, pp. 206–7.)

189

Of course, the structuralist marxist sociology of the 1970s was not the only source of assumptions about teachers' incorporation into the state. The sociology of occupations, imbued with functionalist assumptions about professionalism, stresses teachers' dependence on benevolent state patronage and sees the growth of state education provision and teachers' enhanced professional status as symbiotically linked (Tropp, 1957; Parry and Parry, 1974; Hoyle, 1974, 1980). Studies of teachers' influence on education policy-making also stress consensus and partnership between teachers and the state (Kogan, 1975; Briault, 1976) or see teachers as using their professional expertise as a basis for negotiation with the state (Archer, 1979).

The issue of teachers' class position has also been treated in such a way as to contribute to the idea of their incorporation into the state. Discussions rooted in functionalist approaches to professionalism stress teachers' efforts to dissociate themselves from the working class (Bergen, 1982), while much neo-marxist class analysis condemns teachers as unproductive labourers and excludes them from the working class (Ginsburg *et al.*, 1980). Debates on the class position of teachers in the mid to late 1970s either focused on their contradictory class location (Poulantzas, 1977) or assigned them to a 'new' middle class (Carchedi, 1975). Pluralist perspectives on policy-making, drawing on uncritical conceptions of professionalism, ignore the issue of class altogether.

Whatever the analytical approach, much historical and sociological writing supports the assumption that teachers identified with, or were incorporated into, the state. They were excluded from the working class, and even colluded in its oppression through their role in social reproduction.

It is impossible to review all the material which contributed to this orthodox view of teachers as semi-professional, lower middle-class state agents (see Ozga and Lawn, 1981 for a review of relevant sources, and Lawn and Ozga, 1981 for a more developed critique of them). However, it is important to stress the range and quantity of such material, and its (conscious or unconscious) support for a perspective on teachers which informs such disparate topics as teachers' life histories (Sikes *et al.*, 1985), management training for teachers, (Hoyle, 1981) and both conventional and critical histories of education (Tropp, 1957 Centre for Contemporary Cultural Studies, 1981).

It is possible to challenge these assumptions about teachers in a number of different, though related, ways. One is through the adoption of a labour process approach to teachers' work (Lawn and Ozga, 1981; Connell, 1985; Ozga and Lawn, 1988; Ozga, 1988a), which focuses on their position as state employees, and on the antagonistic relations between them and their employer. This approach has particular relevance in the current context of changes in the control of teachers' work: in, for example, the abolition of their negotiating rights, the imposition of a contract, the prescription of content in the national curriculum – which has led some commentators to consider the applicability of the proletarianisation thesis to teachers (Apple, 1986; Apple and Teitelbaum, 1986; Ozga, 1988b; Ozga and Lawn, 1988).

Another challenge to assumptions about teachers has come from more sophisticated approaches to the state, which reject its characterisation as a neutral or benevolent arbiter, but which also avoid over-deterministic assumptions about the extent of its powers by distinguishing between its function in the political, economic and social spheres, and by exploring the tensions and contradictions generated by the need to fulfil these functions simultaneously (Corrigan, 1980; Dale, 1981a; Grace, 1987). Critical approaches to professionalism, too, have allowed for the development of analyses which focus on the ideological and control functions of professionalism (Johnson, 1972; Larson, 1977). Historians of education, perhaps especially feminist historians, have begun to uncover 'lost' aspects of teacher history (King, 1987; Danylewycz and Prentice, 1986; Lawn, 1987a) which reveal teacher involvement in radical politics, in working-class alliances, and demonstrate the complexity of teacher–state relations, especially when the significance of gender and class relations in teaching is properly considered (Copelman, 1985).

All these approaches complicate and challenge assumptions about teachers' incorporation into the state. Taken together, they provide a coherent alternative perspective: the focus on the state as employer and on proletarianisation re-opens the issue of teachers' class position, the significance of professionalism is revealed as its contribution to control of the workforce, similar to 'responsible autonomy' (Friedman, 1977), and instances of workforce resistance may also be recognised.

The historical discussion below of particular periods in what may be regarded as 'an extended war of position' (Grace, following Gramsci, 1987, p. 195) between teachers and the state should be placed in the context of the total approach to the study of teachers and the state. Its purpose is to act as a corrective to over-determined views of teachers, and to make the point that teacher–state relations are implicitly problematic, and demand a strategic response from the state. Historical investigation allows us to see how that strategic response has varied (often in response to teachers' political actions, or to economic crisis, or both), and to place the current move towards strong central state control in context.

FROM CENTRAL CONTROL TO INDIRECT RULE AND BACK AGAIN

The Revised Code

The establishment of a state system of education in England and Wales required that, along with growing responsibility for the provision of schools, the state assumed growing responsibility for the provision of teachers, for their training and regulation. Before 1862, teachers – who could be certified, uncertified or apprentice teachers – were engaged and paid by the managers of the schools in which they taught. With the introduction of the revised code, school managers received a single block grant, the amount of which depended partly on the results of examinations carried out by HMI – hence 'payment by results'.

The revised code was intended to be cheap and efficient, but its over-arching aim of 'educating our masters' lay behind the narrowness of the curriculum and its rote-learning methods. Teacher initiatives had raised the quality of working-class education, the code provided more 'appropriate' education, as Grace explains:

> Despite existing mechanisms of surveillance and screening, the system had perversely developed its own dynamic which had resulted in forms of curriculum development, forms of teacher initiative and forms of cultivation of intelligence which had never been intended for working class schooling. The costs of the enterprise had risen dramatically and new subjects had been introduced into the curriculum. Elementary school-

teachers had become more confident and assertive. As standards within the provided system rose the dreadful prospect that working class education might soon surpass in quality that provided by many middle class private schools suggested, as one writer put it, that there would be 'an inversion of the orders of society'. In short, the system in practice had turned out to be altogether too good for the working class. (Grace, 1985, p. 7)

The responsibility for this distortion of the schooling system lay with the teachers, who had become an over-paid and over-confident vested interest in education. Lowe, President of the Board of Education, argued that without the code 'a state of things will arise that the control of the educational system will pass out of the hands of the privy council and of the House of Commons into the hands of the persons working that educational system' (Tropp, 1957, p. 87). Control over the system was reasserted through the application of the principles of a market economy to elementary schools:

The Code would define the product required, the inspector would assess the extent to which it had been achieved, the teacher would be paid in relation to his or her measured efficiency in production . . . The dominant principle was now to be that of efficient pedagogic work production with an emphasis on 'basics'. (Grace, 1985, p. 8).

Reaction to the Code

Two important points can be made about reaction to the code. The first was that not even the central agents charged with its delivery were unanimously in favour of it – Matthew Arnold, a member of the Inspectorate, being its most famous critic. Criticism grew with the perception of Britain's comparatively poor economic performance in the 1870s. Second, the operation of the code provoked resistance from teachers, and was probably the single most significant factor in the development of an organised, unionised, teaching force: the National Union of Teachers (NUT) (then the National Union of Elementary Teachers) was founded in 1870. Thus a period of strong political reaction produced a system designed to define the limits of elementary education and of elementary teaching, and this in turn produced a strong reaction from elementary teachers, one which fostered their sense of identity as a group, despite divisions, especially gender divisions, among them. By equating schools with factories and teachers with workers, the state revealed to teachers the advantages of organisation, and of direct action for the improvement of working conditions. By treating elementary teachers as state servants, the state encouraged them to identify with those whose children they taught, rather than strive unsuccessfully for social promotion.

Evidence of this includes local strikes (in which teachers formed alliances with other workers) and teachers' involvement in radical politics, for example, in the Teachers' Labour League. Until recently, such evidence has been largely ignored, or confined to footnotes. (Lawn, 1987a; Tropp, 1957; Seifert, 1987).

The extent to which teachers became involved in, or sympathetic to, radical politics is, of course, difficult to establish. Teachers did provide a considerable amount of support for the emergent Labour Party, and it was concern about their potential drift to the left, in a period when the Conservatives could no longer take for granted that they were the 'natural party of government', which led the state to identify the management of the teaching force as a political problem.

Some teachers, in the early years of this century, worked in alliance with local trades councils for improvements in their pay and conditions (Thompson, 1927, p. 197), and also made demands, in conjunction with parents and trade unionists, for more educational provision, and for access to education that was more than mere vocational training.

The state consistently attempted to preserve the class-based distinction between elementary and secondary schooling, a distinction resisted by some organised teachers and by some progressive school boards. The 1902 Education Act abolished school boards and created local authorities, run by professional administrators, who formed a barrier between teachers and the class whose children they taught. The 1902 Act reinforced the elementary/secondary split, and laid the obligation on the inspectorate to see that it was adhered to.

Teachers continued to question the division, however. In 1907 the NUT published a pamphlet called 'Higher Education and the People's Children: an appeal to the people against the policy of the Secondary Schools Branch of the Board of Education'. The pamphlet argued against the class segregation which was proposed through the establishment of higher elementary schools and against stringent controls on the elementary school curriculum, condemning this as part of 'a deliberate policy on the part of the Board to discriminate against the children of the working classes' (Simon, 1965, pp. 267–9).

In the aftermath of the 1914–1918 war, and especially in the post 1920 period, when that bi-partite division of educational provision based on social class came under strain, technical justification of such division based on the assessment, through testing, of intellectual ability was invoked. The role of education as a means of maintaining class division grew enormously in importance, as did the need for the state to ensure the co-operation of its teachers. This co-operation could not be relied upon in a period when the NUT had steadily increased its membership and engaged in two long local disputes, while campaigning throughout England and Wales for better working conditions and improved pay (Thompson, 1927, pp. 217-26). Between 1918 and 1920 the affiliation of the union to the Labour Party was discussed. H. A. L. Fisher, then President of the Board of Education, warned that 'an embittered teacher is a social danger' (Grace, 1987, p. 203) and sought ways of reducing that danger.

LICENSED PROFESSIONALISM

The strategic response adopted by Fisher centred round the encouragement of teacher professionalism, within limits. Teachers, including elementary teachers, were to be encouraged to think of themselves as professionals, through the fostering of their responsibilities in certain areas – pedagogic expertise, for example, and identification with the service:

> The National Union of Teachers had played a most valuable part in watching over the material interests of the profession . . . but as the state takes a more and more direct interest in the material conditions of the profession, and as these material conditions become more and more improved, then I hope that the activities of the National Union of Teachers, which is such a

powerful instrument for influencing opinion in this country, may be more and more concentrated upon what I may call the spiritual and intellectual aspects of the teachers' work. (Fisher, 1919; quoted in Lawn, 1987a, p. 69)

Fisher's policy foundered because of the disparity between professional rhetoric and the worsening economic climate which led to the implementation of severe cuts in the level of central support for education in 1922 – a cut of £18 million out of a total allocation to the Board of Education of £50 million. These cuts, and a review of teachers' salaries, superannuation and pension rights aroused fierce opposition from teachers. Teachers continued to drift towards the Labour Party (Lawn, 1987a), and the NUT was involved in a protracted salary campaign which involved most of its local associations in extended disputes or strikes. Thus the teaching force presented an immediate and pressing problem to Baldwin's government.

Baldwin's President of the Board of Education was Eustace Percy, appointed in 1924. According to Lawn (1987b), Percy's correspondence with backbenchers reveals considerable concern about teachers in the Labour Party and the activities of the Teachers' Labour League. Some MPs demanded that teachers take an oath of allegiance, and a Subversive Teachings Bill was suggested, but Percy had a clear perception of the dangers of overt central control in a period when the Conservative Party could no longer assume electoral victory: 'What could be worse . . . than to encourage a conception that teachers are servants of a government in the same way as Civil Servants, and therefore must teach in their schools precisely what any Labour Government may tell them to teach' (Percy quoted in Lawn, 1987b, p. 230).

It was this appreciation of the dangers of a highly centralised system which produced a certain relaxation in curriculum controls over elementary teachers. In 1926 the Board of Education changed the basis of curriculum control from prescription to suggestion, establishing the 'modern principle of curriculum autonomy' (Grace, 1985, p. 10). White's convincing analysis of the motivation of the Conservatives in de-regulating the curriculum concludes:

If Parliament still controlled the content of education, the Socialists would change the Regulations . . . they would be able to introduce curricula more in line with Socialist ideas. To forestall this it was no longer in the interests of the anti-Socialists, including Conservatives, to keep curriculum policy in the hands of the state . . . If they would devise a workable system of non-statutory controls, the Conservatives had everything to gain and nothing to lose from taking curricula out of the politicians' hands. (White, 1975, p. 28)

What we see here is a strategic response by the state to a number of related problems – the danger of an over-centralised system falling into the 'wrong' hands, the drift of some teachers leftwards and economic problems. It is also important to note that licensed professionalism was underpinned by *curricular* autonomy.

The strategic response went further, and included reorganisation of the education system, but on a different basis from the overt controls of the 1902 Act. Martin Lawn has argued that in restructuring the education system Percy was strongly influenced by Lugard's colonial administrative system of 'indirect rule'. This system essentially involved a degree of decentralisation and co-option of local leaders. However, decentralisation existed within the framework of discreet, but strong, central authority which retained overall strategic control, though the mode of application differed according to local custom and circumstance.

Percy's contribution to the administration of education lay, tactically and strategically, in releasing the central authority from direct control of the system. This allowed it to appear as a broker or referee, talking of cooperation and understanding between government and people, which for all intents and purposes meant local authorities and their teachers. Until a local crisis or national emergency appeared, the central authority appeared to be neutral in the system it was controlling (or perhaps more fairly, trying to control). (Lawn, 1987b, p. 234)

Within the strategy of 'indirect rule', the concepts of teacher professionalism and the 'partnership' between central and local state and the teachers are crucial. They fostered the shared meanings and relationships on which indirect rule depended. It was a sophisticated strategy; and, as the colonial parallel demonstrates, though durable, ultimately doomed as the 'natives' resisted co-option and pushed their autonomy beyond its pre-ordained limits.

The 1944 Education Act marks a crucial point in the history of indirect rule. Although it is often characterised as the cornerstone of 'partnership' and teacher autonomy, it is perhaps better understood as an attempt by the state to re-assert control (Ranson, 1985; Shipman, 1984; Fenwick, 1985), but one that was thwarted by resistance from teachers and local education authorities, who were able to maintain their autonomy in a situation of crisis caused by expanding demand, post-war economic uncertainty and major reorganisation (Lawn and Ozga, 1986).

The political and social context of 1944 permitted teachers to defend their 'licensed autonomy' (Dale, 1981b) and resist more direct rule. They were in a strong market position in the period following 1944, when there was a shortage of qualified teachers, public demand for increased educational opportunity, allied to demands for a more just and egalitarian society, acceptance of a human capital approach to investment in education, and the growth of pedagogic expertise, whether associated with intel-ligence testing or based on child-centred methods. A further important factor was that which had initially provoked the centre in promulgating licensed autonomy – the strength of organised teachers.

Throughout the 1950s and 1960s all these factors combined to strengthen teachers' claims to autonomy and to force the state to maintain the rhetoric of indirect rule, that of partnership and professionalism. There are indications, however, that the con-cerns discussed earlier (restricting working-class schooling, limit-ing professional autonomy, and so on) remained, but were forced into the background by political and social 'consensus' in favour of educational expansion and professional expertise. For example, in 1962 the Minister, David Eccles, attempted to set up the Curriculum Study Group in his own department, staffed by his officials. This attempt to re-assert central control over the curriculum was defeated by organised teacher and local educa-tion authority opposition, which resulted in the establishment of the teacher-controlled Schools Council.

The central state was more successful in recovering control of teachers' pay when, in 1965, the Burnham Committee was reconstituted so as to give the Secretary of State veto powers and the DES formal representation (Ozga, 1988b). However, it was only with the threat of economic crisis, in the late 1970s, that the centre began to move away from indirect rule.

BACK TO CENTRAL CONTROL

The end of the 1970s and the 1980s saw a period of economic contraction and concern about educational standards linked to questions of competitiveness and national performance which echoed the historical conditions we have just reviewed. We have witnessed a similar reaction: greater control over educational content (which, it could be argued, restricts the type of education available to the majority to vocationally oriented education) and a greater control over the activities of teachers. The idea of relaxed controls over curriculum has, once again, given way to the need to prescribe centrally (presumably the fear of a Socialist curriculum is no longer a concern of the Conservatives who, after three consecutive election victories, may be confident of once again constituting 'the natural party of government').

The criticisms of teachers which have come from within government and from the 'New Right' also echo the old arguments, castigating teachers for their professional self-interest, their monopolisation of provision, their constant expansion of the curriculum and demands for greater resources. The contradictory elements in professionalism which weakened teachers, especially those associated with status and expertise, left them vulnerable to such criticisms. Teachers had been encouraged to think of themselves as 'experts', and this came between them and parents. That division, fostered by a particular professional ideology, permitted the state to co-opt parents into a new 'partnership' for the 'reform' of the education system. The capacity of teachers to resist such initiatives was weakened by the failure of education policy designed to eradicate inequality; it was becoming apparent to teachers that education could not, after all, compensate for society. Furthermore, teachers were having to cope with simultaneous decline in both resources and pupil numbers. All these factors combined to create favourable circumstances for the reassertion of control over teachers, through policy initiatives which covered training (both pre-service and in-service), performance, payment, conditions of service and curriculum.

The eventual outcome of such initiatives, together with the so-called Great Education Reform Bill proposals, will be a segregated system of education in which resource-starved state schools, staffed by de-skilled teachers, offer a vocationally oriented core curriculum, and opted-out schools and the city technology colleges offer different versions of élite education. The historical parallels are all too obvious.

CONCLUSION

How far can we go in developing such parallels? The historical material outlined above emphasises the importance of recognising not just state strategies but teachers' responses to them. The revised code failed because of teacher resistance and the threat of teacher militancy, combined with teachers' consistent attempts to expand educational provision beyond predetermined limits. Overt central controls failed in 1862, in 1902 and in 1944. Are the factors which led to historical failure present in the current context? Or are there significant differences between these periods and the 1980s, which make overt controls more likely to succeed, and if so, what are they?

These questions demand further exploration, using the insights gained from historical study and from the approaches to the study of teacher–state relations outlined at the beginning of this chapter. For example, it is worth considering the significance of the teachers' strikes in Scotland, England and Wales in 1985–87. That long and hard campaign could be evidence that, once again, underpaid teachers form a 'social danger'. Without the subtle response of Fisher or Percy, more confrontation between teachers and the state seems inevitable. In the absence of the management strategies of indirect rule, how is teachers' co-operation in the great 'reform' of education to be achieved? (Presumably through the creation of a managerial stratum, with separate pay, conditions and negotiating rights, and responsibility for supervision and appraisal of the teaching workforce. These managers will be men, while the workforce is predominantly female.)

The significance of the gender division in teaching has been explored by feminist historians, who have uncovered the exclusion and marginalisation of women in male-dominated teacher unions (Copelman, 1985; King, 1987; Corr, 1988), and who have discussed the intersection of class and gender in teaching. The connections between proletarianisation and the gender composition of the teaching workforce need further study, within a framwork sensitive to the impact of patriarchal relations on work (Danylewycz and Prentice, 1986) and which recognises strategies of resistance employed by women (Lawn, 1988).

The next few years promise to be a very interesting period in the extended 'war of position' between teachers and the state. We need more work which uncovers what teachers felt, thought and did in the periods reviewed here; we need a fuller account of teacher history, so that we can better undestand what is happening to teachers now.

REFERENCES

Althusser, L. (1971) 'Ideology and Ideological State Apparatuses', in B. R. Cosin (1972) (ed.), *Education, Structure and Society* (Harmondsworth: Penguin).
Apple, M. (1986) *Teachers and Texts* (London: Routledge & Kegan Paul).
Apple, M. and Teitelbaum, K. (1986) 'Are Teachers Losing Control of Their Skills and Curriculum?' *Journal of Curriculum Studies* 18.
Archer, M. (1979) *Social Origins of Education Systems* (London: Sage).
Bergen, B. (1982) 'Only a Schoolmaster: Gender, Class and the Effort to Professionalize Elementary Teaching in England 1890–1910', *History of Education Quarterly*, Spring.
Bourdieu, P. (1973) 'Cultural Reproduction and Social Reproduction', in R. Brown (ed.) *Knowledge, Education and Social Change* (London: Tavistock).
Bowles, S. and Gintis, H. (1976) *Schooling in Capitalist America* (London: Routledge & Kegan Paul).
Briault, E. (1976) 'A Distributed System of Educational Administration', *International Review of Education*, 22, (4).
Carchedi, G. (1975) 'On the Economic Identification of the New Middle Class', *Economy & Society*, Vol. 4, No. 1.
Centre for Contemporary Cultural Studies (1981) *Unpopular Education* (London: Hutchinson Education).
Connell, R. W. (1985) *Teachers' Work* (London: Allen & Unwin).
Copelman, D. M. (1985) 'Women in the Classroom Struggle', unpublished Ph.D. Thesis, Princeton University.
Corr, H. (1988) 'Politics of the Sexes in English and Scottish Teachers' Unions 1870–1914', Paper to BSA Annual Conference, Edinburgh, March.
Corrigan, P. (ed.) (1980) *Capitalism, State Formation and Marxist Theory* (London: Quartet Books).
Dale, R. (1981a) 'The State and Education: Some Theoretical Approaches' in *The State and the Politics of Education* (Milton Keynes: The Open University Press).

Dale, R. (1981b) 'Control, Accountability and William Tyndale' in R. Dale, G. Esland, R. Fergusson and M. MacDonald, *Education and the State, Volume 2* (Lewes: Falmer Press).

Danylewycz, M. and Prentice, A. (1986) 'Teachers' Work: Changing Patterns and Perceptions in the Emerging School Systems of Nineteenth and Early Twentieth Century Canada', *Labour/Le Travail*, Vol. 17 (Spring).

Fenwick, K. (1985) 'Changing Roles in the Government of Education', *British Journal of Educational Studies*, Volume 33.

Friedman, A. (1977) *Industry and Labour: Class Struggle at Work and Monopoly Capitalism* (London: Macmillan).

Ginsburg, M., Meyenn, R. and Miller, H. (1980) 'Teachers' Conceptions of Professionalism and Trades Unionism: An Ideological Analysis', in P. Woods (ed.), *Teacher Strategies: Explorations in the Sociology of the School* (London: Croom Helm).

Grace, G. (1985) 'Judging Teachers: The Social and Political Contexts of Teacher Evaluation', *British Journal of the Sociology of Education*, Vol. 6, No. 1.

Grace, G. (1987) 'Teachers and the State in Britain: A Changing Relation', in M. Lawn and G. Grace (eds), *Teachers: The Culture and Politics of Work* (Lewes: Falmer Press).

Hoyle, E. (1974) 'Professionality, Professionalism and Control in Teaching', *London Educational Review* 3 (2).

Hoyle, E. (1980) 'Professionalization and De-professionalization in Education', in E. Hoyle and J. Megarry (eds) *World Yearbook of Education 1980* (London: Kogan Page).

Hoyle, E. (1981) 'The Process of Management', in *Management and the School* (Milton Keynes: Open University Press).

Johnson, T. (1972) *Professions and Power* (London: Macmillan).

King, S. (1987) 'Feminists in Teaching: The NUWT 1920–40', in M. Lawn and G. Grace (eds), *Teachers: The Nature and Politics of Work* (Lewes: Falmer Press).

Kogan, M. (1975) *Educational Policy-Making: A Study of Interest Groups and Parliament* (London: Allen & Unwin).

Larson, M. S. (1977) *The Rise of the Professions: A Sociological Analysis* (Berkeley: University of California Press).

Lawn, M., (1987a) *Servants of the State: The Contested Control of Teaching 1910–1930* (Lewes: Falmer Press).

Lawn, M. (1987b) 'The Spur and the Bridle: Changing the Mode of Curriculum Control', *Journal of Curriculum Studies*, 19 (3).

Lawn, M. (1988) 'Skill in Schoolwork: Work Relations in the Primary School', in J. Ozga (ed.), *Schoolwork: Approaches to the Labour Process of Teaching* (Milton Keynes: Open University Press).

Lawn, M. and Ozga, J. (1981) 'The Educational Worker, A Reassessment of Teachers', in L. Barton and S. Walker (eds), *Schools, Teachers and Teaching* (Lewes: Falmer Press).

Lawn, M. and Ozga, J. (1986) 'Unequal Partners: Teachers under Indirect Rule', *British Journal of the Sociology of Education*, Vol. 7, No. 2.

Ozga, J. T. (1987) 'Studying Education Policy Through the Lives of the Policy-Makers: An Attempt to Close the Macro-Micro Gap' in S. Walker and L. Barton (eds), *Changing Policies, Changing Teachers* (Milton Keynes: Open University Press).

Ozga, J. T. (ed) (1988a) *Schoolwork: Approaches to the Labour Process of Teaching* (Milton Keynes: Open University Press).

Ozga, J. T. (1988b) 'The Politics of Teaching', Part II of *Educational Organizations and Professionals* (E814) (Milton Keynes: Open University Press).

Ozga, J. T. and Lawn, M. (1981) *Teachers, Professionalism and Class* (Lewes: Falmer Press).

Ozga, J. T. and Lawn, M. (1988) 'Schoolwork: Interpreting the Labour Process of Teaching', *British Journal of the Sociology of Education*, Vol. 9, No. 3.

Poulantzas, N. (1977) 'The New Petty Bourgeoisie', in A. Hunt, (ed.) *Class and Class Structure* (London: Lawrence & Wishart).

Purvis, J. (1980) 'Women and Teaching in the Nineteenth Century', in R. Dale *et al.* (eds), *Education and the State, Volume 2* (Lewes: Falmer Press).

Ranson, S. (1985) 'Contradictions in the Government of Educational Change', *Political Studies*, Vol. 33, pp. 25–34.

Riseborough, G. (1985) 'Pupils, Teachers' Careers and Schooling' in S. Ball and I. Goodson (eds), *Teachers' Lives and Careers* (Lewes: Falmer Press).

Seifert, R. (1987) *Teacher Militancy: A History of Teacher Strikes 1896–1987* (Lewes: Falmer Press).

Shipman, M. (1984) *Education as a Public Service* (London: Harper & Row).

Sikes, P., Meason, L. and Woods, P. (1985) *Teacher Careers, Crises and Continuities* (Lewes: Falmer Press).

Simon, B. (1965) *Education and the Labour Movement* (London: Lawrence & Wishart).

Thompson, D. (1927) *Professional Solidarity among the Teachers of England* (Columbia University Press).

Tropp, A. (1957) *The Schoolteachers* (London: Heinemann).

White, J. (1975) 'The End of the Compulsory Curriculum', in *Curriculum: The Doris Lee Lectures*, Studies in Education, Volume 2 (Institute of Education, University of London).

10 Urban Politics and the Rise of the Labour Party, 1919–39

Mike Savage

In this chapter I will use two local case studies to examine the reasons why the Labour Party became a mass political party between 1914 and 1939.[1] The speed of Labour's growth was in many respects remarkable. Having only won a small proportion of the vote before the First World War, it was in a position to form a government (albeit briefly) in 1924, and by 1929 it won 35 per cent of the vote, 287 seats and formed a government as the largest single party. Even after a major setback in 1931, when the split between the Prime Minister MacDonald and the rest of the Party saw Labour win only 50 seats, by 1935 it had once again secured 35 per cent of the popular vote.

Hitherto most explanations of the rise of the Labour Party have centred around a debate between those historians who see the emergence of Labour as largely a product of political change alone, and those who relate it to changes in class relations in the workplace. In this chapter I will argue that it is necessary to supplement these accounts with an examination of conflicts around the public provision of services. At the local level there were major conflicts over the provision of housing, health and education in the inter-war years. These often involved working-class residents organising on a neighbourhood basis to demand public services. What I will show is that where the Labour Party was able to join in such campaigns it usually attracted higher levels of electoral support than when it remained aloof from them.

I shall start by briefly discussing two accounts of the rise of Labour. First, I will argue that writers who maintain that the rise of the Labour Party was largely a product of trade union growth tend to overestimate the role of trade unions in providing a base for popular electoral support for Labour. Second, I will discuss why public services became such a central political issue in the inter-war years. Then I shall move on to my two case studies of

Preston (in Lancashire) and Slough (in the Home Counties) to illustrate how, in two contrasting places, the rise of the Labour Party was related to struggles over public services. I use case studies since most public services were provided by the local state at this time and hence in order to examine the role of conflicts over service provision in affecting political alignments it is necessary to focus on this level.

TRADE UNIONS AND THE RISE OF THE LABOUR PARTY

There are two dominant interpretations of the rise of Labour between 1900 and 1940. The first argues that changes in the labour process helped to develop new forms of working-class consciousness which led to higher levels of trade union membership and to new forms of political mobilisation (Price, 1986; Burgess, 1980; Hinton, 1983). For Price, as for earlier writers such as Hobsbawn (1964) and Hinton, the decline of craft autonomy and the emergence of the 'mass collective worker' was of critical importance in leading to class solidarity and general support for independent Labour politics.

On the other hand other historians have argued that the rise of the Labour Party was simply a product of political changes. The most influential of these accounts is that of Matthew *et al.* (1976) who argue that the rise of Labour could largely be attributed to the effects of the 1918 franchise extension which enfranchised many previously excluded working-class voters. The same approach has been extended in the work of Reid (1985). He argues that it is misguided to explain the emergence of the Labour Party in terms of changing structures of work. He reasserts the 'autonomy of politics' and the changing character of the state in facilitating the rise of the Labour Party (see also the paper by Knox in the same volume).

Although these two accounts seem to differ fundamentally in their conceptualisation of working-class politics, they share one assumption in common, that the rise of the Labour Party is closely related to the fortunes of the trade union movement. In Price's work the rise of new unionism from the 1880s is evidence of the growing capacity of the unskilled general workers to organise, a tendency caused by the changing character of the productive process. In Reid's work it was the changing relationship between the trade unions and the state forged in the First World War which was of key importance. War-time experience of state intervention in industry persuaded unions and their members that the state could be an important lever to improve working-class conditions more generally, and so facilitated greater support for a working-class political party. In both accounts the Labour Party's fortunes are seen as tied up with the fortunes of the trade union movement.

The Labour Party did draw on trade unions for finance, organisational support and personnel. Also, many members of trade unions were attracted to the Labour Party because of their general commitment to the trade union movement. However, I will argue that there were other social factors which also helped the Labour Party, arising out of neighbourhood mobilisation over the provision of public services. Let me start to develop this point by indicating why it is inappropriate to explain the rise of the Labour Party in electoral terms purely by reference to the role of trade unions.

First, surveys of voters have rarely found that trade unionism is a major correlate of Labour voting (though there is some evidence that it has been increasing in importance in this respect since the 1960s). Franklin (1985) calculates that only about 6 per cent of the variance in the Labour vote could be explained by trade unionism in the mid 1960s. Now, of course, detailed surveys only go back to 1964, a period well after that which interests us, though still a period when 'class politics' seemed very much evident. However, a survey carried out by Mass Observation in Bolton in the 1930s showed that many trade unionists had no strong political interests.[2]

Another way of probing the relationship between union membership and Labour politics is to examine whether trade union members 'contracted in' to pay the political levy in large numbers. In fact, in 1937 only 51 per cent of union members paid a political levy: a high but by no means overwhelming number (Cole, 1948). Undoubtedly others would have voted Labour, but it is nonetheless interesting that their commitment did not stretch as far as giving financial support. Some unions had very low rates of contracting in – the Amalgamated Engineering Union (AEU) had only 24 per cent.

Psephologists have also devised other ways of accounting for political support, which do not rely on surveys. This is aggregate data analysis, where voting patterns in constituencies are measured against those constituencies' social characteristics in order to analyse the associations between them. This work has convincingly shown that areas of Labour strength are those areas where large numbers of working-class people live closely together, implying that it is the 'neighbourhood' links among the working class which produce high levels of Labour support. Miller (1977) showed that such a phenomenon, the 'neighbourhood effect', goes back as far as 1918.

A final general problem relates to the periodisation of Labour's rise in electoral popularity. Many studies emphasise the rise of Labour in the early 1920s, with the period of intense industrial conflict which came to an end with the General Strike of 1926 (Cronin, 1984; Burgess, 1980; Hinton, 1983). Yet Labour's electoral support peaked in the later 1920s when trade union membership was falling away very rapidly. The rise of the Labour vote was only of modest proportions in the early 1920s when industrial conflict was rife, and as Cook (1975) shows, in many municipalities Labour was unable to consolidate its local election successes of 1919, losing seats in considerable numbers until the mid 1920s. Yet although union membership halved in the 1920s, from over 8 to 4 million, Labour voting grew to reach 37 per cent by 1929. Similarly, in the pre-war period, the time of major industrial conflict in the Syndicalist upsurge of 1911–1914 was not a period when the Labour Party did well electorally (Shepherd and Halstead, 1979).

While no one would deny that trade union loyalties were an important basis for the emergence of the Labour Party, the points above do indicate that the rise of Labour cannot be seen merely as a political reflex of trade union growth. This leads me to my main theme: that in the inter-war years the political struggles arising out of service provision by the local state also proved to be a crucial area in which the Labour Party could drum up support. I will first examine why the provision of public services should have become such a pressing issue in this period.

THE POLITICS OF SERVICE PROVISION IN THE INTER-WAR YEARS

Many sociologists have argued that issues arising out of the public servicing of human needs become a pressing issue in late capitalist societies. T. H. Marshall's influential discussion of the rise of 'social citizenship' is one of the most well known. The problem with such accounts is that they assume a teleological process where the 'rise' of citizenship automatically extends itself and steadily encompasses more issues under its rubric. Urry (1981) develops this argument, however, by suggesting that in late capitalism struggles over 'reproduction' come to the fore, replacing those based around 'circulation' concerned with legal equalities and freedoms. Having achieved the suffrage and formal democratic freedoms after 1918 the working class could move on to struggle in other areas. The working class were hence in a position to use new-found political muscle to demand the provision of public services.

The extension of democratic freedoms did then allow working-class people to mobilise effectively to demand public services. But why should they choose to struggle for public services at all? As Gordon's contribution to this volume shows, in the period before 1914 the Labour movement did not envisage women's role as domestic servicers and housewives being changed. Thane (1985) also demonstrates the lack of working-class interest in public welfare provision before 1914. The most important contribution to this point is made by Saunders (1984; 1986), who argues that contradictions in the nature of service provision in Victorian Britain led to the emergence of state services after 1900. He argues that in Victorian society services were provided on the market, but this system had a major weakness: workers on generally low wages could not afford the high costs of consuming services provided on this market basis, and hence they looked more to state service provision as an alternative.

Saunders' argument is, however, misleading since service provision before 1900 was not provided on a market basis but on a mutualist one, where groups of people provided for their own service provision through co-operative societies, medical clubs and the like (Savage 1987, ch. 2). Hence there was no real contradiction since workers on low wages could still have services provided if they put in time to provide them through their own mutualist efforts. Mutualist provision did, however, have its own contradictions relating to gender differences. They drew on a pre-existing 'public sphere' facilitiating contacts and resource mobilisation. Since this public sphere was primarily based on male institutional structures it frequently ignored women's needs.

Many of the mutualist societies made little attempt to cater for women's needs. The most notable example of this were the medical aid societies of South Wales which provided good services for men but were helped to preside over very poor childbirth services (Savage 1987, pp. 30–1). Women did have their own forms of sharing and communication (Ross, 1983), but these had no financial resources or institutional basis.

The introduction of the female franchise in 1918 (extended to women under 30 in 1928) gave women the potential to mobilise politically for the first time, and demands to force state intervention in the area of service provision served to ease their domestic burdens (see Mark-Lawson *et al.*, 1985; Mark-Lawson, 1987 for further discussion of this line of argument).

I have suggested that by the inter-war years the potential for popular mobilisation over the provision of public services had increased. I will now turn to my case studies to show how this fed through and affected the fortunes of the local Labour movements. I deliberately chose two contrasting towns in order to bring out the similarities and differences. On the one hand, Preston in Lancashire was an old industrial town with well-established trade unions, where the Labour Party had achieved a measure of success before 1914. Slough in Buckinghamshire was, however, a product of inter-war economic development, massive in-migration, and with weak trade unions. In Preston I will show that the origins of the Labour Party did lie in the policies pursued by the union movement, but during the 1920s they took a back seat as the mobilisation of women became more significant, and a new politics demanding an expansion of public services developed. In Slough I will show that it was not until the Labour Party came to terms with demands for housing provision that it became a major electoral force. In both places therefore I will show that the ability of the local Labour Party to join in struggles over public services, often related to the mobilisation of women, was a critical factor behind the Party's fortunes.

THE LABOUR PARTY IN PRESTON 1900–18

Preston was a town which developed in the nineteenth century based upon a staple industry – cotton textiles. By the later nineteenth century it was beginning to wane, losing out to the more specialised producers in other parts of Lancashire and abroad. Nonetheless cotton remained the single largest employer, especially of women, until the 1930s and Preston was famous for its fine quality production of cloth. From the turn of the century the local economy began to diversify, particularly with the growth of newer forms of engineering such as vehicle production and electrical engineering. Unionisation in the cotton industry was extensive and by 1918 both the weaving sector and the smaller spinning trade were virtually 100 per cent unionised. The engineering industry had been badly organised before the War, with the Amalgamated Society of Engineers being very weak, but the Workers Union had one of its strongest branches in Preston's new engineering firms, and all the engineering unions were able to come out of the War with unprecedented levels of unionisation. Alongside these two dominant employers was a range of small craft industries in building and clothing, and these had always been relatively well unionised and active in the Preston Trades Council, which was founded in 1866 (Savage, 1987; 1988a).

It might have seemed that such a strong presence would serve as a secure base to launch Labour politics. In the Victorian period this had not proved the case, as many union members were known to support the Conservatives in an area well known for its working class Conservatism (Joyce, 1980; Kirk, 1983; Clarke, 1971). Nonetheless this legacy of Toryism was thrown off dramatically quickly after 1900. The Labour Party won one of the two parliamentary seats in 1906, and gained several seats on the local council between 1903 and 1908. The trade unions were undoubtedly very important in causing this realignment, since the threat to their legal status implicit in the Taff Vale case of 1901 encouraged many of the leaders of local unions to ditch the Tories and support Labour (Pelling, 1968). Similarly the proposals of the Conservatives in 1905 to abandon free trade seemed to many workers in the town to hit their job security, since they felt that if other countries imposed tariff barriers in retaliation the export trade would be severely hit.

This point seems to support the trade union interpretation of the rise of Labour. The interesting implication of Labour's growth, however, was that the Tories responded by mobilising at the level of the neighbourhood. The Primrose League was especially notable here, and it developed ward branches and had 2000 members by 1910 (see Savage, 1987, ch. 6). On this new basis the Tories successfully regained their dominant political position in Preston after 1910.

Before 1918 the rise of Labour owed little to demands for public service provision. However, the growing mobilisation of the Conservatives in the wards was to presage developments in the inter-war period where the concerns of local trade unions had less effect in shaping patterns of local party support, and the issues changed to how the local parties could cater for the needs of residents for public services.

THE FAILURE OF TRADE UNION POLITICS IN PRESTON 1918–39

The Labour Party did extremely well in Preston in the immediate period after the First World War. In 1918 Tom Shaw won one of the parliamentary seats for the Labour Party, and in the 1919 local elections Labour won seven of the twelve seats. Writers such as Burgess (1980), Cronin (1984) and Hinton (1983) have seen this as evidence that war-time changes in the workplace and the general growth of trade unions led through to cause political change. What this account fails to recognise, however, is the extent to which war-time experience acted to fragment as much as to unify the working class, and the sectionalism which resulted did not help the Labour Party's electoral position.

The most notable example of this was in the hostility of the Labour Party to women's paid labour, a concern greatly intensi- fied in the First World War (Braybon, 1980; Walby 1986; Savage, 1987). The fact that the Labour Party in Preston was so dominated by trade unions, and that the union representatives had a majority of seats on the executive meant that their hostility to female labour fed through into the Labour Party. They refused to allow a women's section until 1923 (it was one of the last constituency parties to do so), ran no women candidates in local elections until the mid 1920s, and in their policy statements disparaged the need to take women's issues seriously – and in particular showed little interest in local state provision of services (Savage, 1987, pp. 165–73).

The alienation of women from the Labour movement in Preston was skilfully seized upon by local feminists organised in the Women's Citizens' Association (WCA). The WCA actively campaigned over women's employment rights, opposed the marriage bar on women council employees, and demanded full 'technical and industrial' education for girls so that they would not be disadvantaged in the labour market. The Labour Party were unsympathetic to them. When the WCA approached the Labour Party asking one of their candidates for a free run in the ensuing local elections, the Labour Party refused, and subsequently the WCA steadily moved more closely into an alliance with the Conservatives. These WCA candidates began to raise issues concerned with public service provision in their election campaigns. In 1929 a WCA candidate declared that 'the Town council . . . was directly concerned with people's homes' and many points came up which called for the understanding of women – such as education, housing, maternity, child welfare and so forth (Savage, 1987, pp. 171–2).

From 1920 leading women members began to stand as municipal candidates, always in opposition to Labour, stressing the need for women to be fully represented, and for public service provision to be extended. There were victories over Labour candidates in 1920 and 1921. The Conservatives began to co-operate with the WCA, recognising the political gains to be made. This alliance reached the stage that by 1923 the three female candidates, all WCA members, stood with Conservative support against Labour candidates. The Labour Party made no attempt to put forward women candidates of their own. Two of the three women were successful, and they performed much better than male Conservative candidates. Labour's local election performance fell back from its 1919 high point and by the mid 1920s they were failing to make any inroads into the Conservative majority, though Labour was more successful at the parliamentary level where the restriction of the female vote before 1928 helped Tom Shaw to retain the parliamentary seat.

The problems in winning over women to the Labour Party were seen also in the tensions between craft workers and unskilled workers. There were major disputes of this sort in the 1919 foundry dispute, and in 1922 during the major engineers' lockout. In both these cases the skilled unions were able to force the Trades and Labour Council to take punitive action against the unskilled unions, and in 1922 this so antagonised the General and Municipal Workers' Union (GMWU) that they contemplated opposing all official Labour candidates with their own nominees in the local elections. Furthermore the growth of unemployment in the 1920s and especially the 1930s caused tensions between the trade unions, who were seen as representing wage earners, and the unemployed. The trade unions refused to provide any facilities for the unemployed and the local churches and charitable institutions were able to wean many of the unemployed away from the Labour Party by their vigorous involvement in providing for the unemployed (Savage, 1987, pp. 180–7).

Hence the hold of the trade unions on the local Labour Party proved to be an electoral liability by the mid 1920s. In the pre-war period it had helped to launch the Labour Party but by 1925 it could not sustain local electoral support. After their failure in 1920 the Labour Party blamed their lack of ward committees, and the Party began to realise that it needed to mobilise in the wards. In 1923 the Organisation Sub Committee made a far-reaching decision to mobilise more actively in the neighbourhoods, forming ward committees, and deciding to carry on more active political work at the Labour Clubs. Membership of the Party was based on ward organisation after the introduction of a stamp scheme in 1924, whereby members could pay their subscriptions once weekly to a visiting collector. This had the effect of building up regular contacts between party members at their homes and by 1938 there were 1357 individual members. More generally lectures were held in the wards, annual Labour galas held, and there were also frequent ward socials, ward picnics, Labour choirs, whist drives, hiking clubs and Labour balls (Savage, 1987, p. 173).

The growth of ward organisation was closely linked to the development of women's sections. It was agreed to form a women's section in 1923 and the women's sections were developed on a ward basis. In 1925 they organised a women's week with meetings held in Labour clubs, and as a result of good publicity 'strong and virile [sic] women's sections have been formed, 7 branches having a membership of nearly 500', which was to rise to 635 by 1928. In 1929 the women's sections were officially 'complimented on their activities' by the Labour Party (Savage, 1987, pp. 173–4).

The hold of the unions was steadily eroded throughout the 1920s. An increasing number of executive committee members were not from trade union backgrounds. Most of the finance was raised from campaigning activity rather than by trade unions.

The emergence of women's involvement also led to the development of a politics based around demands for improvements in local service provision. In place of the conservative trade union oriented policies of the immediate post-war years, a new popular statist politics emphasising that consumers' needs could only be met by local state intervention emerged in the years after 1925. The women's sections were extremely influential in supporting these new concerns. In 1928 the women's sections organised a conference on nursery schools and this demand was taken up shortly afterwards by local Labour candidates, though previously the Party had no policy on them. They also supported open air schools and cheap slipper baths, both of which were to become major election themes. In 1931 the women's sections held a conference on the 'socialisation of medical services', marking an abrupt shift from the former emphasis upon supporting voluntary medical care, geared as it was to the male wage earner. There were also demands for the provision of municipal lodging houses for working women, and for public wash-houses – again a demand taken up by Labour candidates.

From the mid 1920s the Labour Party became enthusiastic supporters of municipal enterprise to benefit the householders. In 1925, following the municipalisation of the electricity supply, the Labour Party advocated its provision in all homes. There was also a greater emphasis placed on municipal housing built for low rent, which contrasted with their previous advocacy of council houses built to sell. As recently as 1923 the Party had refused to set up a Tenants Defence League, but their concerns with tenants' issues increased thereafter. They successfully campaigned for lower council rents, a campaign in which some of the Labour Clubs took a prominent part (Savage, 1987, ch. 7).

There was then a far-reaching shift in Labour Party organisation and policy in the later 1920s. This tapping of female and neighbourhood bases of support, leading to a consumer oriented statist politics, also generated unprecedented levels of electoral support. The popularity of Labour in this period, so often interpreted as simply a sympathy vote for the miners' defeat in the 1926 general strike (for example, Cronin, 1984), should be linked to these wide-ranging changes in the character of Labour politics. One symptom of this was the growing significance of the female vote. The Labour revival in 1925 in the local elections was attributed by Councillor Ellison to 'the splendid efforts of the party workers and particularly of the women'. In the 1929 general election most of the canvassers were women, and 'Councillor Morris says that a very considerable proportion of young married women of Preston – those of 21 upward who have been enfranchised – have thrown in their political lot with Labour' (*The Times*, 30 August 1928). The role of neighbourhood organisation was also vital. Membership of the Labour Clubs rose steadily to reach a peak of around 2000 in 1929. Those wards with particularly strong Ward Committees, notably Fishwick, tended to become the safest Labour seats in local elections.

The Preston case shows that although trade unions were a major force behind the emergence of the Labour Party before 1914 they proved an unstable base for the Party in the 1920s. The Labour Party's rise in electoral popularity in the later 1920s was linked to the growth of women's involvement in the Party, and their adoption of a politics which supported state intervention to help consumers.

THE ANATOMY OF LABOUR WEAKNESS: THE CASE OF SLOUGH

I will now examine a town which contrasts with Preston on many counts. Preston was a typical nineteenth-century industrial town with an old established working class: Slough was a product of the 'second industrial revolution' and did not expand till after 1918. Preston had a well-established Labour movement before 1914, but Slough's was weak until the later 1930s. I will demonstrate that despite these differences the Labour Party was subject to similar processes to those in Preston. In particular, it was only when they came to terms with the politics of local service provision that they made a significant electoral breakthrough.

Between 1918 and 1939 Slough grew more spectacularly than any other British town. In 1901 Slough had only 7400 population, but in the inter war-years it expanded dramatically to 60 000 by 1938, largely a product of the demand for Labour brought about by the new firms on the Slough Trading Estate (Allen, 1951; Savage, 1988b). The new workers came from a variety of sources, but the two major groups were the Welsh (about 16 000 of them had moved to Slough by 1935) and those from the North East

(*Slough Observer* 15 January 1932; Chegwidden and Myrddin-Evans, 1934). Most were from a working-class background.

Despite this rapid influx of working-class residents support for the Labour Party actually declined from 1919 until the mid 1930s, before a modest resurgence in the later 1930s. In 1919 Labour shared in Labour's national popularity, winning three of the four Urban District Council seats in that year, but support fell away in the early 1920s. In contrast to Preston it signally failed to rally in the later 1920s, although this was the period when mass working-class immigration was under way. No Labour councillors were elected between 1927 and 1929. The situation improved slightly in the 1930s and the occasional Labour councillor was elected, but it was not until 1935 that a major breakthrough was achieved, with Labour winning three of the seven seats. This revival was consolidated in 1937 when Labour won two seats and the Independent Labour Party won another. In the inaugural borough elections in 1938 Labour's rise was confirmed, for although it only won four of the 24 seats it won 43.2 per cent of the vote (excluding one uncontested ward, where the independent candidates may have had Labour sympathies). At the parliamentary level the same situation was to be found. Despite the mass influx of working-class voters the Labour vote crept up only slowly throughout the 1920s from 14 per cent in 1922 to 18 per cent in 1929, before expanding rapidly in the 1930s to reach 35 per cent in 1935 (*Slough Observer*, various).

One explanation of the weakness of Labour might have been the overall weakness of the trade union movement, and this is part of the answer. There is no question that for much of the inter-war period trade unions were extremely weak in the town. In 1935 the Trades Council reported that of the 15 000 workers on the Estate, the 'overwhelming majority' were non-unionists (TUC, 26 February 1935).[3] Yet while the weakness of trade unionism was an important factor behind the early weakness of the Labour Party in Slough, it cannot explain the rise of Labour after 1935, since trade union membership remained low even after Labour support had grown considerably. Despite many campaigns to improve unionisation, in 1934 the Trades Council had only 648 members (out of over 20 000 eligible) and this rose only marginally to 1549 by 1936, and to about 3000 by 1938. Even during the Second World War Slough remained a black spot. One union organiser could still claim that 'workers in the District were anything but trade union conscious' (*Slough Observer*, 23 April 1944).

Whiting (1985), in a study of Oxford, argues that the development of Labour Party support in the later 1930s was related to industrial conflict in the motor industries, particularly in the Pressed Steel dispute of 1934. In Slough, however, there was no overt industrial conflict throughout the 1930s, and indeed employer paternalism actually seemed to be increasing its hold in the late 1930s with the successful promotion of the Slough Social Centre in 1938, which provided a wide range of leisure facilities (see Eagger, 1965). Many firms also gave holiday pay, organising sports and social clubs, canteens and the like. Thus Labour's electoral rise did not coincide with any marked outbreak of industrial militancy or any erosion of employer paternalism.

The central reason for the Labour Party's weakness before the later 1930s lay in their lack of interest in the politics of service provision. Here they were decisively outgunned by the local Ratepayers' Associations which managed to get remarkably high levels of popular support, and used this base to sustain Conservative dominance electorally. In Slough, the most pressing social problems lay in housing provision. For a while a large amount of flimsy private housing was built for owner occupiers, but it became apparent in the later 1920s that working-class owner occupiers could not meet their outlays, and many fell behind on mortgage repayments and rates. Only public housing seemed to offer a solution, but it was the Ratepayers' Associations rather than the Labour Party which most vigorously campaigned for the provision of cheap housing which would not overburden the rates.

The Ratepayers' Associations grew steadily on a ward basis in the late 1920s and were able to organise road associations in some areas. It was Farnham Ratepayers' Association which led the campaign for new council house building (*Slough Observer*, 31 March 1929; 7 March 1930; 31 March 1933). Farnham was a major working-class area, built next to the Trading Estate, where there had been major speculative house building in the later 1920s. The Labour Party had been left standing by the rapid mobilisation and indeed had accepted the council's original position that no council houses could be built (*Slough Observer*, 31 March 1933). Yet the Ratepayers' Associations soon had several thousand members and gained majorities in the 1930 elections. The result was a major public house building programme, resulting in the creation of the 350-house Manor Park Estate in 1930, and the building of a further 1500 houses by 1939.

The growth of Labour support from the mid 1930s was primarily based upon the fracturing of this alliance. In part this was because of tensions over the extent to which further council housing was needed after the initial crisis had passed and unemployment eased. In 1932 the Secretary of Slough Ratepayers' Association resigned when he felt council housing had gone 'far enough' and there was no need for further development. Burnham Ratepayers' Association decided to oppose further development when they felt that many new council house tenants were not being replaced at their old houses, leaving rates uncollected. Membership fell away, and the organisations, though still dominating the local councils, became less active (*Slough Observer*, 29 July 1932; 4 November 1932).

In the mid 1930s a sudden escalation of housing-based conflict gave the Labour Party a new opportunity to develop a sympathetic stance towards the provision of public services. It was, however, still slow to respond. Once again the Farnham area was at the centre of things. Many of the houses built for owner occupation had been given up when their owners could not afford the repayments, and indeed the adjacent Manor Park Council Estate attracted many of them. Many houses passed into the hands of a large London estate management agency for private renting, and initially they set reasonably cheap rents of 12/6d. A Tenants Defence League was formed to represent these tenants in 1934.

The Labour Party did not prove interested in supporting their cause. However, the Independent Labour Party did. The ILP had been a part of the mainstream Labour movement before 1914 (see Gordon's chapter in this volume), but it grew more disillusioned with the Labour Party, especially because of the moderation of the 1929 Labour government, and in 1932 it disaffiliated, deciding to run its own electoral candidates under more left wing auspices. It seized upon the Tenants Defence League as a good way to drum up support and the Chair of the League was an ILP activist, as was another noted member, Ruth Harrison, who was a teacher at the local nursery school.

This Tenants Defence League was rapidly embroiled in a major conflict. In 1936 the LWS estate company decided to increase rents by 2/6d a week. Both the Farnham Residents' Association and the Tenants Defence league opposed the rent increase. The

Ratepayers' Association, trying to maintain its support in the area held a number of meetings demanding the traditional solution of further council house building to lower the demand for housing and hence alleviate the market pressure on private rent levels. At a mass meeting of the Ratepayers' Association with 200 attending, when a vote showed that the majority of the attenders were tenants, Councillor White declared that 'your only hope in the long run is . . . for the council to get control of the production of sufficient working class houses in this area'. It was, however, the Tenants Defence League which organised a remarkably successful rent strike and carried the day; and after one month's resistance the LWS company capitulated and abandoned the proposed rent increase (*Slough Observer*, 14 February 1936; 20 March 1936).

After this conflict there was a renewed wave of council house building, yet the hold of the Ratepayers' Association was slipping. The Labour Party, which had not been active in the rent strike, failed to dislodge their candidate for Farnham, and indeed Labour only got 35 per cent of the vote on a remarkably low 15 per cent turnout in 1936. Yet the longer-term consequences were more dramatic as the ILP used the basis of the Tenants Defence League to expand their organisations in the neighbourhoods. They produced a regular newspaper and organised local meetings in the Tenants' Hall. In 1937 Ruth Harrison stood as ILP candidate in a ward never won before by the Labour Party, and to everyone's astonishment won the seat. Whereas the Labour Party had never won more than 150 votes, she polled 544 against her opponent's 477. She had made a deliberate appeal to women voters, many of whom had been mobilised in the rent strike (*Slough Observer*, 17 April 1936).

The mobilisation around housing issues in a campaign led by a woman hence broke the hegemony of the local Ratepayers' Associations, after all the efforts of the Labour Party had been in vain. This success in turn had the effect of jolting the Labour Party into realising that they needed to counter the ILP presence. The ILP attempted to make a compact with the Labour Party to avoid rival candidates. This failed but when the Ratepayers' Association won back Farnham as Labour and the ILP split their vote the need for co-operation became apparent, and in the political reorganisation surrounding the incorporation of Slough in 1938 many leading ILPers were persuaded to join the Labour Party. In turn, the Labour Party lost its sole reliance upon trade unionism as it opened itself up to other pressures. A number of other Tenants Defence Committees were formed, and the Labour Party became more attuned to the politics of service provision.

Thus the growth of the Labour Party in Slough in the later 1930s was primarily related to patterns of mobilisation and conflict arising out of housing, rather than through trade union agitation and workplace conflict. Although the unions remained weak, the Labour Party had succeeded in securing considerable support by 1939 on the basis of neighbourhood support, and through the catalyst's role played by the ILP. As in Preston, by 1939 the Labour Party relied more on the issues arising out of issues of local service provision than it did from work based conflict.

CONCLUSIONS

Despite the dramatically different character of Preston and Slough a similar process has been observed, though at different periods and in contrasting ways. A Labour Party based initially on trade union bases of support had to come to terms with new political demands arising for the provision of services. In Preston the greater breadth of unionisation allowed a trade union party to command more support than was the case in Slough, where only a small proportion of the workforce was unionised, but even in Preston there were enough non-unionists and enough workers antagonised by the unions' sectional demands to make Labour support unstable after 1920. In both cases Labour had to respond to the political mobilisation of their opponents in the neighbourhood, though in Preston the Party was able to respond directly to the Conservative ward organisation, while in Slough the Labour Party made few determined efforts to do so until the popularity of the ILP made them aware of the electoral viability of such a step.

In both places the issues of service provision became the backbone of the campaigns waged by the 'new' Labour parties: demands for state housing, health services and education. And, as we have seen, in both places it was the mobilisation of women which brought these issues to the fore. The role of the Labour Party women's sections have been overlooked by many historians who have seen them as little more than subordinate bodies to the Constituency Labour Parties, but in Preston at least there is good evidence that many policy issues actually originated from these sections. There was no parallel to the role of Preston's women's sections in Slough, but there was a major mobilisation of women in the rent strike in Farnham, and Ruth Harrison was a leading force behind the revitalisation of working-class politics.

The Labour Party owed its origin to the conflicts arising from the workplace. The trade unions continued to be vital support institutions. Yet during the inter-war years a slow and uneven process can be found where the Labour Party came to campaign less on trade union based issues (at the local level at least), and more on issues concerned with the provision of public services. In some areas, such as Clydeside, these concerns developed in the years of the First World War and the well-known rent strikes (Melling, 1983). In other areas, such as South Wales, the transition took longer. But in all cases these demands coincided with the mobilisation of women, who used their new-found political muscle to prioritise new concerns. It was through these developments that the Labour Party began to gain its association with state welfare policies in the period after 1945.

NOTES

1. This is a much shortened version. More detail, especially on Slough, can be found in Savage (1988c).
2. The Mass Observation Archive at Sussex University has this survey in its 'Worktown' files.
3. My thanks to the TUC for giving me access to these files. Further material from them can be found in Savage (1988b).

REFERENCES

Allen, C. R. (1951) 'The Growth of Industry on Trading Estates 1920–1939 with Particular Reference to the Slough Trading Estate', *Oxford Economic Papers*, 3.
Braybon, G. (1980) *Women Workers in the First World War* (London: Croom Helm).
Burgess, K. (1980) *The Challenge of Labour* (London: Croom Helm).
Chegwidden, T. and Myrddin-Evans, G. (1934) *The Employment Exchange Service of Great Britain* (London: Macmillan).
Clarke, P. F. (1971) *Lancashire and the New Liberalism* (Cambridge University Press).

Cole, G. D. H. (1948) *A Short History of the Labour Party from 1914* (London: Routledge & Kegan Paul).

Cook, C. (1975) 'Liberals, Labour and Local Elections', in C. Cook and G. Peele (eds), *The Politics of Reappraisal* (London: Macmillan).

Cronin, J. (1984) *Labour and Society in Britain 1918–1979* (London: Batsford).

Eagger, A. (1965) *Venture in Industry: The Slough Industrial Health Service* (London: Lloyd Duke).

Franklin, M. (1985) *The Decline of Class Voting in Britain* (Oxford: Clarendon).

Hinton, J. (1983) *Labour and Socialism* (Brighton: Wheatsheaf).

Hobsbawm, E. J. (1964) *Labouring Men* (London: Allen & Unwin).

Joyce, P. (1980) *Work, Society and Politics* (Brighton: Harvester).

Kirk, N. (1983) *The Growth of Working Class Reformism in Mid-Victorian England* (London: Croom Helm).

Mark-Lawson, J. (1987) unpublished Ph.D. thesis, Department of Social Policy, University of Lancaster.

Mark-Lawson, J., Savage, M. and Warde, A. (1985) 'Gender and Local Politics: Struggles over Welfare 1918–1939', in L. Murgatroyd *et al.*, *Localities, Class and Gender* (London: Pion).

Melling, J. (1983) *Rent Strike: People's Struggles for Housing in Industrial Scotland* (Edinburgh: Polygon).

Miller, W. (1977) *Electoral Dynamics in Britain since 1918* (London: Macmillan).

Pelling, H. (1968) *A Short History of the Labour Party* (London: Penguin).

Price, R. (1986) *Labour and Society* (London: Croom Helm).

Reid, A. (1985) 'Politics and the Division of Labour 1880–1920', in H. Momsen and H. Huring (eds), *The Development of Trade Unionism in Great Britain and Germany* (London: Allen & Unwin).

Saunders, P. (1984) 'Beyond Housing Classes', *International Journal of Urban and Regional Reasearch*, Vol. 8, No. 2.

Saunders, P. (1986) *Social Theory and the Urban Question* (2nd edn) (London: Hutchinson).

Savage, M. (1987) *The Dynamics of Working Class Politics: The Labour Movement in Preston 1880–1940* (Cambridge University Press).

Savage, M. (1988a) 'Women's Work in the Lancashire Cotton Industry', in J. Jowitt and A. McIvor (eds), *Employers and Labour in the English Textile Industries 1850–1939* (London: Routledge).

Savage, M. (1988b) 'Trade Unionism, Sex Segregation and the State: Women's Employment in 'New Industries' in Inter-War Britain', *Social History*, Vol. 13, No. 2.

Savage, M. (1988c) 'The Social Bases of Labour Politics in Britain 1919–1939', *Occasional Paper*, No. 14, Department of Sociology, University of Surrey.

Shepherd, J. and Halstead, J. (1979), 'Labour's Municipal Election Performance in England and Wales 1900–1913', *Bulletin of the Society for the Study of Labour History*, No. 39.

Slough Observer, various.

TUC (various), correspondence to the TUC organisational committee on unionisation in Slough.

Thane, P. (1985) 'The Labour Party and State Welfare', in K. D. Brown (ed), *The First Labour Party 1906–1910* (London: Croom Helm).

Urry, J. (1981) *The Anatomy of Capitalist Societies* (Basingstoke: Macmillan).

Walby, S. (1986) *Patriarchy at Work* (Cambridge: Polity).
Whiting, R. (1985) *The View from Cowley* (Oxford: Clarendon).

Acknowledgements
I would like to thank the editors of this volume for their helpful advice on the preparation of this chapter.

11 Women and Working-Class Politics in Scotland 1900–14

Eleanor Gordon

INTRODUCTION

Recent interpretations of women's relationship to the various organisations and political associations of the nineteenth- and early twentieth-century labour movement stress the objective constraints on women's participation, rather than, as previously, the inherent apathy or docility of women. In particular the low level of trade union organisation among women has been attributed to their subordinate position in the labour market, where their employment was characterised by low status, low pay and poor conditions. Although such accounts provide a better understanding of the obstacles to women organising, they still accept the traditional assumption that women were apathetic and docile and focus on women as the 'problem'. Consequently this approach has paid insufficient attention to the structures, policies and practices of the organisations of the labour movement and the extent to which they failed to provide a supportive framework for women. (See Gordon, 1985; 1988 for a discussion of this in relation to Scottish trade unionism.)

The early history of women's organisations, such as the Co-operative Women's Guild and the Women's Labour League, and the history of the Independent Labour Party (ILP) demonstrate the receptiveness of women to political issues which related to their concerns and were important materially and politically to their daily lives. It also demonstrates, however, the political limitations of the familial ideology of the labour movement, and of the view of women as primarily homemakers. Not only did it lead to the neglect of the interests of the many women workers who did not conform to this stereotype, but it neglected them as a group who could be mobilised in the class struggle.

WORKING CLASS POLITICS IN THE EARLY TWENTIETH CENTURY

In the pre-war years, despite the challenge of the Labour Party, the Liberals still held sway in national electoral politics. However, it should be emphasised that the national franchise was extremely limited, only about 60 per cent of adult males were enfranchised, and, of course, no women had the vote. At local level, partly because of the wider franchise, political life could assume a different hue and socialist politics and ideas often had an altogether more flourishing and vigorous existence, even if they were not always translated into electoral success. Local elections, municipal school boards, and parish councils were frequently contested and sometimes won by committed socialists of different creeds. By 1914 there were only two Labour MPs in Scotland, but about two hundred Labour councillors, although Labour did not have control of any town council, and was still very much a minority party. There was a flowering of socialist or more broadly labour organisations which spearheaded a number of campaigns attracting widespread popular support among the working class. The broader social issues which were raised, and where socialists were to the forefront of struggles, ranged from the housing question and unemployment to school meals and the medical inspection of school children. A new socialist culture was emerging which found organisational expression through the formation of Clarion Clubs, socialist Sunday schools, socialist rambling clubs, socialist orchestras and choirs and a plethora of political education classes.

The socialist movement of the early twentieth century divided into two different ideological camps; one which had its intellectual roots in both early utopian socialism and radical liberalism and which has been characterised as ethical socialism; and one whose intellectual touchstone was the writings of Karl Marx, and which is referred to as scientific socialism (MacIntyre, 1980). In Scotland the major representative of labour socialism or ethical socialism was the ILP, which was in fact the most influential of all the socialist organisations in Scotland. The marxist tradition was represented by the Social Democratic Federation (SDF) and the Socialist Labour Party (SLP), although in terms of membership these organisations were tiny.

The common denominator for each of these organisations was

the emphasis they placed on education and propaganda as a means of disseminating their ideas, and frequently they shared political platforms in order to do this. The reputedly sectarian SDF was equally involved in this socialist current, with John MacLean's lectures on history, marxist economics and public speaking attended by socialists of a variety of different creeds. Even the courses for women co-operators and their speakers' classes, which were held under the auspices of the politically moderate co-operative union, were taught by the marxist MacLean. The public meetings organised by the Clarion Scouts and the ILP were addressed by speakers drawn from the wide spectrum of left-wing politics, and were attended by hundreds, while socialist literature was widely distributed by the Reform Bookclub and the Civic Press.

Clearly socialist politics and propaganda reached a wide audience and, more important, political activity involved a broader constituency than the formal membership of the different socialist organisations. Therefore the lacklustre performance of labour candidates in electoral politics belied the fact that at local level there was a vibrant network of socialist organisation, propaganda and agitation.

WOMEN AND LABOUR POLITICS

What was novel about working-class politics in this period was the extent to which some of the political associations of the labour movement attempted to involve women in political activity. The Women's Co-operative Guild and the Women's Labour League, which was effectively the women's section of the Labour party, were formed principally to introduce the principles of co-operation and labour politics to women, while the dominant organisation of the Labour coalition in Scotland, the ILP, contained a fair contingent of women in its ranks.

The ILP displayed many of the political traits of radical liberalism, and indeed it is often portrayed as the heir to the traditions of Scottish liberalism, particularly in its prime target for vilification – landlordism. The ILP's belief in the neutrality of state insitutions led to its policies centring on an electoral strategy which sought to colonise both local and national political institutions with the representatives of labour organisations.

However, the ILP was distinguished by its willingness to engage in direct and radical struggles of an extra-parliamentary nature, and by its fostering of organisations of local democracy such as ward committees and tenants' defence associations (Smith, 1984). It directed its agitational work towards local issues, emphasising the importance of grass roots involvement, while casting the net of its educational activity to include women and children. The ILP stressed the importance of enlisting women to the socialist cause because of their role as moral guardians of children: 'When we win the men for the socialist cause, we do no more than that, when we get the women, we get at the same time all the men and women of the next generation' (*Forward*, 6 November 1909).

The inclusion of women and children in the educational, recreational and cultural life of labour organisations was a relatively new departure which not only went some way towards breaking the sexual segregation of the cultural and leisure associations of the working class, but also served to reconstitute them on the basis of a family-wide appeal, rather than a purely masculine one. Socials, dances, choirs, 'at homes', day trips and concerts enabled the participation of family members on a wider basis than had been possible in the leisure associations of the Victorian labour movement.

The ILP was also alone of the socialist groups in supporting the extension of the franchise to women on the same basis as men, although little was done in the way of active support or promoting a campaign for women's suffrage. Support took the form of devoting long articles to the 'Woman Question' in the pages of *Forward*, which was effectively the voice of the ILP.

The activities of the labourist or ethical wing of the socialist movement embraced many more women than the small number who were formally affiliated to these organisations, and it was these women who spearheaded the campaigns which were such a prominant feature of local politics in the pre-war and war years. However, the ambit of socialist activity seems to have excluded working women. Although many of the active ILP women were working class, few of them seem to have been wage earners, and overlapping membership of trade unions and political organisations was restricted to a tiny handful of women, such as Kate McLean, the Scottish organiser of the National Federation of Women Workers and a member of the ILP, and Agnes Pettigrew, secretary of the shop assistants' union and active in the Women's Labour League and the ILP. Even women's organisations, such as the Scottish Co-operative Women's Guild (SCWG) and the Women's Labour League (WLL), were dominated by housewives rather than wage-earning women. The SCWG was aimed specifically at housewives and more particularly at the wives of better-off sections of the working class. According to the Scottish Guild's first historian and former president, Mrs Buchan, its original purpose was to enable 'the women of the co-operative movement to meet together in friendly converse and by so doing, help to break the monotonous existence of even a comfortable and desirable home' (Buchan, 1913, p. 64).

The WLL established its first Scottish branch in Glasgow in June 1908. Its first president was Lizzie Glasier, sister of Bruce Glasier, editor of *Labour Leader*. The correspondence of the Glasgow League indicates that positions of responsibility in the organisation were occupied by middle-class women. In letters to the Town Clerk from two members of the League responsible for preparing schemes for the relief of unemployment among women, the addresses given were in the prosperous Hyndland and Kelvindale district of the city. Many of the League's activists seem to have been drawn from the ILP. Miss Hanman, a member of the branch's press committee, claimed that within two months of the formation of the Glasgow branch it had 'a membership of 60 or 70 including the best working women in the ILP' (*Woman Worker*, 18 September 1908). The WLL, in common with the women's co-operative guild, saw their main function as recruiting housewives to the labour movement and regarded enlisting women wage-earners as 'the supplementary side to the interesting of the working wives and mothers in our cause' (*Woman Worker*, 3 July 1903).

It appears that, with the exception of a small number of women who were prominent in the trade union movement, working women seem to have been absent from the networks of political organisations which flourished in the pre-war years. There were obviously objective constraints which imposed limitations on their full participation, as Hannah Mitchell, an activist in the Lancashire Radical Suffrage Association, remarked. 'No cause can be won between dinner and tea, and most of us who were married had to work with one hand tied behind us' (Liddington and Norris, 1978, p. 16).

Women workers shared their exclusion with unskilled male workers who similarly were not well represented in the formal political organisations of the labour movement. The ILP membership was predominantly skilled manual workers, although it attracted a fair amount of clerks, supervisory workers and professional people, and the small membership of the SDF tended to draw on the same social background. Although there is little concrete information on the membership of the SLP, it clearly did not expect to recruit members among the poorer sections of the working class, believing that 'it was useless going to slum districts as the people there seemed to be hopeless' (Challinor, 1978, p. 36).

Given the absence of unskilled and semi-skilled men from the political associations of the labour movement, it is perhaps not surprising that wage-earning women, the vast majority of whom were classed as unskilled, were also absent. And yet the ILP attracted substantial numbers of working-class housewives, while the SCWG and the WLL were formed principally to introduce labour politics to women.

The received view of women workers is that they were quiescent, submissive, and unable or unwilling to organise industrially. However, in the twenty or so years before the First World War women workers played an important part in the 'New Unionism' of 1889–91 and in the labour unrest of 1910–14 (Gordon, 1985). Between 1890 and 1914 women workers in Scotland were involved in over two hundred officially recorded strikes. It was usually the case that women were not organised in a union when they took action, although it was increasingly the case that trade union recognition became incorporated into their demands in the course of a strike.

The demands of women workers were primarily instrumental; however, many of the disputes indicate that underlying basic material grievances there were more intractable issues relating to dignity, self-respect and self-assertion (Gordon, 1985). In addition, women workers were involved in significant disputes which had widespread ramifications. One of the longest strikes of this period involved Ayrshire net workers who were in dispute for over five months in 1913. The strike sparked off a number of claims from other workers which had Kilbirnie 'seething with discontent'. A number of men's trade unions increased their membership, and a branch of the ILP was formed in the town.

The strike also generated an unprecedented level of solidarity and contributed to the mobilisation of labour in the area on a class-wide basis rather than a purely sectional one. A strike of women textile workers in Kirkcaldy in 1911 had similar ramifications, sparking off a number of disputes among tram workers, policemen and other factory workers, and leading to the formation of a number of union branches among previously unorganised male workers.

There is also evidence that the suffrage issue enjoyed wide support among women workers. The predominantly female Dundee Union of Jute and Flax Workers passed several resolutions in support of women's suffrage, including a resolution condemning the imprisonment of suffragettes who had demonstrated in the House of Commons (Dundee Union of Jute and Flax Workers, minutes, 23 October 1906). On one occasion a speaker from the Women's Social and Political Union (WSPU) was invited to address the women members of the Union; however, there was dissension from the male members within the committee of the Union over forging closer links with the WSPU and an invitation to send a delegate to a WSPU conference in the Gillfillan Halls in Dundee was left to lie on the table (ibid., 25 June 1907). Support for women's suffrage was not unanimous within the committee with some of the male delegates arguing in favour of the adult suffrage position. Even after the Labour Party had changed its policy to opposition to any proposed extension of the franchise which did not include women, some male members of the committee remained intransigent in their advocacy of adult suffrage (ibid., 7 January 1913).

The long strike of the Ayrshire net workers originated over a demand for an increase of 6d per net but soon broadened out to include a demand for recognition of their union. The strikers' demands were often expressed in terms of gaining equality with men and this theme was perhaps stoked by the employers' refusal to recognise women's unions which gave a feminist edge to the dispute, evinced by the comment made by one striker and given general assent, 'Wait till we get a vote' (*Forward*, 14 June 1913) and the perhaps hopeful remark by the correspondent in *Forward* that the strikers were 'keen suffragists, and for the most part socialists too' (ibid.).

Given the militancy of many women workers and their support for the suffrage question, their absence from the political associations of the working class cannot be easily attributed to apathy or lack of receptiveness to broader social and political issues. It may, therefore, be the case that the explanation for their absence lies in the policies and practices of the socialist movement itself rather than in the imputed weakness of women workers.

IDEOLOGIES OF FEMINISM IN THE LABOUR MOVEMENT

The organisations which made efforts to recruit women related to them in their capacity as homemakers, and addressed them as the 'wives, sisters and sweethearts of male workers' (*Woman Worker*, 12 June 1908). Meetings were often held during the day as the assumption was that women would not be involved in waged labour. Women's involvement in politics and wider social questions was based on the belief that it would develop their qualities as homemakers as well as infusing the 'purifying and elevating' influence of women into political and social life. The attitude to women workers was underpinned by the overarching assumption that women's employment was temporary, that married women's work violated the 'natural' division of labour between the sexes and that women's primary role was in the domestic sphere.

The largest of the women's organisations, the SCWG, had as its primary objective the promotion of the ideals and principles of co-operation among women with the aim of making them 'better wives, better mothers and better members of society', and to train them 'to take their place in the home, in the social circle and in the Co-operative Society' (SCWG, Annual Reports, 1906).

Although women's province was defined as the home and thus their primary duties and responsibilities related to the family, the SCWG maintained that this should not preclude women from participation in public life, arguing that 'the hand that rocked the cradle was directed by a brain that notwithstanding she had to be the wife and mother and responsible for the home, was yet able to spare the time and the will to help her sister-worker' (Buchan, 1913, p. 13). Moreover, it was argued that political life would be enriched by women's contribution as they possessed a number of valuable qualities, both moral and practical, which derived from their role as homemakers and mothers. Mrs Buchan, president of the Guild for several years, argued that guildswomen were more conversant with the 'inner workings of the movement' than the men, as their role as 'Chancellors of the Exchequer' in the home imbued them with the root principles of co-operation (SCWG, Annual Reports, 1909).

For male co-operators the particular virtues which women possessed were regarded as ideally suited to the role of moral campaigner and it was believed that their major contribution to the movement would centre on schemes for the 'moral and social elevation of the poorer members [of society]' and 'the elimination of sin and crime' (SCWG, Annual Reports, 1910). Women co-operators were exhorted to regard themselves as 'a worker, a missionary for the cause of women's progress' and to support 'all questions especially relating to women' (SCWG, Minutes 1901).

In Scotland the other main working-class women's organisation, the WLL, was dominated by women of the ILP and consequently its political ideology and conception of the role of women was largely derived from this organisation. Although the ILP subscribed to the belief that women's suffrage was part of the struggle for equal rights for women, sexual equality was defined as the recognition of the equal value of motherhood and the centrality of the home and the family to the health of the nation:

> First let our citizenship be recognised, and we are on the only safe and sure road to the enthronement of motherhood equally with fatherhood as the guiding principle of our national life. Then will woman, the mother and the homemaker, set about her beneficent work in the land, unhampered – no longer 'unofficially'. (*Forward*, 16 January 1909)

The destruction of the home and the undermining of the importance of the family were regarded as the product of unfettered capitalism and an index of its brutality, while the task of defending the home and the family was assigned to the socialists and incorporated into the working-class struggle. Defence of the family was interpreted as the defence of the 'natural' sexual division of labour which located women in the home. By drawing women into the labour force, capitalism was regarded as violating the natural order of things and destroying the 'natural' qualities of women. In an article fulminating against the extent of married women's work in Dundee and deriding a scheme for the provision of day nurseries, Tom Johnston, the editor of *Forward*, asserted: 'The husbands stay at home dry nursing, the women go out to earn wages. What an inversion of civilisation! What a damning indictment of capitalism!' (*Forward*, 19 October 1912).

Therefore while the ILP alone of the early twentieth-century labour movements displayed an active commitment to the 'Woman Question', its definition of feminism involved elevating the status and role of mothers and reasserting the ideology of separate sexual spheres. The ILP did have a vision of their new Socialist Commonwealth which involved the transformation of family life and the role of women. However, it was a vision which was still grounded in the ideology of the complementarity of gender relations. An editorial in *Forward* argued that when women got the vote: 'Where man has rigged a scaffold and a gas pipe, woman will plant a flower . . . the inevitable tendency will be . . . to drastic Housing and Temperance legislation' (*Forward*, 19 November 1910).

The introduction of women into politics and public life was viewed as a means of democratising and humanising society by incorporating the particular qualities of women developed by virtue of their role as wives and mothers:

> Soon for the first time, we shall set abuilding that new society, built on a true Democracy, and which absorbing as it must the finer women feelings, and the social spirit, gives to Humanity its one last hope of rearing on Earth that happy, joyous free life, for which we have struggled and yearned down the centuries. (ibid.)

Woman's entry into politics was also viewed as part of her duties as a wife and mother. Thus the WLL urged women to take an interest in the sanitary and education committees, in the provision of school meals and a whole range of similar issues on the basis that 'though "Woman's place is in the home", she cannot fulfil her duties there unless she looks beyond its four walls, and takes her part in public affairs which affect the home and children closely' (*Woman Worker*, 19 June 1908).

The success of organisations such as the Women's Co-operative Guild, the Women's Labour League and the ILP in attracting women illustrates the generally untapped potential of women's political involvement, and the importance of addressing issues which reflected the interests and the concerns of women if they were to be drawn into political life.

By addressing women primarily as homemakers, these organisations clearly endorsed the view of separate sexual spheres. Although acceptance of a separate sphere for women was clearly not incompatible with a public role, there were difficulties in reconciling a belief in the complementarity of gender roles with a belief in complete equality between the sexes. Despite the rhetoric of the ILP, the fragility of its commitment to women's rights and equal status was evident in its reluctance to select women as candidates in elections, and in the observation of a leading ILPer that it was not 'considered good form for women to appear on the platform at co-operative or other working class meetings' (Dollan, 1923, p. 48).

Essentially women's place in the labour movement was based on their status as wives and mothers and while it drew many women into political activity and extended their public role, it was in a way which reinforced existing gender divisions and confirmed the home as the natural domain of women.

The Social Democratic Party is usually depicted as a sectarian and dogmatic organisation which was isolated from the mainstream of the labour movement. However, the SDF in Scotland could not be accused of isolationism as they participated fully in the socialist culture of the pre-war years, due largely to the efforts of John MacLean to reach the widest possible audience with his education classes. MacLean, the leading light of the SDF, also rejected the mechanical version of marxism prevalent at the time which minimised the role of working-class organisations and activity in effecting change. In Scotland, therefore, the SDF had a greater impact on the Scottish working class than it did south of the border, although its membership was still tiny and restricted mainly to skilled workers.

The SDF had little to say on the specific issue of the 'Woman Question'; therefore its conception of women's role and the relations between the sexes can only be inferred from its political diagnosis and its vision of an alternative social and political order. Maclean only referred to a socialist future where classes would be abolished and no mention was made of sexual inequalities, the sexual division of labour, or the role of women in a socialist society. However, there is an indication that MacLean subscribed to the view that married women's province was the home and not the workplace when he exhorted women strikers in Neilston to form a union: 'We strongly advised the Nitshill lassies to get into a union, and stay in until they got married' (*Woman Worker*, 14 June 1910).

Further evidence of the SDF's commitment to the family and the notion of the home as the haven of working men from the rigours of competitive capitalism is contained in a speech given by one of its members at a rally in Dundee. Condemning Dundee's industrial system which employed so many married women, he railed:

A home ought to be the holiest of holies. The man who performed his honest duties ought to be able to say – here is my altar of love, here shall I rest, here shall I withstand the vile temptations . . . of the world . . . But what did they do – went home and gave the baby a bottle – went home and let the wife go out and earn the dollars. (Walker, 1979, p. 60)

The Women's Trade Union League (WTUL) and the National Federation of Women Workers (NFWW), which performed pioneering work in the trade union organisation of women, had a similar conception of the role of women. Married women's presence in the labour force was regarded by the non-socialist members as a flaw in capitalism, a temporary breakdown in social organisation which could be remedied without the transformation of the social structure, while for the socialist women in these organisations, it pointed up the inefficiency of capitalism. Although they were dedicated to the task of organising women workers, their firm belief was that husbands should earn enough to support a wife and children at home and in comfort, and their ultimate aim was to shake married women out of the labour market.

WORKING WOMEN

Clearly the political ideologies of the socialist, co-operative and trade union movements, and their conceptions of women's role within this framework, conditioned their response to women workers and their struggles. The WTUL and the NFWW recognised that the double burden of women workers made it more difficult for them to become involved in trade union affairs and that there was a need for special organisational apparatus and propaganda directed specifically at women. However, their commitment to the prevailing ideology of domesticity ensured that they made no attempt to tackle the conditions which created these difficulties and were content to confine their concerns within the traditional boundaries of trade union issues. They made no demands around the question of women's productive role such as birth control, maternity rights and child-care facilities. This contrasted with the approach of Russian women socialists to organising women. In an interview in *Woman Worker* in 1909, Alexandra Kollontai argued that to organise women successfully, it was necessary to address questions which specifically affected them and she mentioned that maternity rights was one of the issues which Russian women socialists had taken up (*Woman Worker*, 19 May 1909).

Adherence to the ideology which conceived of women as primarily dependants militated against the WTUL campaigning on the right of single women to work for the same wages as men, and from organising to facilitate employment for the many women with dependants who needed to work. There was an implicit belief that women's proper sphere was the home. Indeed a long-term objective was the realisation of a family wage which would remove married women's work from the labour market.

Although the WLL was active in campaigns to alleviate unemployment among women, organising demonstrations, setting up a shelter for unemployed women, and petitioning Glasgow Council to set up a Women's Distress Committee, the League's support for women's right to work was confined to spheres which were regarded as 'women's work', and did not pose any threat or competition to male employment. For example, members of the League devised schemes for training in domestic work and hygiene, elementary sick nursing, campaigned for the establishment of a municipal workshop, and the creation of 'similarly suitable employment' such as needlework, agricultural fieldwork and market gardening (Special Committee, 1909).

A common theme running through the labour movement's pronouncements on women workers was a conception of them as essentially weak and powerless and in need of the protection of others. When Mona Wilson resigned from secretaryship of the League in 1903, the committee agreed that they had to find an organiser who could rouse the 'underpaid and helpless women workers', although they claimed it was a task which was 'well-nigh hopeless', and Lady Dilke spoke of 'the joy of knowing that by our efforts we have brought the feeble, the ignorant and the lonely to feel that they are not alone' (Hamilton, 1925, p. 76).

This partly explains the turn to legislative work taken by the WTUL. Increasingly it looked to Parliament rather than trade union action to promote changes in industrial life, and their priorities became the anti-sweating campaign and, allied to it, the campaign for Wages Boards and a minimum wage.

The ILP could also be active in support of the struggles of women workers, but it was in their capacity as victims rather than as a way of developing their capacity for self-organisation. Its support was fuelled by the belief that capitalism had plucked these women from their natural territory and stripped them of their natural 'womanly attributes'. George Barnes, an ILP Member of Parliament, addressed the women strikers of Kilbirnie, denounced their employers, and pledged his support for their cause on the basis that it was the iniquities of capitalism which forced them to do 'men's work' (*Forward*, 14 June 1910).

The ILP also saw its task as establishing the ideal of a family wage as a reality and attacking every example of its violation. It was on this basis that they related to women workers and elicited their support for socialism. There were obviously women workers for whom this policy had great appeal and who were in accord with the ILP's conception of women's role. A letter to *Woman Worker* from a married woman weaver expressed her support for socialism on the basis that:

one of the most cruel and brutal conditions is that which married women have to live under when the time comes when they have to endure that sacred duty which should be the glory of superb womanhood. A mother has to go to the mill up to the time of childbirth because her husband's wages will not keep them. Then consider the heartache that mother must endure when she has to take her baby between 5 and 6 o'clock in the morning out to nursery in all kinds of weather. This is the system that brutalises, instead of bringing out the instincts of motherhood. (*Woman Worker*, 26 June 1908)

There were many working women, however, who defended their

right to work, supported equal pay and were critical of the position taken by many trade unionists and socialists, who sought to exclude women from certain occupations. A female printer from Edinburgh wrote to *Forward* complaining about the support given to legislation to exclude women from working at the pit-brow by John Wheatley, a leading ILPer and founder of the Catholic Socialist League:

> If at present time you prohibit women working at dangerous, unhealthy or unfit industries then I contend you take them wholly from the entire labour market. I challenge your readers to show me one industry where the conditions of work all round are such as could be said is fit for our future mothers? (*Forward*, September 1911)

She went on to decry the hypocrisy of men who wanted to exclude women from male trades, but did not care about the drudgery and toil involved in other work such as domestic service. She defended the right to work and condemned women's containment to the domestic sphere:

> It is said prohibition would have the effect of raising the wages of men and so enabling the women to remain at home. Even were such a state possible I doubt very much that it is desirable. Women as well as men are human beings and have the same instincts and longings just as men. She wishes to express herself in other ways than being just a toy, a pet, a doll . . . Women no longer believe her one niche in life is motherhood, she longs to do her share of the world's work, to assist in its education, add to its store of literature, art and science. (ibid.)

For many women workers the demand for the right to work and equal pay was based on necessity rather than a challenge to the ideology of a male breadwinner. The experience and the economic necessity of working engendered a more pragmatic acceptance of this ideology among working women who might have accepted that men had a greater eligibility to work, but who also recognised that they had the right to earn a living wage. Thus 400 Edinburgh women compositors' response to the men's union's call for a ban on the further recruitment of female labour argued that '*We women* feel the fact that women have been employed in Edinburgh as compositors for nearly forty years gives women a claim on the business' (Cockburn, 1983, p. 156).

The commitment of the ILP, however, to the ideology of separate sexual spheres and the sanctity of the family frequently led them to support sectional trade union struggles to exclude women.

The only socialist organisation which related to women as workers rather than homemakers was the Socialist Labour Party whose emphasis on industrial struggle and class unity precluded a conception of an arena of struggle other than the workplace. Their diagnosis of all problems as class problems clearly shaped the SLP's attitude to women's suffrage and the more general issue of women's rights. Although they frequently proclaimed their belief in the equality of the sexes and women's social, political and economic emancipation, they remained implacably opposed to women's suffrage arguing:

> Socialism is in full accord with the Suffragist movement insofar as it is a protest against the present social status of women. Socialism is in accord with the Suffragists' exposure of the contemptible and superficial arguments of the anti-feminists . . . When all is said, however, Socialism and Suffragism remain at emnity because of the basic difference in their principles . . . under the existing system of society any changes of laws giving the same opportunities to women as to men, would only benefit those women who belonged to the privileged or propertied class in society. Socialism in fact is a revolutionary movement . . . The SLP holds that the Suffragist movement is of great interest and importance to the women of the bourgeoisie, but of none to women of the working class. (*Socialist*, January 1909).

Although the SLP prescribed the equal access of women to the means of production as the basis of independence and equality, in practice they subscribed to the ideology of a family wage under capitalism, accepting that if women were married their wages would be supplementary to the men's. They attributed this to the fact that married women themselves were content to work for less money because they had other means of support, claiming that single and widowed women 'suffer from the competition of many less helpless wives and daughters whose necessities only force them to aim at supplementary earnings' (ibid.). Thus women themselves were blamed for their low wages – this position being a variant on the theme that there are certain groups of workers who are willing to work for lower wages, and ignoring the powerful ideological and social factors which determined women's earnings.

The SLP were reticent about outlining a detailed blue-print for the new socialist order, and despite their constant assertions about the equality of the sexes, they give little indication of how the role of women and men might be transformed by socialism or what constituted equality. They were certainly sensitive to attacks on socialists being anti-family and argued that while it was impossible to predict the detailed results of freedom for women:

> This much can be said. If the home in its true sense is also an ideal, if monogamy in its true sense is also an ideal, these are ideals which will only be possible of realisation under Socialism. There is nothing in Socialism incompatible with that true home life which capitalism destroys. (*Socialist*, October 1909).

The refusal of the SLP to view women as other than members of an oppressed and exploited class, whose historic mission was the overthrow of capitalism, meant that they did not subscribe to the stereotypical image of women workers as passive, and were quick to acknowledge women's combative qualities. Their rejection of the sectionalism of craft unionism and insistence on the common interests of the working class led them to champion women's right to work in the face of campaigns to exclude 'cheap female labour'. They took the Edinburgh compositors to task when they demanded that machine composition be solely undertaken by male union labour, accusing them of being reactionary and divisive:

> What economic or social argument can be put forward to justify the claim that the trade is yours? Whatever the justification there may have been in the past when a high degree of ability may have been necessary to acquire and work at the trade, that reason has forever passed away, if it was ever more than a trade guild superstition. (*Socialist*, July 1910)

However, their dismissal of reforms which they considered mere palliatives and their refusal to acknowledge the specific problems of women as distinct from the class question meant that they did nothing in practice to advance the right of women to work and indeed could be obstructive on this issue. Thus they attacked the Women's Freedom League for advocating maternity benefits because 'the intention of the capitalist is to secure a healthier and more capable community of workers' (*Socialist*, June 1919).

As the issue of women's rights was subsumed under the class struggle, the SLP did not attempt to relate to women workers as women but as wage earners whose entry into the labour force made their interests identical with other wage earners. Therefore they made no special effort to organise women workers and did not conduct any campaigns based on the specific interests of women workers, such as advancing their right to work. Women were recruited to the struggle for socialism as wage earners, therefore all non wage-earning women were ignored, as were the real differences in the historical experience of diverse sections of the working class.

CONCLUSION

With the exception of the SLP, the political organisations of the working class in the pre-war years had a conception of women's role in terms of the domestic sphere and their primary commitment to the home and the family. The housing struggles of the war years and the campaigns around school meals, the medical inspection of school children, and a range of issues are testimony to the fact that this position encouraged a definition of feminism which exploited the potential for the broadening of political consciousness and political engagement within the parameters of the existing sexual division of labour. Although this ideology generated political struggles and propelled women into public life, it reflected and reinforced the fragmentation of the working class along gender lines by confirming women's association with domestic labour and reinforcing patterns of job segregation which confined women to a well-defined sphere of 'women's employment'.

The idealisation of family life and the central place accorded to women in the spiritual and moral development of the working class were in stark contrast to the serious material disadvantages imposed on those women who did not conform to the stereotype of the woman dependent on the earnings of a male breadwinner, who were forced to sell their labour for a wage which was assumed to be supplementary.

The image of women as homemakers treated women as a homogeneous group with identical experiences and needs, and denied the validity of their experience as waged labour. Women's place in the labour movement was based on their status as wives and mothers and there was no attempt to harness them to the struggle for socialism in their capacity as workers, or to encourage them to identify or organise as workers. This not only reinforced their marginality in the labour market, but contributed to the marginality of working women from working-class politics by failing to recognise them as a potential political constituency.

REFERENCES

Buchan, A. (1913) *History of the Scottish Co-operative Women's Guild, 1891–1913* (Glasgow).

Challinor, R. (1978) *The Origins of British Bolshevism* (London: Croom Helm).

Cockburn, C. (1983) *Brothers* (London: Pluto).

Dollan, P. (1923) *Jubilee History of the Kinning Park Co-operative Society*.

Dundee Union of Jute and Flax Workers, Committee Minutes (Dundee Archives and Record Centre).

Gordon, E. (1985) 'Women and the Labour Movement in Scotland, 1850–1914', unpublished Ph.D. thesis, University of Glasgow.

Gordon, E. (1988) 'The Scottish Trade Union Movement: Class and Gender, 1850–1914', *Journal of the Scottish Labour History Society*, No. 23.

Hamilton, M. A. (1925) *Mary MacArthur* (London: Leonard Parsons).

Liddington, J. and Norris, J. (1978) *One Hand Tied Behind Us* (London: Virago).

MacIntyre, S. (1980) *A Proletarian Science* (Cambridge University Press).

Scottish Co-operative Women's Guild Annual Reports (Scottish Co-operative Society, Shieldhall).

Scottish Co-operative Women's Guild, Minutes.

Smith, J. (1984) 'Labour Traditions in Glasgow and Liverpool', *History Workshop Journal*, 17, Spring.

Special Committee on Relief of Unemployment among Women, Minutes (Strathclyde Regional Archives).

Walker, W. (1979) *Juteopolis* (Edinburgh: Scottish Academic Press).

Newspapers

Forward 1906–13.
Socialist 1908–10.
Woman Worker 1908–09.

Index

Aids, 32, 46, 50, 69
Amalgamated Engineering Union, 206

Benn, A., 81
Beveridge, William 6, 89, 92, 96–116
Booth, Charles, 166–7, 170
Branthwaite, R. W., 165, 168–70, 173, 180
Briggs, A., 77
Brod, H., 53–5
Butler Josephine, 62

capitalism, 53–5, 97, 99, 127–8, 154, 189, 207–8, 232, 235, 237, 240
Carlen, P., 181–2
censorship, 67, 69
Charity Organisation Society, 173
child abuse, 9
child allowances, 3, 106, 107
childbirth, 209
citizenship, 77–8, 90, 97, 99, 102, 113–16, 133, 183, 208
civil service, 5, 50, 51, 66, 78, 196,
civilising process, 15–19, 26–7
  and status of women, 17, 27
Clarion Clubs, 225
class
  composition of the labour
    movement 228–9
  consciousness, 205, 230
  differences, 42, 120–1, 123, 173–4
  images, 43
  imposition of values, 128, 173–4
  inequality more visible, 83, 86
  inequality reduced, 79, 100, 104, 110, 113
  middle class, 'new', 190
  relations 43, 58, 96–7, 190, 191, 204, 217
  segregation in education, 194–5
  working class, disassociated from, 190
  working class, respectability, 173–4

working class women, 'the problem of', 171–4
colonial administration, 197–8
Cominos, P., 181–2
Committee on Physical Deterioration, 1903, 61
Conservative Party, 45, 109, 196–7, 199, 210–11, 212, 217
Contagious Diseases Acts, 43, 50, 62
cooperative societies, 208, 226
community, 127–8
Criminal Law Amendment Act 1885, 61, 62–3
The Custody of Children Act, 64
cuts in government spending, 196

D'Emilio, J., 55
divorce, 61
doctors, see also professions, 148, 153
domestic violence, 179
duelling, 17–19

education, 64, 120, 172–3, 189–201, 214, 226, 236
  Board of Education, 194–6
  curriculum control, 196–9
  Education Act 1870, 64
  Education Act 1902, 194
  Education Act 1944, 198
  elementary/secondary split, 194–5
  H.M.I.s, 192
  local education authorities, 194, 198
  for motherhood, 172–3, 236
electrification, 214
Elias, N., 15–17, 19, 26–7
employment,
  labour process, 191, 205
  of married women, 232–3, 235, 237
  marriage bar, 66, 212
  Select Committee on the Bill for the Regulation of Factories 1831–32, 141
  wages, 103, 128, 139, 208, 236, 240
  women's right to work, 238–9

women's employment, 64, 66–8, 137–56, 178, 183, 229
women's exclusion from, 9, 18–21, 90, 154, 211, 238
women workers, received view, 229
engineers, 206, 210
eugenics, 60, 123, 124, 169–72

Fabians, 103, 171
Factory Acts, 137–55
factory inspectors, 151–2
family, 42, 52–3, 55, 97, 100, 105–8, 123–4, 130, 154, 171, 224, 227, 231–5, 240, 241–2
family allowance, 109
family wage, 130, 237, 239
fathers, 64, 65
feminists, 33, 53, 59, 62, 119, 133, 137, 191, 200, 230, 233
state feminism, 125
feminity, 13, 24, 28
Fisher, H. A. L., 195–6
Foucault, Michael, 38–9, 42
franchise, 205, 209, 215, 225, 227, 230
functionalist, 190

gender, *see also* employment, of married women; employment, marriage bar; employment, women's; employment, women's exclusion from; employment, women's right to work; morality, of women *and* sex differences
and class, 4, 10, 58, 137, 139, 201
divisions and inequality, 4, 6, 7, 8, 17, 18–21, 41, 64, 79, 90, 97, 99–100, 105–8, 126–31, 140–8, 152–4, 174, 183–4, 200, 208, 227, 231–42
and sexuality, 41–2
General Mannerheim League for Child Welfare, 123
General and Municipal Worker's Union, 212
Grace, G., 191, 192–3, 195
Grafton, P., 91

Habitual Drunkards Act 1897, 163

Harris, J., 98, 100, 101, 105, 106, 107
health, 141, 143–50, 153, 214, medical aid societies, 209
health visitor, 64
heroism, 13–28
honour, 14, 17–18, 25
home help, 6–7, 127
homosexuality, *see* sexuality
housing, 101, 214, 217–20

income tax, 103–5, 111–16, 122
Inebriates Act 1898, 7, 163, 175, 176, 180
inequality, *see* class, gender and race
infant welfare movement, 64, 123, 141–3
infant mortality, 143, 145, 174
inflation, 111
Interdepartmental Committee on Social Insurance and Allied Services 1942, 97–8

kinship, 127

Labour Clubs, 215
Labour Party, 90, 98, 109, 194, 196, 205–21, 225–41
electoral support, 204, 206–7, 214–15
The Independent Labour Party, 9, 216, 218–20, 224, 226
Socialist Labour Party, 239
women candidates, 212, 234
women's section, 211, 213, 220–1, 226
mobilisation of women, 209, 214–15, 219, 221, 226–42
laissez-faire, 149, 171
Lawn, M., 194, 196–7
local politics, 101, 207–21, 225
London County Council, 175–81

MacDonald, Ramsay, 204
MacKinnon, C. A., 52, 57, 58–9
magistrate, 175, 181
maintenance, 63, 106, 109
marriage bar, 66, 212
married man's allowance, 106
Marshall, T. H., 85
marxist, 190

masculinity, 4–5, 13–28, 52–7
  duelling, 17–19
  heroism, 13–28
  honour, 14, 12–18, 25
  wimp, 14–15
Mass Observation, 206
mass media, 52, 68
maternity allowance, 111, 128, 131, 236
Maternity and Child Welfare Act 1918, 64
means test, 103, 105, 108, 115
medical aid societies, 209
medical inspection, 61, 172
Committee on Medical Inspection and Feeding of Children Attending Public Elementary Schools, 61
midwives, 64
minimum wage, 103
morality, women's, 142, 146–7, 167
moral panic, 57, 148, 163
Mort, F., 63, 67
motherhood, 60, 64, 128, 140–2, 169, 172–4, 232–3

National Federation of Women Workers, 227
National Union of Teachers, 193, 194–6
National Union of Elementary Teachers, 193
National Insurance Bill 1911, 105
national health, 109, 113, 214
nationalism, 96, 99, 100–2
networks, women's, 127–31, 208–9
the New Right, 45, 199
Notifications of Births Act 1907, 64
nurseries, 214, 233

parenthood, unfit, 64, *see also* motherhood and fathers
paternalism, 217
patriarchy, 19–20, 52–69, 115, 137, 139, 154–6
pension, 107–8, 110–13
pluralist, 190
police, 62
  police court, 175

political parties,
  Australian Labor Party, 6, 98–104, 110–12
  Conservative Party, 45, 109, 196–7, 199, 210–11, 212, 217
  electoral support for Conservatives, 210, 217
  electoral support for Labour, 214, 206–7, 214–15
  Finnish Agrarian Party, 125, 225
  Finnish Liberal Party, 125, 225
  Finnish Social Democratic Party, 125
  Independent Labour Party, The, 9, 216, 218–20, 224, 226
  Labour Party, 90, 98, 109, 194, 196, 205–21, 225–41
  Social Democratic Party, 234
  Socialist Labour Party, 239
  Swedish People's Party, 125
  United Australian Party, 101
  women candidates, 212, 234
  women's section, 211, 213, 220–1, 226
  mobilisation of women, 209, 214–15, 219, 221, 226–42

pornography, 57, 60, 68
Post Office, 50, 51, 66
population problems, *see* eugenics
the Primrose League, 210
prisons, 176, 179, 181–2
punishment of women, 181–2
professions,
  as state agents, 65, 123, 148, 153, 189–201
proletarianisation, 190, 200, 201
prostitution, 43, 46, 50, 175, 179, 182
public/private, 53, 128, 231

race,
  and citizenship, 102, 111
  inequality, 99
  racism, 43–4
Ratepayers' Association, 217
rape, 24, 27
reformatories, 8, 163–83
religion, 38–9, 45, 53
  Sunday schools, 225

respectability, 173–4
Riseborough, G., 189
Lord Rosebery, 171
Royal Commission on Divorce and
    Marital Causes, 61

Select Committee on the Bill for the
    Regulation of Factories 1831–32,
    141
sex experts, 31–2, 57, *see also*
    professions as state agents
sexual differences, 41–2, 139, 143–8,
    168–9, 171, 181–3, 231–4, 236–8
Sex Disqualification Removal Act
    1919, 66
sexual harassment, 51, 57, 59
sexuality, *see also* Aids, morality,
    prostitution, pornography, rape
    and chastity, 173
    and class, 42–43
    and consumerism, 54, 68
    desexualisation, 56, 67
    heterosexuality, 68, 69
    history of, 32–48
    homosexuality, 36–7, 45, 46, 50, 55,
        65, 67, 68, 69
    and power, 38–44
sexual liberation, 54
slipper baths, 214
Social Darwinism, 171
Social Democratic Party, 234
socialist, 225–42
social security, 6, 96–116
    White Paper on Social Security
        1944, 109
social work, 173–4
Society of Engineers, 210
state, *see also* civil service and welfare
    state
    centralisation, 80, 105, 196–7, 110,
        111, 199–200
    colonial administration, 197–8
    definition, 1–2, 138, 191
    free trade, 210
    and gender 19–21, 79, 81, 97, 105–8,
        114–15
    intentionality, 3, 9, 10, 44, 80, 81,
        83, 92, 97, 139, 195–201
    and sexuality, 3–4, 5, 40–4, 50–69

and violence, 4–5, 19–21, 27
and women's employment, 7, 9, 64,
    66–8, 90, 119–21, 128, 137–56
Stedman Jones, G., 183
Subversive Teaching Bill, 196
suffrage, 227, 230
Syndicalists, 207

teachers, 8, 65, 189–201
    Teachers' Labour League, 194, 196
    National Union of Teachers, 193,
        194–6
    National Union of Elementary
        Teachers, 193
    Subversive Teaching Bill, 196
Thompson, D., 194–5
Titmuss, R., 85, 87
trade unions, *see also under individual
    names*, 8–9, 105, 122, 193–4
    contracting in, 206
    in the cotton industry, 206
    and the Labour party, 204–21
    male domination, 200
    and married women working, 235
    'new unionism', 229
    strikes, 200, 207, 214, 229–30
    Taff Vale, 210
    trades councils, 194, 210, 212
Townsend, P., 85–6

unemployment, 103, 104, 213, 236

war,
    cold war, 93
    and democracy, 90, 94
    decentralisation, 87
    evacuation, 85–6
    Falklands, 21, 92
    history of, 15–17, 19, 21–7
    hospitals, 87
    World War I, 60, 61, 64, 66, 67,
        89–90, 183, 206, 211, 221
    World War II, 75–94, 96–116, 120
wash-houses, 214
welfare state,
    definition, 76–82
    history of, 4, 6–7, 75–116
    in Australia, 6, 96–116
    in Finland, 6, 119–31

in Sweden, 6, 93
and warfare, 6, 82, 96–116
Wilson, Elizabeth, 82, 106–7, 110, 114
Women's Citizens' Association, 211–12
Women's Cooperative Guild, 9, 224, 226–8

Women's Labour League, 9, 224, 226, 228–33
Women's Social and Political Union, 230
Women's Trade Union League, 235
Workers' Union, 210